YEAR-ROUND
GARDENING
PROJECTS

YEAR-ROUND
GARDENING
PROJECTS

Drawings by Elayne Sears

Projects by

Oliver E. Allen ◆ *Nancy Bubel* ◆ *Thomas Christopher*

Teri Dunn ◆ *Thomas Fischer* ◆ *Lee Reich* ◆ *Janet H. Sanchez*

STOREY

Storey Books
Schoolhouse Road
Pownal, Vermont 05261

Articles and drawings are from *Horticulture* magazine's monthly "Step-by-Step" column.

Cover and interior drawings © Elayne Sears
Edited by Pamela Lappies
Cover design by Woodward Design and Meredith Maker
Text design and production by Meredith Maker
Production assistance by Design + Format
Indexed by Northwind Editorial Service

Printed in the United States by R. R. Donnelley
10 9 8 7 6 5 4 3 2 1

Library of Congress Cataloging-in-Publication Data

Year-round gardening projects / Elayne Sears ; projects by Oliver E. Allen . . . [et al.].
    p.   cm.
    "The articles are arranged by season, as they appeared in
Horticulture"—Introd.
    Includes index.
    ISBN 1-58017-039-0 (pbk. : alk. paper)
    1. Gardening. I. Sears, Elayne. II. Allen, Oliver E. III. Horticulture.
SB453.Y4 1998
635—dc21   97-51994
                                               CIP

When the world wearies and ceases to satisfy,
there is always the garden.

Table of Contents

Contributing Authors

Elayne Sears is an accomplished freelance illustrator whose work regularly appears in many country living and gardening magazines, including *Horticulture, Country Journal, National Gardening,* and *Adirondack Life.* Sears has also illustrated many books for Storey Communications, Inc., including *A Country Wisdom Journal, Garden Way's Joy of Gardening, Country Wines, Feeding the Birds, Successful Small-Scale Farming,* and our series of *Wildflower Gardener's Guides.* Her work is also featured in the *Better Homes & Gardens Step-By-Step Successful Gardening* series, *The Wise Garden Encyclopedia, The Encyclopedia of Organic Gardening, Rodale's Illustrated Encyclopedia of Perennials, Let's Get Growing, The Weekend Garden Guide, The Lives of Whales and Dolphins,* and *The Lives of Birds.* An avid gardener, Sears lives on a small farm in the Adirondacks with her husband and two children, three horses, numerous peacocks and chickens, and a mule.

Oliver E. Allen is a former editor for *Life Magazine* and Time-Life Books. He now works as a freelance editor, and writes for magazines including *Horticulture, American Heritage,* and *Audacity.* Allen is the author of nine books, including *Gardening with New Small Plants, The Vegetable Gardener's Journal,* and Time-Life titles including *Wildflower Gardening, Decorating with Plants, Pruning and Grafting,* and *Shade Gardens.* He lives in New York City.

Nancy Bubel is a freelance writer and gardening columnist for *Country Journal.* Her writing has appeared in *Horticulture, Organic Gardening, Family Circle, Woman's Day* and other magazines. Bubel has written nine books, including *Root Cellaring (Garden Way Publishing), The New Seed Starter's Handbook, Garden Projects, The Country Journal Book of Vegetable Gardening,* and *The Adventurous Gardener.* She lives in Wellsville, Pennsylvania.

Thomas Christopher was Horticulturist for Columbia University for ten years, and is now a freelance garden writer. His work appears in publications including the *New York Times, Horticulture, Town & Country,* and *Natural History.* Christopher is the author of *Waterwise Gardening, Compost This Book!,* and *In Search of Lost Roses,* winner of the Garden Writers Association of America's 1990 "Quill & Trowel Award of Excellence." He lives in Middletown, Connecticut.

Teri Dunn is an editor and award-winning writer. Formerly Associate Editor for *Horticulture Magazine,* she is now a Senior Copy Writer for Jackson & Perkins Co., Medford, Oregon. While at *Horticulture,* Dunn edited the "Step-by-Step" series from which *Gardening Techniques Illustrated* is derived. She lives in Medford, Oregon.

Thomas Fischer is Senior Editor at *Horticulture* magazine where, in addition to his editing duties, he has written more than 30 gardening articles. He holds a Master's degree in English Literature from the University of Chicago. Fischer lives in Jamaica Plain, Massachusetts.

Lee Reich is a horticultural consultant, writer, and lecturer. He holds Master's degrees in Soil Science and in Horticulture from the University of Wisconsin and a Doctorate in Horticulture from the University of Maryland. A frequent contributor to a variety of gardening magazines, he is also the author of *Uncommon Fruits Worthy of Attention: A Gardener's Guide* and *A Northeast Gardener's Year.* Reich lives in New Paltz, New York.

Janet H. Sanchez holds a Master's degree in Anthropology from California State University. A freelance garden writer, she is a frequent contributor to *Horticulture* and *National Gardening* magazines. Sanchez is the author of *Lawns, Groundcovers & Vines* from the *Better Homes & Gardens Step-By-Step Successful Gardening* series. She lives in Santa Rosa, California.

Introduction

Dear Gardener,

When *Horticulture* asked me in 1987 to illustrate their monthly Step-by-Step column, I had no idea of the gardening journey I was about to embark on. Now, some eighty Step-by-Steps later, I feel pretty confidant about attempting most gardening projects. I have, in fact, tried a lot of those in this book and been gratified with the results — thanks to the authors, some of the most respected garden writers around, and the experts at *Horticulture* who carefully edited every step. The gardening information herein is simply the best available.

Since each article was originally intended to stand alone, you will find some procedures repeated from time to time, especially those involving soil preparation and amendments. It doesn't hurt to be reminded not to neglect the most basic foundation of a great garden! The format allows you to quickly study a subject and be off to the garden without doing further research. The articles are arranged by season, as they appeared in *Horticulture*, although some chores can be done any time of year and others extend from one season to the next.

Thanks to my family and all my gardening friends who have helped me over the years by digging, troweling, raking, and planting while I sketched furiously or snapped photos. I've tried to represent gardeners as real people and as all kinds of people, young and old. Thanks to my editor at *Horticulture*, Sarah Boorstyn Schwartz, for all of her good suggestions and for never asking me to remove a beard or clean up a gardener!

Whether you're starting seeds, moving a tree, installing a pond, or dividing perennials, check it out here before you start, and happy gardening.

Elayne Sears

Spring

That God once loved a garden
We learn in Holy writ.
And seeing gardens in the Spring
I well can credit it.

— Winifred Mary Letts

Unpacking Mail-Order Plants

Thomas Christopher

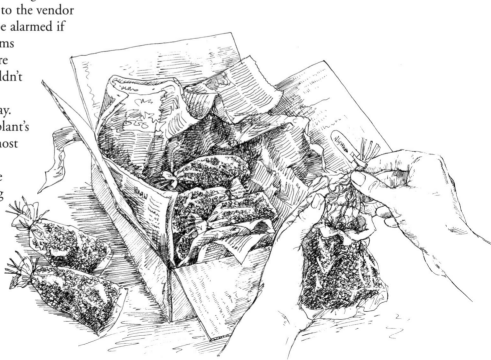

IN LATE WINTER I'm already watching for the arrival of my spring order of perennials. I buy most of my perennials by mail. This requires more planning than when I pick up container-grown plants at the garden center, but ordering by mail does offer advantages. Mail-order nurseries usually offer greater selections of cultivars than local nurseries do, and they save me time as well. With catalogs, I can do my shopping in the evening and keep the daylight hours for outdoor work.

Mail-order gardening does involve one complication. To keep the cost of postage to a reasonable level, nurseries routinely ship plants bare-root — that is, without soil. If dug while dormant and moved to cold storage, the plants will survive long periods without any loss of vitality. However, trouble may begin after they leave the nursery. If the shipper's truck is warm, plants may break dormancy and begin growing in the box. If the trip is prolonged, the plants may dehydrate. Either condition will prove fatal if it persists for more than a day or two. You can guard against this type of damage by paying to have your order shipped by air-freight or by United Parcel Service, thus shortening the trip. But your treatment of the plants upon their arrival is also crucial to success.

1. FIRST AID Open the box of plants as soon as it arrives. If the plants aren't in good condition, promptly return them to the vendor for replacement or credit. Don't be alarmed if you find last year's foliage and stems withered and brown (the plants are dormant, after all), but they shouldn't be broken or shredded, and there should be no sign of mold or decay.

Often a careful search of a plant's crown, the spot where the lowermost leaves join the stems, will reveal dormant buds. They may be quite small and well hidden, but as long as they are plump and firm, the plant is healthy. In many cases you'll find no signs of life in the upper part of the plant. Check its roots, which should be packed in organic mulch and wrapped in plastic. Gently peel the plastic back from one or two of the bundles. If the roots are undamaged, the plant will almost surely revive once planted outdoors.

If the packing material around the roots is dry, trickle in a little water, enough to moisten but not soak the roots. Unless you intend to plant right away, don't disturb the protective wrapping any more than necessary. To store the plants for two or three days, just replace the plants in the shipping carton and set it in a cool, dimly lit space, such as an unheated garage.

2. TEMPORARY QUARTERS Unfortunately, nurseries sometimes prove more prompt than the season, and their plants may arrive while your garden soil is still half-frozen and soggy. Digging soil in that condition will destroy its structure, and you may have to wait several weeks before it dries sufficiently to be worked.

Bareroot plants can't wait that long. If you can't plant them into the border within two or three days, you must furnish them with a temporary home. In the gardener's vernacular, this is called "heeling in." Dig a trench a half spade-length deep in some well-drained, sheltered spot — the side of a south-facing slope is ideal. Fill it with a mixture of one part builder's sand and one part peat moss. The dormant perennials can be planted there until the garden soil is workable and you can transplant them to their final location.

3. PREPARATION FOR PLANTING Whether you are heeling perennials into a prepared trench or planting them directly from the shipping box into the bed or border, you should prepare them for the move. Unwrap the plants and gently remove all packing material. With a sharp pair of shears, snip off any broken roots. Then set the plants to soak for an hour or two in a weak solution of soluble fertilizer (no more than quarter strength) to get them off to a good start.

4. PLANTING Treat bareroot perennials as you would any other perennial, with one exception: Do not let their exposed roots dry out. Carry the plants to the garden in their bucket of fertilizer-water, and don't remove them until you are ready to set each one in the soil. Once they are planted, water them well. Then cover them for two or three days with an overturned bushel basket. Shielding the plants from the wind protects them from dehydration while the roots, at long last, awaken.

Spring Lawn Care

Oliver E. Allen

ALTHOUGH THE MAJOR WORK in renovating or reconditioning a lawn should be done in the late summer or early fall in most parts of the United States, a few simple steps taken in the spring will enable you to get your lawn off to a strong start for the new year. For while winter's cold toughens grass and strengthens its roots, it may also leave a lawn looking ragged. Most greenswards, therefore, benefit from additional preparation at the start of the season.

The best time to ready your lawn for the new year is in early spring, after the ground has thawed but before heavy rains have made it soft or muddy, and before the grass itself has started to grow. The soil should be moderately dry and workable.

1. TEST FOR PH If you have had your soil tested for pH within the past year, there is no need to repeat the process, as the results should be good for at least a couple of years. But if you have not done so, take care of it now. The most foolproof method is to take soil samples from several spots in your yard, place these in separate containers, label each sample, and send them to the nearest cooperative-extension office for analysis. The results will include recommendations for correcting any imbalance. The trouble with this route is that agents tend to be terribly busy, especially in the spring, and may take several weeks to respond.

A quicker (if less precise) alternative is to buy a soil-testing kit from a garden center and do the job yourself. The kits are easy to use and the results close enough for most purposes. Be sure to test a number of samples from different spots in your yard. If the outcome suggests that ground limestone should be added (to reduce acidity), buy it now but do not apply it until you have completed the next two steps.

2. RAKE OR SWEEP THOROUGHLY Most lawns will have accumulated twigs, patches of leaves, and even small branches during the winter. Now is the time to remove them, plus any thick layers of thatch, either by using a mechanical sweeper or a special thatching rake. If you rake, be sure to do so gently lest you uproot existing grass shoots or dislodge pieces of sod, which may have been loosened by the winter's frost heaves. Gently tamp down any loose sods with your foot. Do not use a weighted roller on them; rolling, once considered to be a standard spring operation, is now deemed harmful in most situations, as it compacts the soil unduly.

3. PATCH BARE SPOTS Repair any places where the grass has worn away, either by laying down sod (available at garden centers) or by seeding. Sod gives more immediate results, but it can be used only in places that receive full sun. To install sod, remove enough soil where you are

patching so that the sod will be level with the surrounding turf, scarify, or loosen, the new surface, lay in your sod, tamp it down by foot or with a roller, then water well; repeat the tamping and watering every other day or so for the next two weeks, or until you are certain the new grass is growing well. To seed the same area, scarify its surface, scatter seed on it, dust the area with fertilizer, cover the seed by raking the soil lightly with your rake turned upside down, then water with a gentle spray, taking care not to dislodge any seed; keep the soil moist by watering occasionally until the new grass has sprouted and reached a height of at least two inches (5 cm). You can use the same seed for patching as you have used on the rest of the lawn, but you may prefer to use one of the recently developed perennial rye grasses. They sprout faster and more copiously than ordinary grasses and will blend well with other strains.

  With the lawn cleaned and patched, you can now apply any ground limestone that has been recommended. Be sure to spread it evenly over the entire lawn.

4. FERTILIZE LATER While tradition dictates that you apply fertilizer to your lawn as soon as you have readied it in the spring, there is no need to do so immediately (except for the spots that have been seeded). Even without fertilizer the grass should begin growing vigorously when warm weather arrives; it needs no extra stimulus. Better to wait until the main surge of growth has passed and you have already mowed the lawn once or twice — until late May, say, or early June. A generous feeding at that stage will be especially beneficial to the roots of the grass and should provide your carpet of green with the necessary nourishment to last through most of the summer.

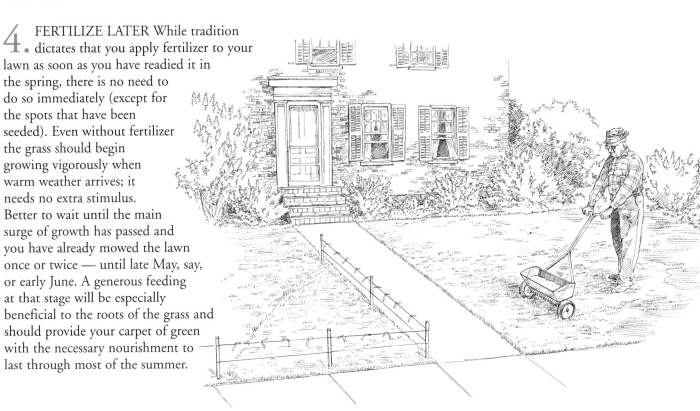

Building Raised Beds

Janet H. Sanchez

MY HUSBAND and I have built many raised beds over the years. Raised beds provide plants, especially vegetables, with ideal conditions in which to grow. The deep soil in these beds allows maximum root growth, drains easily, and warms up earlier in spring. Also, water and fertilizer can be concentrated where they are needed.

The simplest raised beds are made by piling soil into the areas designated for planting. There are several advantages, however, to using beds bounded with boards. If your soil, like ours, is heavy clay or full of rocks, you can set these bottomless boxes on top of the problem soil and fill them with improved, fertile soil. The boards will prevent the good soil from eroding away. The boards also provide a solid place to attach a trellis for climbers such as peas or morning glories, or a framework for bird netting or shade cloth. And if you line the bottom of a raised bed with chicken wire, you can easily control gophers and other marauding rodents.

Finally, when enclosed, raised beds give a garden an organized look. Three or four will permit crop rotation. Try arranging several to form an interesting pattern. Installing paths around them — mulched, graveled, or planted to lawn — will keep your feet out of the mud and enhance the overall design.

1. GATHER SUPPLIES Rot-resistant redwood or cedar is ideal for building raised beds. Local lumberyards may offer other relatively durable softwoods such as tamarack or cypress; look for two-inch (5 cm) rough- or utility-grade planks. We've even used one-inch (2.5 cm) plywood recycled from a construction project. Although it rotted after five or six years, it was economical, and using it may have helped save a tree or two. Avoid using pressure-treated wood or water-repellent wood preservatives, as there are questions about the safety of these products when used near edible plants.

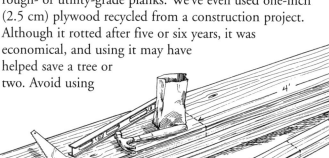

It's best to make these boxes no wider than four feet (1.2 m) so that you can reach the middle of the bed easily. Length can vary, though those longer than 10 feet (3 m) ought to have stakes along their sides to prevent bulging, as should ones of any size constructed of one-inch (2.5 cm) plywood. Plan to make your boxes at least 12 inches (30 cm) deep to allow plenty of room for roots.

To make the four-by-eight-foot (1.2 by 2.4 m), 12-inch-deep (30 cm) box shown here, you'll need three boards that are eight feet long, one foot wide, and two inches thick. Also, have on hand a four-foot (1.2 m), two-by-four-inch (5 by 10 cm) piece of lumber and about a pound (.45 kg) of 12d or 16d galvanized nails.

Use two of the eight-foot (2.4 m) boards for the sides of the box; cut the remaining one in half to form the ends. To make the corner posts, cut the two-by-four (5 by 10) into four segments, each one foot (30 cm) long.

2. CONSTRUCT THE BOX Build the box on a hard, level surface, such as a patio or a driveway. To make one side, lay one of the eight-foot (2.4 m) boards flat, and place a corner post (with the four-inch [10 cm] side flat against the board) under each end. Line up each post carefully so that its edge is parallel with the end of the board and fasten the pieces with four or five nails. Arrange the nails in an off-set pattern to help prevent the wood from splitting. Repeat this step with the other eight-foot (2.4 m) plank and the remaining two corner posts.

Next, stand one of the sides, complete with corner posts, on edge and line one of the end boards up with it.

Drive three nails through the end board into the sawed end of the long board and three or four more nails through both end board and corner post. You have now finished half of the box.

Nail the other end board in place, then sandwich the remaining eight-foot (2.4 m) side between the ends and nail it into place to complete the box.

3. POSITION THE BOX With a helper, carry the box to its permanent site. When placing the raised bed, remember to allow at least 30 inches (76 cm) between it and other structures so that there is room to maneuver a wheelbarrow or lawn mower. And for maximum sunlight, orient it with the long sides running from north to south.

Use a carpenter's level to check that the top of the box is even all the way around. If not, move the box aside temporarily and dig trenches to accommodate the sides that are too high. The box will settle unevenly if you try to level it by placing it on built-up soil or fill.

4. PREPARE THE BOX FOR PLANTING Loosen the top few inches of soil at the bottom of the box to aid drainage. If you need to foil rodents in your garden, cut a piece of chicken wire or hardware cloth about four inches (10 cm) larger than the inside dimensions of the box. Lay the wire inside the box, bend the edges up against the sides, and secure it to the boards and corner posts every few inches all the way around with staples or bent-over nails.

Now, fill the raised bed with equal parts of compost and good topsoil. (Look under "Topsoil" in the Yellow Pages for sources.) Water the bed well and be prepared to add a little more soil before planting, as some settling will occur.

Making a Compost Pile

Janet H. Sanchez

COMPOSTING GIVES A GARDEN new life from old by recycling fallen leaves, grass clippings, and other organic materials into humus, a dark crumbly substance that enriches and improves the soil. As our landfills fill up, it is increasingly necessary to deal with garden debris right in our yards rather than dispose of such potentially useful materials.

Given a year or more, a pile of organic leftovers will decompose all by itself. However, with a little extra effort, you can create optimum conditions for the microorganisms responsible for decay by giving them the mixture of air, water, and nutrients they need. When these microorganisms are flourishing, a pile heats up quickly, killing most weed seeds and disease organisms. In only a few months, the compost will be ready for use.

1. STOCKPILE INGREDIENTS Your compost will heat up more quickly if you collect the ingredients in advance and assemble the pile all at once. Collect the materials you'll need for several weeks, storing them in small piles, bags, or trash cans.

Although there is no exact recipe for making compost, decay-producing organisms appreciate a diet of roughly equal amounts of high-carbon and high-nitrogen materials. Carbon-rich materials are dry or brown, and include straw, leaves, small prunings, sawdust, and shredded newspaper. Materials high in nitrogen are fresh and often green like grass clippings and young weeds. Kitchen scraps such as vegetable peelings, crushed eggshells, and coffee grounds are high in nitrogen as well. Avoid meat scraps, fats, and dairy products, which may attract rodents. Farm animal manures are a useful nitrogen-rich material, but don't use dog or cat droppings, which may carry diseases.

For even faster finished compost, cut thick materials such as vines and broccoli stems into small pieces. If you have a lot of leaves, shred them with a mower first.

2. PREPARE THE WIRE BINS Wire bins help keep a composting operation tidy. I like to have two side by side so it is easier to turn the compost when the time comes. Make sure the bins are within reach of a hose. Placing them on open ground, rather than on pavement, allows excess water to drain away and soil organisms to enter the pile.

The bins should be four feet (1.2 m) in diameter since smaller piles don't have enough mass to heat up. As for height, most gardeners find that three-foot (.9 m) fencing is tall enough — it's difficult to heft material over a higher enclosure.

Anything from poultry netting to snow fencing will make good bins. Set up the wire in a circle. Bend back any projecting pieces, and fasten the two ends together in three or four places with lengths of flexible wire. If you are using one-inch (2.5 cm) poultry netting, drive several four-foot (1.2 m) wooden or metal stakes into the ground just inside the perimeter of each bin to provide extra support; sturdier sorts of fencing will stand on their own.

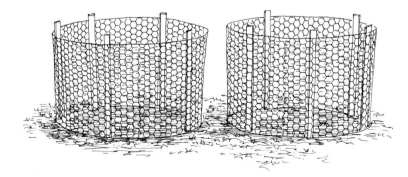

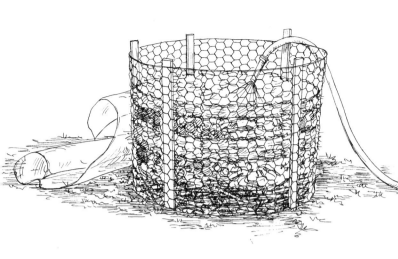

3. MAKE THE PILE Start the pile by placing several inches of a coarse material such as sunflower or cornstalks in one of the bins. This allows some air to enter the bottom. Then alternate the carbon- and nitrogen-rich materials in four-inch (10 cm) layers. Exact measurements aren't critical, but try to keep the layers equal.

Water as you progress, making the pile damp but not soggy. When you are finished, cover the pile loosely with a piece of plastic or fiberglass to keep the moisture level constant.

4. TURN THE PILE In a few days, the pile will become hot, reaching 130° to 150°F (54° to 65.5°C) in the center. After another five to seven days, the temperature will peak and the pile will begin to cool. It will shrink considerably and become fairly compact.

At this point, you need to replenish the air supply required by the microorganisms at work in the interior. Using a spading fork or pitchfork, transfer the partially finished compost into the second bin, making sure that the coarser materials that were at the outside of the original pile are now at the center of the new one. Water if needed. The job will be easier if you peel off the wire frame and set it aside first.

The pile will heat up again, although not as much as before. Let it sit and finish decaying slowly or, if you wish, turn it one or two more times at two-week intervals to hasten the composting process.

5. USE THE FINISHED COMPOST Begin using your compost when most of the materials have broken down and are no longer recognizable. It may be fairly coarse. Spread it as is on the vegetable garden or around ornamentals, or sift it through a half-inch (1.25 cm) mesh screen to produce a finer material. The coarse residue left after sifting makes a good starter for a new pile. If you wish to store some of the finished compost for future use, cover it so rain won't leach out the nutrients.

Building a Cold Frame

Janet H. Sanchez

A COLD FRAME is simply a box with a transparent cover or lid that is used to protect plants during the colder months. During the day the sun's rays heat the air and soil within the frame, creating a favorable environment for plant growth. At night, stored heat keeps the temperature inside the box warmer than the outside temperature, reducing the chance of frost or freeze damage.

The usefulness of a cold frame far outweighs the modest expense and effort involved in its construction. In spring, it provides an ideal environment for hardening off annual flower and vegetable seedlings started indoors. Come summer, the same structure (its cover replaced with lath or shade cloth) can serve as a nursery for young biennials or perennials. Many gardeners extend their vegetable harvest into late fall by sowing fast-growing greens directly in a cold frame in late summer. I've also used my cold frame to overwinter rooted cuttings and potted bulbs destined for early-spring forcing.

1. SELECT A COVER An old window sash or storm window works well as a cover or top — its size will determine the cold frame's dimensions. If you don't happen to have one on hand, recycled windows are often available at salvage yards or garage sales.

Alternatively, you can make a cover out of clear sheets of acrylic or fiberglass sandwiched between narrow strips of wood and reinforced at the corners with metal corner plates. You can even use inexpensive polyethylene film stapled to a similarly reinforced wooden frame, although the film usually lasts for only a year or so. (Some hardware stores carry thicker, longer-lasting 10-mil plastic.)

When choosing a cover, be certain that it isn't too wide; otherwise you won't be able to reach the plants easily. Two and a half to three feet (.8 to .9 m) is a convenient width, while a length of at least four feet (1.2 m) will allow your cold frame to accommodate a variety of plants.

2. BUILD THE COLD FRAME Plan to have your frame slope from about 18 inches (46 cm) high at the back to 12 inches (30 cm) at the front. This design gives your plants headroom yet allows rainwater to run off and helps trap sunlight.

The box itself can be built of inch-thick (2.5 cm) redwood or cedar, both of which are naturally rot-resistant. More economical (albeit less durable) choices are five-eighths-inch-thick (1.6 cm) pieces of plywood or common lumber.

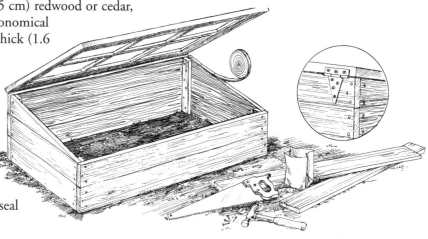

For strength, reinforce the corners of the box with vertical one-by-two-inch (2.5 by 5 cm) posts, making sure the posts are flush with the top of the box. Use galvanized nails to construct the frame, or screws if you plan to disassemble it for seasonal storage.

Attach the cover to the back of the frame with galvanized steel T-hinges and screws, and apply weather stripping around the edges to help seal the crack between the frame and the cover.

3. CHOOSE A SITE Place your cold frame in a spot that is protected from harsh winds by trees, shrubs, a fence, or a wall. A south-facing exposure is ideal for maximum sun, but in a pinch, an east- or west-facing location will do. It's also a good idea to locate the frame fairly close to the house, since you will want to check on your plants frequently and have easy access to water.

4. OPERATION Ventilation is vital to prevent the small volume of air in your cold frame from overheating and killing your plants. As a general guideline, it's wise to prop open the cover a few inches when the interior temperature reaches 70° to 75°F (21° to 24°C). Open it wider if the temperature continues to rise. I've found that a minimum-maximum thermometer is the best way to track temperature fluctuations inside the cold frame.

If you aren't going to be around to check the frame during the day, invest in a nonelectric vent controller that automatically opens and closes the cover at a preset temperature. However, be aware that the strongest models can raise only 20 pounds (9 kg).

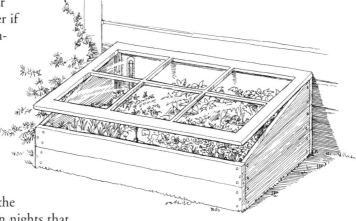

As for the plants, keep them moist but not soggy. In warm weather daily watering may be necessary, especially for young plants in small pots. To help prevent disease, water in the morning so the foliage has a chance to dry before evening. On nights that threaten to be unusually cold, toss an old blanket or piece of carpet over the frame to further insulate the plants inside.

How to Plant Potatoes

Nancy Bubel

POTATOES ARE ONE of the first food crops you can plant in spring. Like peas, spinach, and onion sets, they are planted as soon as the ground is dry enough to dig. If your garden is slow to thaw, don't worry. As long as you get the crop planted four weeks before your last frost, it should do well.

To start your potato patch, buy "certified" seed potatoes, which have been inspected to assure they are disease-free. Don't plant home-grown potatoes with the corky blemishes typical of scab (or with symptoms of other diseases), because this disease will pass on to the next generation. And don't plant potatoes purchased from food markets — they are not reliable for use as seed potatoes because they have been sprayed to retard sprouting.

Seed-potato cultivars like 'Kennebec' and 'Norland' are commonly available in hardward stores and garden centers, where you may also be able to find old favorites like 'Green Mountain' and 'Cobbler'. You'll probably have to mail-order special kinds like 'Butte', an excellent baker, and 'Yukon Gold' and 'Yellow Finn', both golden-fleshed cultivars.

1. ENCOURAGE SPROUTING I like to presprout seed potatoes before I put them in the ground. Exposing them to light encourages them to form nubs of growing shoots from the eyes (each eye is a dormant bud). Plants treated by "chitting," as this process is called, root quickly and mature earlier than those without sprouts. Chitting is simple: Just spread the potatoes in a sunny indoor place for two to three weeks before planting.

2. CUT AND DRY Cutting removes the dominance of the eyes grouped at one end of the potato and encourages all of them to sprout. About a week before planting time, cut each large seed potato into pieces weighing about three or four ounces with one to two eyes each. Spread the pieces out in a single layer for a few days. The dried flesh is less likely to rot than raw cut surfaces once planted out in the cold, wet soil typical of an early-spring garden.

Why not plant a whole potato? Because the many eyes on a large potato will grow into a multistemmed plant that bears many small potatoes. There are two exceptions: You may leave small (egg-size) potatoes whole, and some mail-order potatoes for seed are shipped as marble-size plugs cut from whole tubers. The latter look skimpy and often develop more slowly, but the resulting plants have usually made satisfactory yields in my garden.

3. PREPARE A FURROW Potatoes like loose, well-drained soil. Wait until the soil has dried enough to be workable, so it will be well broken up into fine crumbs. Soggy soil studded with clods discourages the growth of any plant or seed.

Hoe each furrow about three or four inches deep. Rows in the garden should be 30 to 36 inches (76 to 91 cm) apart, wide enough to permit tilling, hilling, or mulching between them. If you plant in a raised bed, the furrows can be closer, about a foot (30 cm) or so apart. I have had good luck planting potatoes in a series of two or three rows in a 30- to 36-inch-wide (76 to 91 cm) raised bed.

In any case, enrich the furrow with an inch or two (2.5 or 5 cm) of compost, well-aged manure, or bagged dehydrated manure. (Do not use fresh manure, as it may encourage disease.) Mix it with the soil in the bottom of the furrow.

4. PLANTING Set the seed-potato pieces in place about 10 or 12 inches (25 or 30 cm) apart in the furrow. (In the rich soil of a raised bed, you can plant them slightly closer.) Plant them cut-side down, so the eye will be uppermost, and press them firmly into the soft soil. Then rake about three inches (7.5 cm) of fine loose soil over them. Mark the row so you won't dig it up to plant radishes before the leafy sprouts appear.

5. HILLING UP The new crop of potatoes will form above, not below, the seed potatoes you planted. Hilling up the row gives them an easily penetrated mound of soil to grow into and prevents greening from exposure to the sun. (Green potatoes are unfit to eat because they contain the toxic alkaloid solanine.)

Hilling is easier if done right after rototilling the paths between the rows or beds, when the soil is loose and deeply worked. If you garden with hand tools, use a garden fork to loosen the soil first.

Use a hoe or rake to draw up the loose soil from the aisles, banking it high over the potato plants but leaving four or five inches (10 or 12.5 cm) of stem and leaf uncovered.

Layering a Rhododendron

Oliver E. Allen

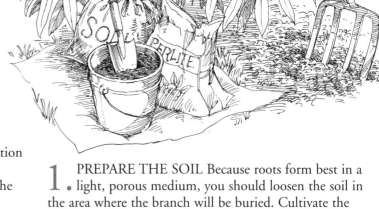

SOME PLANTS MULTIPLY themselves by putting down roots from pendulous branches that touch the ground. The forsythia is one of the most notorious examples — it roots so readily it can become invasive if left untended. The phenomenon is known as layering, and it can be used as a remarkably simple way to propagate plants — especially woody ones — for which neither seeds nor cuttings are satisfactory methods. An elegant rhododendron that you'd like to duplicate would be a prime candidate. What you do, in effect, is bury a section of a branch in the ground. If you follow certain precautions roots form, and before long you can cut the new plant loose to exist on its own.

The botanical key to the process is a cut that you make in the branch before burying it. The wound interrupts the flow of nutrients, causing sugars to accumulate, and this seems to promote the formation of roots. The parent plant supplies some nourishment to its offspring until you separate the two and is in no way harmed by the exercise.

Although several kinds of layering are practiced (such as air layering, in which the wound is enclosed in sphagnum moss and wrapped with plastic but the branch is not buried), so-called ground layering is the simplest. The job is best begun in the early spring when the ground can be worked but before new growth has started. To layer a rhododendron you will want to select a healthy, young shoot low enough on the plant to be bent to the ground; the older and woodier the branch, the less likely it is to root. To be sure of results, try layering two or three shoots (so long as you can find young, low ones predisposed to layering). The only supplies you need are root-promoting powder (available in any garden center), a forked twig or short length of heavy wire, some peat moss (or compost or leaf mold) and sand or perlite, and a sharp knife.

1. PREPARE THE SOIL Because roots form best in a light, porous medium, you should loosen the soil in the area where the branch will be buried. Cultivate the soil; break up any lumps; add a good heap of peat moss, compost, or leaf mold, plus some sand or perlite; and mix thoroughly. Remove enough of the resulting mix to leave a shallow hole three inches (7.5 cm) deep.

2. WOUND THE BRANCH Using your knife, make a cut about halfway through the branch on its underside, preferably near a node or branching point and six to eight inches (15 to 20 cm) from the end. Do not flinch; a common mistake is to make the cut too shallow to induce root growth. Wedge a sliver of wood (a wooden match stick serves nicely) into the cut to keep it open, and dust the newly bared wood with rooting powder.

3. SECURE AND BURY Lay the branch into the hole with the cut at the lowest point (facing downward) and the end pointing up and out the other side. Anchor the branch using your forked twig or heavy wire (bent like a staple); otherwise the wind will soon dislodge the whole affair. Once the branch is securely pinned, you may want to insert some soil behind the part leading out of the hole to point it more sharply upward, thus giving the resulting plant a straighter stem; but be careful not to bend it so much as to break it. Some gardeners loosely attach the tip of the branch to a stake to guide it vertically. Fill the hole with the soil mix and tamp well with your feet.

4. KEEP THE SOIL MOIST Except for one paramount concern, you need pay no attention to the layered branch for at least a year. The concern — and it is vital — is that the soil around the buried section remain moist. Dryness can swiftly kill young rootlets, and if the ground is dry for even a day as the roots are forming, the new plant may be lost. The solution is to keep a good mulch in place over the layered area (black plastic is a particularly efficient moisture conserver) and to keep an eye on weather conditions during the warm months. During any rainless spell pull back the mulch every other day or so and feel the soil. If it is on the dry side, give it a good but gentle soaking and replace the plastic.

5. SEPARATE THE NEW PLANT For reasons no one really understands, the amount of time needed for new roots to develop varies widely among genera. Rhododendrons root very slowly, and it is likely to take at least a year and more likely two for roots to grow. The trick is in determining when roots have become sufficiently established and when to sever the plant. Since the shoot can put on new top growth without putting down roots, you cannot rely on that measure. One way to check is to lift the staple and gently tug on the shoot. If it offers resistance, roots have formed. Do not expose the rooting area to the air for long or it will dry out. When the roots are well established, sever the supporting branch near the soil line (and then cut the resulting branch stub back to the nearest node or to another branch for appearance's sake). The young plant is best left in place for a month or two after it has been severed to ensure that its roots are well established. At that point it can be transplanted.

Establishing a Hedge

Oliver E. Allen

HEDGES ARE WHAT you might call multipurpose plantings: they are commonly called upon to perform such disparate functions as enhancing a landscape design, providing privacy from prying eyes, barring entry to people or (more commonly) animals, blunting the force of the wind, or simply acting as a background screen for other plants and flowers. They can assume many shapes and aspects, but often the desire is for a formal planting, the hedge's sides and top sheared rigorously and evenly to create a classic smooth-sided green wall.

Many kinds of plants can be used to make a formal hedge — for example, boxwood, holly, hemlock, and yew; each has its enthusiasts. A particularly popular plant, however, is privet, which (1) is easy to shape, (2) grows fast (a good-size hedge can be achieved in just a few years) and reasonably thickly (despite being deciduous), and (3) is tough (hardy in all but the very coldest regions) and resilient. I recall one February blizzard that absolutely flattened my 75-foot-long (23 m) privet hedge. There was barely a sign of it above the snowdrifts. Three months later, rebounding, it was growing lustily at its former uniform five-foot (1.5 m) height. Here, therefore, are some pointers on privet growing.

Because bushy growth from near the ground is essential in formal hedging, your privets must be planted properly and then pruned with what might otherwise seem excessive zeal. But first you need to decide what sort of plants to buy and how many. Get young plants, not more than two or three years old (they will come bare-rooted), and figure on a plant every foot or so. The best times to plant are spring and fall. One caution: If the hedge is to mark the edge of your property, be sure to position it at least two feet (.6 m) inside the line. Good hedges do not necessarily make good neighbors.

1. **DIG A TRENCH** To provide the best growing medium, dig a trench at least a foot (30 cm) deep and a foot and a half (46 cm) wide all along the route of your hedge. Break up the bottom surface with a fork and mix in organic matter into the soil you set aside; then fill up the trench almost to the surface. You can add fertilizer (5-10-5 is a good formula) if you know from a soil test that your soil is extra poor or you want truly swift growth, but it is not absolutely necessary. Tamp down the mix by treading on it lightly — do not compact it.

2. **SET THE PLANTS IN** Set the plants along the center of the trench, working soil around and among the roots. Allow the plants to sit a trifle deep: if the texture of the bark reveals where the soil line has been, lower them about an inch (2.5 cm), but otherwise simply make sure they are well down. To ensure planting in a straight line you may want to stretch a string over the trench or, alternatively, mark the line beforehand with stakes. Fill up the trench most of the way but leave a slight depression in the ground to facilitate watering; tamp again. Apply a good organic mulch and water the entire planting thoroughly. At this point, incidentally, you may want to snake a temporary chicken-wire barrier along the plant line to prevent animals from passing through, keeping it in place until the hedge has achieved its full height and density; by that time the wire will have disintegrated.

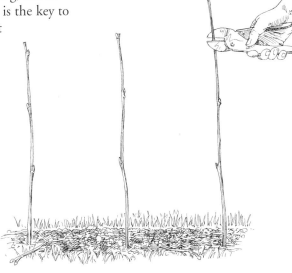

3. PRUNE HEAVILY Now comes the brutal part. Right after planting, cut all your privet plants back to a height of about two feet (.6 m). This is the key to the entire drill, for only when it is cut will privet branch, and you want it to start branching right at ground level. While the hedge will certainly look puny at first, it will soon respond by producing abundant shoots below the point where it has been cut and, because of the rich soil mix you have provided, growing at full tilt.

4. SLOPE THE SIDES As the multiple stems begin to shoot up, start shaping your fledgling hedge by pruning its sides so that they slope inward slightly from base to top. This is another key point: although privet will probably grow adequately in poor light, it will tend to concentrate its growth in its upper reaches and allow its lower branches to die back unless you permit plenty of light to reach the lower half.

5. KEEP PRUNING REGULARLY The fledgling hedge should be cut back again once or twice the first year; each time, remove half to two-thirds of the new growth to promote further branching. Until the hedge reaches its desired full height, continue pruning in this manner two or three times a year (while maintaining the sloping sides). No further fertilizing should be needed, for the privet will grow swiftly enough. When the hedge is at its optimum height you can either shape the top to be rounded or pointed or leave it flat; the decision is entirely a matter of taste, although rounded and pointed tops shed snow better than flat ones.

Thereafter, the hedge should be pruned at least once a year depending on how fast it puts out new shoots. If only one pruning is called for, the best time is in late June or early July after the privet has completed its major new growth for the year; additional shearings can be done earlier in the spring or, if necessary, in September (but not too close to frost time). If despite its annual shearing it gradually gets taller, do not hesitate to cut back into older wood — the privet will take this in stride. And if despite its sloping sides the hedge loses its bottom growth, the remedy is again drastic: cut it all the way down to that initial two feet (.6 m) and start over. Do not fear, the hedge will not die. In no time at all those energetic privet plants will be totally restored to full size and to an eminently satisfying bushiness.

Laying a Flagstone Path

Lee Reich

TO MAKE A FLAGSTONE PATH as durable and solid beneath your feet as it appears to your eyes, each stone needs firm footing on a well-drained base. Base preparation is even more critical where the soil freezes in winter or where the soil is high in clay. And on ground that slopes more than a foot (30 cm) every 10 feet (3 m), you may want to consider putting in steps in conjunction with the path.

Flagstone paving can be made from any type of horizontally layered rock that can be split into flat slabs, or flags. Arizona sandstone, Pennsylvania bluestone, and slate are among such rocks. Artificial flagstone may be made of concrete, cast into slabs, and dyed the yellow, buff, tawny-red, or gray color of natural stone.

In any case, use one- to two-inch-thick (2.5 to 5 cm) flagstone for paving. Irregularly shaped flags lend a casual air to a path, while square and rectangular flags create a sense of order and formality.

1. PLANNING THE PATH In planning a path, consider its purpose. Jogs or curves slow footsteps and might be what is needed where you want to encourage a prolonged look at a choice planting. Where footsteps will be hurried, such as from the back door to the vegetable garden, lay out a straight path. Bear in mind that two people strolling together along a major garden path — even two intimate people — need a path four to five feet (1.2 to 1.5 m) wide. Eighteen inches (46 cm) is adequate for a small, secondary path for one person.

Sprinkle pulverized limestone on the ground to outline the proposed path. For a straight path, guide yourself with strings and stakes. To achieve smooth bends on a curved path, use two garden hoses to mark the edges, and measure across at intervals to keep the path's width constant.

2. DIGGING OUT THE SOIL Remove existing soil to a depth of at least four inches (10 cm). If the site is soggy (especially in winter), allow for more drainage by digging out more soil, up to 12 inches (30 cm) if necessary.

You won't need the excavated soil, so shovel it directly into a wheelbarrow. Sprinkle this excess soil between the layers of a compost pile, or stockpile it for use in potting mixes.

3. ESTABLISHING A BASE Shovel porous drainage material such as coarse sand or stone dust into the excavated area, tamping and smoothing it with a board as you proceed. This material will provide a solid base for the path and prevent water from collecting and freezing beneath the flagstones.

Fill in with enough drainage material so that the topsides of the stones will be a half-inch (1.25 cm) above ground level after they're set in place. Make the center or one side of the path an inch (2.5 cm) higher than the rest so that surface water will run off.

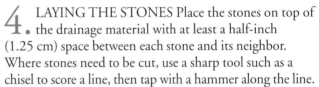

4. LAYING THE STONES Place the stones on top of the drainage material with at least a half-inch (1.25 cm) space between each stone and its neighbor. Where stones need to be cut, use a sharp tool such as a chisel to score a line, then tap with a hammer along the line.

Step back periodically as you work to assess your design, especially when laying randomly shaped stones. A pleasing design is random, but not dizzying, and there shouldn't be continuous joints between consecutive pairs of stones along the length of the path.

Once you are pleased with the layout, settle each stone into place by giving it a few slight twists, then tap it several times with a mallet.

5. FILLING IN BETWEEN STONES Shovel additional sand or stone dust on top of the stones, then sweep the material with a broom to fill the spaces between the stones. Further settle the material into the gaps with a light sprinkling of water from a fine-spray hose. Allow a few days for settling, then repeat the shoveling, sweeping, and watering down.

Plants growing between the stones always give a path a softened appearance. Moss is attractive, but establishing it is chancy — try sprinkling the path daily for a few weeks to encourage wind-borne moss spores to gain a foothold.

Thyme, especially woolly thyme, and chamomile are appealing and easy to establish between stones. Either sow seeds directly, covering them with the sand or stone dust and watering lightly until seedlings take, or insert small plants into slits made with a knife. Once the plants have filled in, no further care is needed except occasional tidying up and weeding. When trod upon, both of these plants yield the additional pleasure of their fragrances.

Planting a Container-Grown Shrub

Thomas Christopher

THE OLDER WRITER who guided my first steps into journalism charged a unique tuition: For every lesson in writing he gave me, I had to dig, ball and burlap, and transplant one of the six-foot-tall (1.8 m) rhododendrons that obscured the lower windows of his house. No doubt that's why I appreciate the convenience of container-grown shrubs so much now.

Rhododendrons and other shrubs that have been raised in containers are far easier to handle than the more traditional balled-and-burlapped (B&B) specimens. Because a container-grown plant's root ball is sheathed in rigid plastic or metal, it is less vulnerable to damage during the trip from the nursery to your yard. And whereas B&B shrubs should be planted immediately, container-grown shrubs can wait a couple of weeks without harm. Finally, the roots of a container-grown shrub suffer less disturbance in the course of transplanting, usually escaping the trauma that afflicts newly planted B&B stock.

As I learned from my mentor, everything has its price. Unless you give a container-grown shrub special treatment at planting time, it may never establish itself in its new home. Instead, it will die a year or two later, seemingly without provocation. Luckily, though, it's not hard to prevent this sad event.

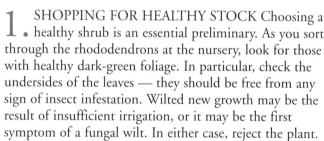

1. SHOPPING FOR HEALTHY STOCK Choosing a healthy shrub is an essential preliminary. As you sort through the rhododendrons at the nursery, look for those with healthy dark-green foliage. In particular, check the undersides of the leaves — they should be free from any sign of insect infestation. Wilted new growth may be the result of insufficient irrigation, or it may be the first symptom of a fungal wilt. In either case, reject the plant.

When you find a specimen you like, have someone at the nursery ease it out of its container so that you can inspect the root ball. You should see roots emerging to encircle a ball of earth. If the soil is entirely hidden by a tangled mass of roots, the shrub has been in the container too long and its growth has been stunted.

2. PREPARING THE PLANTING HOLE Dig a hole at least twice as wide as the shrub's root ball and one and a half times as deep. Sift out any rocks or other debris from the soil removed from the hole. Then blend in an equal volume of organic material such as peat moss or compost (don't skimp). The medium in which your plant was potted is light, loose, and organic, ideally suited to root growth. Unless you thoroughly enrich the hole's soil now, the roots will never expand beyond the original ball and the plant will gradually starve or die of thirst.

3. READYING THE ROOT BALL Tip the plant on its side and slip it out of its container. If it doesn't come readily, slit the container open with a pair of tin snips. Use a sharp knife to make four longitudinal cuts at even intervals around the root ball, slicing about an inch into the soil.

This simple surgery will sever any roots that have grown in a circle around the root ball. Though these girdling roots may not be harming the shrub now, they will gradually strangle it as it grows.

You may also encourage a healthy pattern of root growth at this time by teasing a few of the longer roots loose from the surface of the root ball so that you can direct them outward when you plant.

4. PLANTING Set the rhododendron's root ball into the hole, tucking enough of the amended soil under it to raise the shrub's crown (the point where the trunk meets the roots) to a level even with the surface of the surrounding soil. Be sure not to sink the roots deeper than they were in the container, for even an extra inch (2.5 cm) will smother them.

Backfill around the root ball, tamping down the soil with the handle of your shovel so that no air spaces are left to dry out the roots. Once the hole is filled, use any excess soil to surround the shrub with a dike a couple of inches high; this will trap extra water to keep the roots moist. Fill the dish of soil with water several times to thoroughly soak the roots. Then blanket it with an inch (2.5 cm) of mulch as added insurance against dehydration.

5. WATERING The compact root balls of container-grown shrubs make them particularly vulnerable to drought. The amount of irrigation your rhododendron demands will vary according to the porosity of the surrounding soil, but you'll probably have to water twice a week through the heat of the summer. When you water, water slowly and deeply, for the moisture must penetrate all the way to the bottom of the rhododendron's root system.

Dividing a Shrub

Lee Reich

ANY SHRUB THAT PRODUCES suckers (new shoots originating below ground) can be propagated easily and quickly by division. This method of propagation will provide you with young, vigorous shrubs in place of one that has become old and excessively woody at its center. Spireas respond well to division, as do kerrias, lilacs, oak-leaf hydrangeas, Siberian dogwoods, fragrant sumacs, and many others.

The best time to divide a shrub is in early spring while it is still dormant, just before new growth begins. To do this, you'll need a long-bladed spade and gloves to protect your hands. Before you begin, sharpen the spade with a file. A sharp spade will make it easier to divide the shrub. It also will make clean cuts that heal quickly.

1. DIGGING UP THE ROOT BALL You must first free the shrub — a spirea, in this case — from the soil by severing its roots. Push your sharpened spade down into the soil six inches (15 cm) or so away from the crown, with the blade angled to get under the plant. Work all the way around, levering the root ball upward. As you free the plant from the soil, bounce the handle up and down to shake some of the adhering soil loose. This will make it easier for you to see what you are doing in subsequent steps.

2. TAKING THE CROWN APART This part of the project may be difficult, depending on the size of the shrub. Have additional tools handy in case you need them: an ax, heavy loppers, and a couple of garden forks.

Once the root ball is free, begin separating it into pieces. Each piece should have one or more shoots with some roots attached. Spread the spirea's branches apart so you can look down into the crown, then make cuts with your shovel. If the crown is very woody, you may have to use an ax to get started. Save only those pieces growing around the outer edge of the crown, as they are the youngest and most vigorous parts and make the best new plants.

Pull the pieces away from the crown's center with your hands or insert two garden forks back to back and pull their handles away from each other. Continue cutting and pulling apart the crown, depending on its size and how many new plants you wish to have. Discard the remains of the woody center.

3. TRIMMING THE NEW PIECES Inspect each piece and use pruning shears to cut off any torn roots or underground shoots. Shorten an above-ground shoot if it is so long that the new plant will be top-heavy or unsteady in the wind. Also shorten any lanky roots that may not fit conveniently into a planting hole.

Work quickly to prevent the exposed roots from drying out. Keep the pieces you are not working on covered with a wet cloth or burlap.

4. REPLANTING Depending on how intact their roots are, your new plants may need a year of coddling in a nursery row before being planted in a permanent location. The rich, weed-free soil of a vegetable garden is a good place for a nursery row.

If your objective was to have a revitalized shrub growing in the same spot as the old one, dig out the remains of the old plant and set in one of the new ones. Otherwise, transplant the divisions to other parts of your garden.

In any event, the planting hole must be large enough to accommodate the roots, easily. Spread the roots in the hole, but do not bend or twist them as you plant. Any wayward roots can be trimmed slightly. Sift soil, and amendments if necessary, in among the roots and firm them in place so that they are in intimate contact with the roots.

After you finish, give each plant a thorough soaking to settle it in the ground. If you keep weeds at bay and provide adequate water in the months ahead, you will have sturdy plants by autumn.

Transplanting a Small Tree

Oliver E. Allen

feet long, and two short lengths of old garden hose (or special tree straps, available at some garden centers). Plus some peat moss or leaf mold and, of course, a spade.

1. DIG A PROPER HOLE Contrary to wide belief, the hole for a tree or shrub should not be deeper than the height of the root ball; unless your soil is sandy the hole should actually be two or three inches (5 or 7.5 cm) shallower so that the tree will sit high (or "proud") and be in no danger of sinking below grade — which would probably kill it. In addition, the soil at bottom center should be as compact as the soil within the root ball, lest the tree sink into it after planting. In sandy soils, however, plant grade level or slightly lower to keep the overly fast drainage from drying out the roots. In any case, make the hole's diameter one foot (30 cm) greater than that of the root ball.

NOTHING COULD BE SIMPLER, you say to yourself, as you contemplate planting the handsome five- or six-foot-tall (1.5 or 1.8 m) balled-and-burlapped dogwood you have brought home from the nursery. Just dig a nice deep hole, pop in the tree, and fill up the hole. It is true that some very tough species may survive such rude handling, but the flowering dogwood (*Cornus florida*) — or its cousin the Asiatic dogwood (*Cornus kousa*) — is not one of them. (Nor are such other favorites as the Japanese maple, the birch, and the beech.) Because your new dogwood has already been the recipient of the shock of having had its roots severely pruned in the balling-and-burlapping process, its transition back into the ground in its new home must be handled with great care. Furthermore, a number of seemingly minor matters, such as the depth of the hole you dig, can prove critical. Surely there is no reason to risk the substantial investment that the tree's purchase represents.

Take note, for example, of the time of year in which you have bought the tree. If it is early spring — an ideal time for acquiring such new plants — the dogwood will adjust most easily, as new growth will not have commenced. Demands on the root system will for a while be minimal. Later in the spring, however, the bursting forth of new leaves means that the roots will be laboring hard to provide nourishment and so may need extra watering for a time. A dogwood bought during summer's heat should be sprayed with an antidesiccant to minimize transpiration (water loss) until its roots take hold. Early autumn is, after early spring, the best time to plant a dogwood, provided it is put into the ground several weeks before the onset of really cold weather.

For proper planting you will need two wooden stakes roughly two-thirds the height of the tree and as thick as its trunk, two lengths of strong wire a couple of

2. MOVE THE TREE CAREFULLY In transporting the tree from your car or curbside to the new hole be sure to lift it by its burlapped root ball — never by its trunk, as this would almost certainly damage it severely by breaking roots near the center. If it is heavy, fashion a sling out of an old tarpaulin and have a friend help you carry it; or use a hand cart; or slide it onto a wide board, place some pipe lengths or similar rollers underneath, and roll it to its new site.

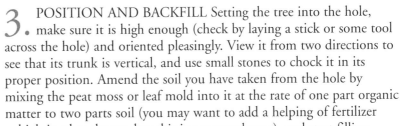

3. POSITION AND BACKFILL Setting the tree into the hole, make sure it is high enough (check by laying a stick or some tool across the hole) and oriented pleasingly. View it from two directions to see that its trunk is vertical, and use small stones to chock it in its proper position. Amend the soil you have taken from the hole by mixing the peat moss or leaf mold into it at the rate of one part organic matter to two parts soil (you may want to add a helping of fertilizer high in phosphorus, but this is not mandatory), and start filling around the root ball. Tamp the soil down as you go, using the shovel handle or your fist. When the hole is about two-thirds filled, cut away the burlap from around the top of the root ball and tuck it down into the new soil (it will eventually decay). Add some more soil, water copiously, and, after the water has receded, fill in any depressions that have been created and complete filling the trench, tamping down with your foot.

4. WATER Using the rest of your leftover soil, construct a dike or saucer around the dogwood to catch water, and add a generous puddle. After the water has subsided, fill the saucer with a good organic mulch like fir bark. For the next several weeks make sure the tree does not dry out — if less than an inch (2.5 cm) of rain falls in a week, add a pailful of water.

5. STAKE IT Until the roots reach out into the surrounding soil you should provide temporary support for your dogwood by driving the two stakes into the ground on opposite sides of the tree about as far out as the dike — they should go in deep enough to reach the firm soil at the bottom of the onetime hole — and connecting them to the tree trunk using the wire lengths. Protect the trunk by covering the wire with your hose lengths or tree straps. After about a year, remove the stakes. By that time the dogwood should be well enough established to need no further attention.

Planting Strawberries

Lee Reich

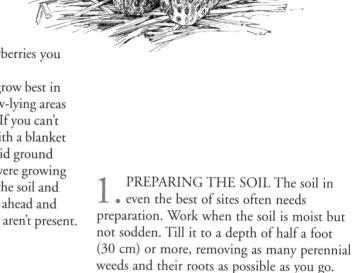

FEW FRUITS ARE AS DELECTABLE as a strawberry grown to perfection and picked fully ripe. They are easy to grow, and if you grow the everbearing types (including the popular day-neutrals), they will reward you quickly, bearing fruit the same season they are planted. The June-bearing types should form strong plants their first season and fruit the following year. Regardless of the type of strawberries you grow, expect a quart (1 litre) of fruit from each plant.

Choose your planting site carefully. Strawberries grow best in moist, well-drained soil in full sun. If you can, avoid low-lying areas where spring frosts are apt to injure the early blossoms. If you can't avoid such a site, you will have to protect your plants with a blanket or plastic sheet when frost threatens. It's also best to avoid ground where grass, tomatoes, peppers, eggplants, or potatoes were growing recently, as these plants harbor pests that may linger in the soil and damage your strawberry crop. If you have no choice, go ahead and plant your strawberries anyway on the chance that pests aren't present.

1. PREPARING THE SOIL The soil in even the best of sites often needs preparation. Work when the soil is moist but not sodden. Till it to a depth of half a foot (30 cm) or more, removing as many perennial weeds and their roots as possible as you go. Doing so now will save you work later, for strawberries have shallow roots that cannot compete with weeds and are easily damaged by hoeing.

Strawberries' shallow roots are also incapable of reaching very far for water or nutrients. To help the soil retain water and to supply some nutrients, spread a two-inch (5 cm) layer of organic matter (peat moss, leaf mold, compost, or well-rotted manure) on top of the bed. Further supplement your plants' diet by sprinkling on a granular 10-10-10 fertilizer at the rate of three pounds (1.3 kg) per 100 square feet (9.3 square m). Throughly mix these amendments into the soil with a shovel or rototiller.

If your soil drains poorly, rake the prepared soil into a raised bed six inches (15 cm) high and two feet (.6 m) wide. If you're making more than one bed, leave 18-inch (46 cm) paths between them.

2. PREPARING THE PLANTS Strawberry plants are usually sold in bare-root bundles. If you cannot plant them immediately, moisten the roots and store the bundles in a plastic bag in the refrigerator.

When you are ready to plant, take a pair of scissors and cut all the roots of each bundle back to four inches (10 cm). Shortening the roots in this manner makes planting easier. Old roots will become nonfunctional anyway as new roots form higher up.

Next, open each bundle and inspect the plants. If they have leaves (they may not), pull off all but two or three of the youngest ones on each plant — this will reduce water loss when the plants are in the ground.

As you work, keep the plants in a pan with a little water in the bottom and drape a damp cloth over them.

3. SETTING THE PLANTS IN THE GROUND An individual strawberry plant requires a square foot (30 cm) of space. Strawberries produce runners (horizontal stems with new plants along their length), so if you set the plants a foot (30 cm) apart, you'll need to trim off all runners as they form. Alternatively, you can set the plants a couple of feet apart and allow the runners to fill the spaces in between. Your first harvest will be greater with the former plan, but you'll have to purchase more plants. (Note that June bearers produce more runners than everbearers do.)

Plant by plunging a trowel straight down into the soil with the concave side facing you. Pull the handle toward you to open a slit in the ground. Fan out the roots and place them in the opened slit, taking care they don't bend as you set them in. Then set the top of the crown just above the soil line. Any deeper and the crown will rot; any

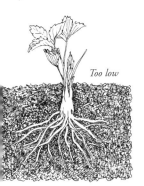 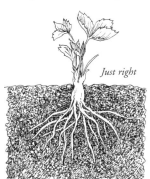 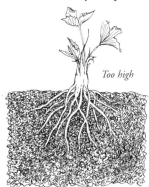

Too low — *Just right* — *Too high*

shallower and the roots will dry out.

Remove the trowel and firm the soil with the heel of your hand to ensure good contact between roots and soil. Give each plant a pint of water to settle the soil and to get it off to a good start. Finally, double check the planting depth.

4. CARING FOR THE PLANTS Strawberries enjoy cool, moist soil, so tuck a two-inch (5 cm) layer of straw or pine needles around each plant. This mulch also will suppress weeds and will keep the berries clean when they appear.

Soon your plants will begin to grow, producing leaves and flowers. Diligently pinch off all flower buds to force the plants to put their energy into growth instead of reproduction. Pinch everbearers for about three months, then stop and allow subsequent flowers to go on to produce berries. Pinch June bearers until flowering ceases in early summer, and expect a bountiful harvest the following year.

Growing Rhubarb

Janet H. Sanchez

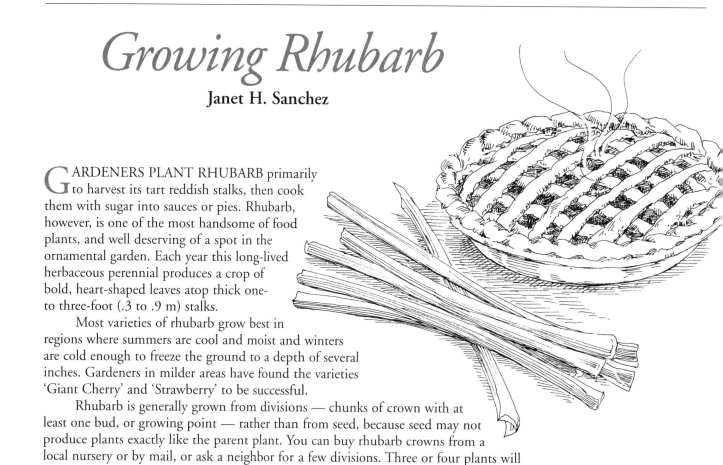

GARDENERS PLANT RHUBARB primarily to harvest its tart reddish stalks, then cook them with sugar into sauces or pies. Rhubarb, however, is one of the most handsome of food plants, and well deserving of a spot in the ornamental garden. Each year this long-lived herbaceous perennial produces a crop of bold, heart-shaped leaves atop thick one- to three-foot (.3 to .9 m) stalks.

Most varieties of rhubarb grow best in regions where summers are cool and moist and winters are cold enough to freeze the ground to a depth of several inches. Gardeners in milder areas have found the varieties 'Giant Cherry' and 'Strawberry' to be successful.

Rhubarb is generally grown from divisions — chunks of crown with at least one bud, or growing point — rather than from seed, because seed may not produce plants exactly like the parent plant. You can buy rhubarb crowns from a local nursery or by mail, or ask a neighbor for a few divisions. Three or four plants will provide plenty of stalks for most families.

1. PREPARE THE SITE Choose a spot in full sun with rich, well-drained soil. Remember that rhubarb is a perennial and will remain in its chosen location for years, so place it out of the way of annual cultivation at the edge of the vegetable garden (preferably on the north side where it won't shade other plants), or take advantage of its ornamental qualities and group several crowns in a flower border. In either case, allow each plant about one square yard (.9 square m).

Careful soil preparation will help your rhubarb remain healthy and productive for many years. Clear the spot of any weeds, being sure to dig out the roots of tough perennial ones. Then loosen the soil to a depth of 10 inches (25 cm). For each plant, mix at least three to four inches (7.5 to 10 cm) of compost or well-aged manure and a handful of fertilizer that is relatively high in phosphorus and potassium (such as 5-10-10) into the soil.

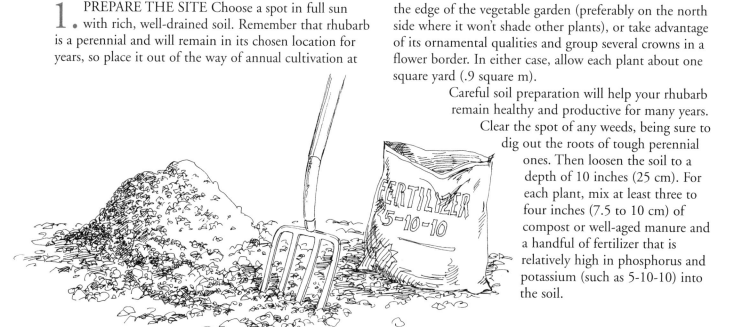

2. **PLANT** Try to plant the crowns as soon as you get them so they don't dry out. It's best to plant in early spring, when the roots are still dormant or the plants are just beginning to leaf out.

Space the plants three feet (.9 m) apart and cover the crowns with only an inch or two (2.5 to 5 cm) of soil. Press the soil firmly around the roots, and water well. As the weather begins to warm, fat buds will push up through the soil, unfurling new leaves.

In a few weeks, when the plants are up and growing, lay down a mulch of straw, straw-laden manure, or composted leaves to help maintain soil moisture and help prevent weed seeds from germinating. Be sure to pull any weeds that do manage to grow. Plan to add more mulch in the fall to help protect the plants over the winter.

3. **CARE** Like most vegetables, rhubarb needs regular irrigation; if rain is lacking keep the soil moist but not soggy. Rhubarb is also vigorous and requires annual feeding for good growth and continued production. Give each plant a handful of 5-10-10 in the spring. A midsummer feeding of fish emulsion or 5-10-10 will also benefit these hungry plants.

Snap off any flower stalks (tall spikes growing from the center) that appear so that the plant will concentrate its energy on producing robust stems, leaves, and roots.

Well-grown rhubarb plants have few insect or disease problems, though you may encounter the rhubarb curculio, a beetle that bores into the stalks and crowns. If you do, destroy infested plants and get rid of any nearby dock weeds, which also harbor this pest.

4. **HARVEST** Let your rhubarb plants grow undisturbed their first year — they need time to become established. You can harvest lightly the second spring after planting, cutting a few stalks from each plant over a period of a couple of weeks. By the third year, the plants should be well developed and you can harvest for about two months each spring. Stop picking when the plant starts producing slender stalks, a sign that its energy is low.

When harvesting, always leave at least half of the plant's foliage to sustain the roots. The stalks are at their best when fairly young, so pick them soon after the leaf expands. Gently pull the stalks from the plant instead of cutting them, because cut stubs may rot.

Only eat the rhubarb stalks; the leaves contain a poisonous glycoside and large amounts of oxalic acid. It is safe, however, to add the leaves to your compost pile, since the harmful compounds will break down in the composting process.

Planting a Raspberry Patch

Lee Reich

NO FRUITS ARE TASTIER or more perishable than perfectly ripe raspberries, a fact that argues for growing them within arm's reach. If you plant the so-called everbearing varieties this spring, you will be able to pick your first berries within months of planting. Summer-bearing varieties yield their first berries the following season. Get your patch off to a good start by purchasing certified disease-free plants. Those dug from a neighbor's patch may seem economical, but they often carry diseases. Choose a site that has full sun and well-drained soil and is as far as possible from other cultivated or wild raspberries. Also, don't plant them where you have recently grown eggplants, peppers, potatoes, tomatoes, or strawberries, which are hosts to raspberry diseases. Clear the area of any sod or weeds before you get started.

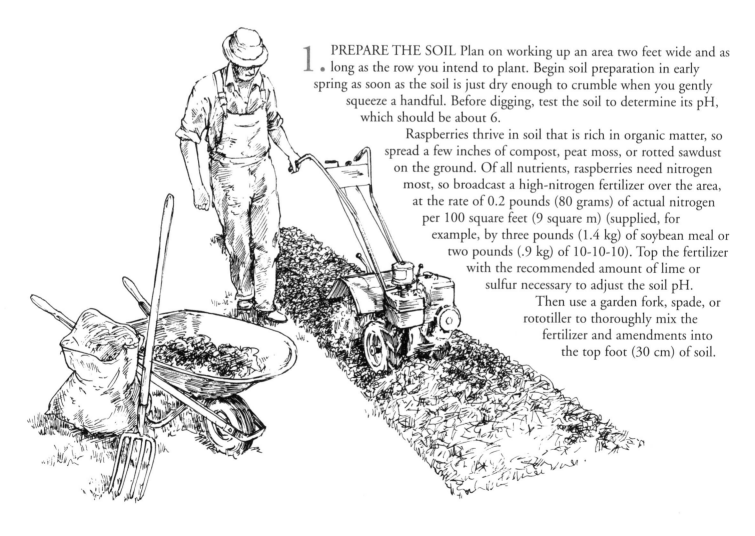

1. PREPARE THE SOIL Plan on working up an area two feet wide and as long as the row you intend to plant. Begin soil preparation in early spring as soon as the soil is just dry enough to crumble when you gently squeeze a handful. Before digging, test the soil to determine its pH, which should be about 6.

Raspberries thrive in soil that is rich in organic matter, so spread a few inches of compost, peat moss, or rotted sawdust on the ground. Of all nutrients, raspberries need nitrogen most, so broadcast a high-nitrogen fertilizer over the area, at the rate of 0.2 pounds (80 grams) of actual nitrogen per 100 square feet (9 square m) (supplied, for example, by three pounds (1.4 kg) of soybean meal or two pounds (.9 kg) of 10-10-10). Top the fertilizer with the recommended amount of lime or sulfur necessary to adjust the soil pH.

Then use a garden fork, spade, or rototiller to thoroughly mix the fertilizer and amendments into the top foot (30 cm) of soil.

2. ERECT A TRELLIS Trellising your plants will keep them upright, thus drier and less prone to disease. It also will put the fruit within easy reach.

You could certainly build a more elaborate trellis, but I have found that the simplest kind consists of a post at each end of the row with two wires strung between them. For the posts, use four-by-fours made from cedar or other rot-resistant wood. Sink them into the ground below the frost line, at least two feet (.6 m) deep, and brace them. If the row spans more than 30 feet (9 m), add posts to the center to keep the wires from sagging.

Use 12- to 14-gauge wire, placing one wire five feet (1.5 m) above the ground and the other two feet (.6 m) above the ground. To facilitate tightening the wires in spring and loosening them in winter, attach a piece of chain to each end of the wires. Run the chains through a drilled hole in the posts, and hold them in place at the desired tension with a large nail.

3. SET THE PLANTS IN THE GROUND As soon as you receive the plants from the nursery, inspect the roots. If they are dry, moisten them. Shorten any lanky roots to 18 inches (46 cm) and cut back any roots that are damaged.

If the ground is not ready, keep the plants dormant in a plastic bag in the refrigerator, or temporarily plant them in moist ground on the cool, north side of your house or garage.

Before planting, soak the roots for a couple of hours in a bucket of water, keeping them immersed until you are ready to set each plant in the ground. Dig holes two to three feet (.6 to .9 m) apart along the row, just large enough to accommodate the roots. Set each plant in its hole, spread out the roots, and backfill with the loose soil, adjusting the planting depth so that the crown is just below ground level. Holding onto a cane, bounce the plant slightly to eliminate air pockets and put roots and soil in intimate contact. Then tamp the soil with your fingers.

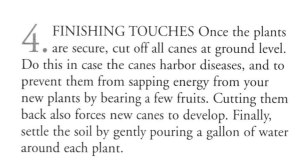

4. FINISHING TOUCHES Once the plants are secure, cut off all canes at ground level. Do this in case the canes harbor diseases, and to prevent them from sapping energy from your new plants by bearing a few fruits. Cutting them back also forces new canes to develop. Finally, settle the soil by gently pouring a gallon of water around each plant.

Layering a Gooseberry

Nancy Bubel

LAYERING IS THE PROCESS of inducing root formation on a plant's branch (or stem) by keeping it in close contact with the soil. Many small fruits layer readily; the process is especially effective for grapes, black raspberries, currants, and gooseberries. Some of these bushes even layer naturally, without any help from the gardener. It was, in fact, the spontaneous rooting of low branches on my gooseberry bush that prompted me to start intentionally rooting more branches. Now, with some nudging from me, that one plant has produced dozens of new bushes over the past few years.

You can start the layering process any time the soil is soft enough to dig in. Spring is an especially good time, because most berry bushes will form roots by the end of the growing season. Be sure to use only disease-free bushes.

You may need to plan ahead, pruning the plant moderately (removing no more than one-third of its top branches) to stimulate the development of lower, bushy branches suitable for layering. In this case, of course, you'd need to wait a season for those low branches to grow before you could start layering the shrub.

1. SELECT A BRANCH Choose a branch that is pliable and close enough to the ground to be bent down easily without breaking. Young branches root more readily than old, woody ones. One with a diameter of one-eighth to one-quarter of an inch (.3 to .6 cm) is fine (somewhat thicker branches are capable of rooting but may be more difficult to maneuver). Remove all leaves from a three- to four-inch-long (7.5 to 10 cm) area along the middle of the branch, the part that will be in contact with the soil. Leave at least three or four inches (7.5 to 10 cm) of leaves at the tip. This portion will not touch the soil; it will become the new plant.

2. NICK THE BARK AND APPLY ROOTING POWDER Wounding the branch's surface brings larger concentrations of the plant's natural rooting hormones to the injured point. Applying a rooting hormone preparation further stimulates the production of roots. I nick or scrape the underside of the branch with a knife. Some gardeners take the time to remove a one- or two-inch-long (2.5 or 5 cm) slice of bark. In any event, it is important not to girdle the plant — take only a strip. If you moisten the bare, scraped surface of the branch with a wet rag, the rooting powder will adhere better.

3. BURY THE ROOTING POINT Keep the branch in close contact with soil to provide the moisture and darkness that promote rooting. Roots will grow more readily into a loose medium than into one that is densely packed, so scuff up some soil to give the branch softer, more aerated ground on which to rest.

Then cover the scraped, treated portion of the branch with several handfuls of loose soil. If the soil under the bush is heavy clay, cover the branch with compost or with a potting-soil mix instead.

Next place a rock or brick over the treated branch at the place where it is covered with soil. This will hold everything in place and help retain moisture. You might want to check on it now and then if the weather is very dry — roots will not develop if the soil dries out completely.

4. CHECK FOR ROOTS AND TRANSPLANT Layered branches started in spring will have formed roots by the end of the growing season. I check my gooseberry starts two to four months after layering.

Remove the rock and tug at the branch. If it seems well anchored, feel for roots in the soft surrounding soil (roots will often be visible once you remove the rock). If the branch has rooted and is producing green leaves, it's ready to grow on its own. Cut it from the parent plant; dig up the rooted section, retaining as much earth as possible around the roots; and transplant the bush into its new home.

It is best to transplant the young bush when it is dormant, in late fall or early spring. However, I have gotten away with potting up little gooseberry plants at other times by coddling them — providing shade, watering well, and covering them with plastic bags for several days to reduce transpiration.

Raising a Clematis

Janet H. Sanchez

THE BEST TIME to plant a clematis is early spring, when dormant bareroot plants are available from mail-order and local nurseries. (A container-grown one can be purchased and planted later in the spring or even in the fall.) Large-flowered clematis hybrids can be grown in a variety of settings, from shade to full sun. Those with purple or red blossoms tend to become sun bleached and are best placed in a location offering filtered sun all day. It is important to choose a spot where the roots will remain cool — the east or north side of a low wall or hedge is ideal.

Clematis climb by twining their slender stems around a wire or other thin support, so if you want to grow one against a wall, you will need to provide a wooden trellis (with narrow crosspieces), sturdy netting, or a network of wire strung through eyebolts for them to grasp. Always set the support in place before planting to avoid disturbing the roots later.

Be forewarned that a clematis may be slow to become established. In its first season, you may see little top growth and few or no blossoms as your plant spends its energy developing roots. With proper care, however, it will take off in the second year, and really hit its stride in the third.

1. PLANTING Soak the roots in a bucket of water for an hour before planting. If the stems are longer than one foot (30 cm), shorten them so the plant will be easier to work with and so you won't inadvertently snap off any at the base. This also encourages the vine to branch freely once it begins to grow.

Dig a hole at least two feet wide (.6 m) and 18 inches (46 cm) deep. Mix some of the excavated topsoil with plenty of organic matter (such as compost, well-aged manure, or damp peat moss) and refill the hole halfway. Stir in a half-cup of 5-10-10 fertilizer and, if your soil is acid, add a sprinkling of lime.

Next, hold the plant in the hole and gently fill in around it with the improved soil. Unlike most plants, a clematis needs to have its crown (the spot where the stem meets the roots) covered by an inch or two (2.5 or 5 cm) of soil. This way, if the top of the vine is damaged, new buds can emerge from the section protected underground. Firm the soil around the plant, then water it in well.

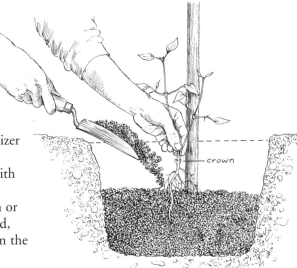

crown

2. CARE Place several inches of compost, leaf mold, or other organic matter in a one-foot (30 cm) circle around the plant to help keep the roots cool and moist. Do not allow the mulch to touch the stem directly, however, since such contact might encourage fungal diseases. If pets or young children are active in your garden, consider shielding the vulnerable lower stems with a collar of wire netting.

Clematis must never be allowed to dry out, so water regularly in dry spells. Once the vine is growing well, feed it with a complete liquid fertilizer, such as 5-10-5. Plan to fertilize again next spring.

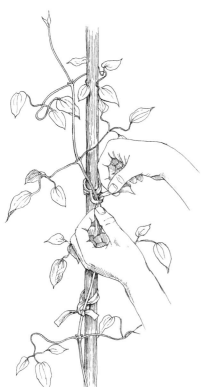

3. TRAINING A clematis may require encouragement to get started upward, but will eventually scramble aloft on its own. To help it on its way, you might need to tie the stems to the support with soft twine as the vine progresses, particularly on smooth ones such as poles, where there is little for the petioles to grasp onto.

If you grow a clematis through a shrub or hedge, provide a stake or length of twine to guide the elongated stems into the lower branches.

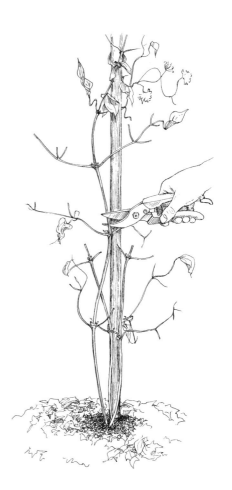

4. PRUNING How much you should prune a clematis depends on when the plant flowers. Those that bloom from mid-June to fall should be pruned back to 12 or 18 inches (30 or 46 cm) starting in their second spring, just as the buds begin to swell. This may seem rather drastic, but summer-bloomers flower only on the current year's growth, so removing the previous year's wood results in more flowers on a stockier plant.

Other clematis bloom between early May and mid-June on old growth, and often again in the fall on new growth. In order to encourage a good display in both seasons, prune this type of clematis lightly in early spring, removing only stems that are obviously dead, and cutting back any weak or unruly ones.

If you aren't sure which type of clematis you have, let the vine grow freely for a year or two while you observe its blooming and growth patterns.

Establishing a Groundcover

Janet H. Sanchez

GROUNDCOVERS are dependable plants that gardeners everywhere count on to blanket the soil with a fairly uniform canopy of dense foliage, suppressing most weed growth from below. They offer solutions to a number of landscaping dilemmas. Some flourish in the shade cast by large trees, while others thrive on hot, steep banks. Most species are easier to maintain than lawns, and many are water-thrifty as well. The plants are available in a variety of leaf shapes and textures, with some featuring flowers and even berries.

Gardeners in cold-winter areas should plant in spring, so the groundcover has an entire season to get established. Those in areas with hot, dry summers and mild winters may want to wait for fall, when winter rains will help get the plants off to a strong start.

1. ADVANCE PREPARATION Even a groundcover with a reputation for being tough can't compete or thrive in weedy soil. Use a sharp hoe to cut shallow-rooted annual weeds, or till the soil and rake out plant remains. Carefully dig out any deep-rooted perennial weeds, such as Bermuda grass and dandelions, removing the roots as well as the tops. Small areas of turf can be sliced off in sections with a sharp, flat spade; you'll need to rent a sod cutter to get rid of larger lawns.

Roughly dig over the site, hauling away rocks and other debris. When you're finished, rake the surface to even it out. On very weedy sites it is a good idea to irrigate at this point and wait a couple of weeks for weed seeds to germinate; the tiny seedlings will be easy to eliminate then, saving you extensive weeding later.

To decide which groundcover to plant for your particular situation, ask someone at your local nursery or get the advice of a professional landscaper. You can also be on the lookout for successful plantings in your neighborhood. Be wary of invasive species that travel quickly beyond their allotted area. If you choose a taller-growing one, keep in mind that it may require shearing every year or so to maintain a leafy, nonwoody appearance.

2. ADD AMENDMENTS A groundcover won't thrive in poor soil. If previous plantings haven't grown well, your soil may have a nutrient deficiency, or the pH may be too high or too low, preventing plants from using available nutrients effectively. You can buy a kit to test the soil yourself or have a professional soil analysis made. Add whatever amendments the test determines to be missing before you plant.

If, as is more commonly the case, your garden soil has no serious problems, you should still take time to improve it. Improve both drainage and soil tilth by spreading three to four inches (7.5 to 10 cm) of organic matter or well-composted manure over the surface. Also broadcast a balanced fertilizer (one with more or less equal amounts of nitrogen, phosphorus, and potassium) at the rate recommended on the label.

Till or dig in all these amendments, then rake the surface smooth and water. Use the rake again after watering to level any low spots that appear.

3. SET OUT THE PLANTS Groundcover plants are commonly sold in small pots, six-packs, gallon (4 litre) containers, or as rooted cuttings in flats. Before setting out those grown in flats, separate the plants by cutting between them with a sharp knife.

You may get conflicting advice about how far apart to set the plants. Choosing closer spacing requires more plants, but the advantage is that the bed will fill in more quickly. Once you've decided on the distance between plants, use a piece of wood cut to the desired length to help you space them evenly.

When planting flat-grown plants or those purchased in smaller pots, set them in holes that are just deep enough for the root ball and slightly wider than their original confines. For larger plants, dig a hole that tapers outward at the bottom to accept the loosened roots, leaving a platform of undisturbed soil in the middle on which to set the root ball. To prevent rot, the crown of each plant should remain slightly above the soil's surface.

When setting groundcover plants into a steep slope where erosion may occur, arrange the plants in staggered rows. Make a small terrace for each plant, creating a basin or low spot behind each one to catch water.

4. WATER AND MULCH Water the plants thoroughly after planting. Then water every few days for the next few weeks, and again whenever the top inch (2.5 cm) of soil feels dry.

It is important to cover the soil between the young plants to help maintain soil moisture and to prevent weed seeds from germinating. Use an organic mulch such as ground bark, straw, or pine needles. Promptly pull any weeds that do appear, and renew the mulch periodically until the groundcover canopy fills in and forms its own living mulch.

Sowing Carrots

Thomas Christopher

WHILE THE HOMELY ROOTS of carrots may lack the élan of arugula or radicchio, they make a vitamin-rich contribution to everything from cakes to soup. As an early crop, carrots flourish right through the lingering cold spells that play havoc with the first sowing of such crops as flageolet beans. If mulched with several inches of straw, a late crop of carrots will stay sweet and crisp in the ground until the arrival of the new year. Carrots are easy to grow, too — if you start them off right. The care you take at planting time will do much to determine the success or failure of this worthy root crop.

1. PREPARING THE BED In the matter of soil, carrots are uncompromising. If the growing root should meet a pebble or a big, hard clump of earth, it will branch or fork. Likewise, if the roots should meet with clay or hardpan, it may stop growing. And although carrots need plenty of moisture, good drainage is essential. If the soil remains perpetually soggy, the roots develop black spots, which decay into unappetizing cavities.

Work the soil well to a depth of at least 10 inches (25 cm), turning it with a spading fork, breaking up any clumps, and removing all stones and pebbles larger than an inch (2.5 cm) in diameter. Add a couple of inches of compost to lighten a clay soil and improve its drainage. This is good medicine for sandy soil as well, since the compost boosts fertility while enhancing the sand's ability to retain moisture.

A final tip: If your soil is heavy, plant shorter varieties such as 'Royal Chantenay', which makes a stubby root five inches long (12.5 cm), or even a beet-shaped carrot such as 'Kundulus'.

2. FERTILIZING Carrots are also particular about fertilizer. Too much nitrogen brings on branching and hairy, fibrous roots. For that reason, nitrogen-rich animal manures are a poor choice for this crop. Instead, sprinkle a thin layer of wood ashes over the soil or apply a commercial 5-10-10 fertilizer at the rate of five pounds (2.3 kg) per 100 square feet (9.3 square m). Both of these downplay the nitrogen while furnishing the potassium and phosphorus that root crops relish. Work the fertilizer in to a depth of four inches (10 cm) with your spading fork, then rake the bed smooth.

3. SOWING THE SEED Timing is not critical when planting carrots, for they'll grow right through the summer in all but the hottest parts of the country. But a cool-weather sowing in early spring does protect them from the larvae of the carrot rust fly, which hatch in warm weather and burrow into the roots.

Stretch a string along the garden bed to mark the row, then lay a board alongside it so that you can step into the bed without compacting the prepared soil. Dig a furrow (a drill in gardener's jargon) three-quarters of an inch (.9 cm) deep along the string, and line the bottom with a quarter-inch (.6 cm) layer of sifted compost. Carrot seed is very fine and therefore difficult to handle, so mix it with clean builder's sand for easier sowing. Sift a fine trail of the seed/sand mixture along the furrow, trying to space the seeds about a half-inch (1.25 cm) apart. You might sow a few radish seeds among the carrots while you're at it. Unlike carrots, which may take three weeks to sprout in cool weather, radishes come up almost overnight, marking the row so that you won't accidentally run a hoe across it before the carrots emerge. By the time the radishes are ready to harvest, the carrots will be ready for thinning; pulling the one crop will help to thin the other. Once you have sown the seeds, cover the drill with sifted compost.

4. WATERING AND MULCHING Soak the planted furrow with a fine shower of water, then cover it with a strip of clear plastic. This polyethylene mulch serves two purposes: It keeps the soil evenly moist and warms it by trapping sunlight. Carrot seed germinates in soils as cold as 45°F (7°C) but performs best in warmer soils; 80°F (27°C) is ideal. Inspect the bed every morning, and as soon as you see any seedlings poking up through the soil, remove the plastic. If the plastic is left in place after the young plants emerge, it will cook your carrots before they have a chance to take root.

Planting a Fruit Tree

Lee Reich

RAISING YOUR OWN FRUIT is immensely satisfying. Imagine, for instance, eating a truly ripe peach, one that makes you jut your head forward with each bite just to keep the juice from dripping down your shirt. You can raise peaches this delicious yourself for a reasonable price and a reasonable amount of effort.

The planting directions that follow apply to all fruit trees. If you decide on a peach tree, pay particularly attention to the site. Peaches demand full sun, freedom from late-spring frosts, and perfect soil drainage. Quick root development is important for any newly planted tree, so plant early in the season, as soon as the soil has dried enough to crumble easily in your hand. A tree planted this spring will reward you with bushels of luscious fruit in the years to come, the first crop appearing perhaps as soon as next summer in the case of the peach.

1. PREPARING THE TREE Fruit trees are traditionally sold bare-root — that is, they are dug when dormant and sold without soil. Whether you buy a tree by mail or from a local nursery, it will need immediate care once it arrives at your home. Unwrap it and soak its roots in a bucketful of water for a few hours. This will plump up the roots in case they have dried out somewhat since having been removed from the ground at the nursery. If you cannot plant the tree immediately after soaking it, temporarily bury its roots in a shallow hole in a shady, protected spot. This "heeling in" will keep the roots moist and delay bud growth until you are ready to plant.

The tree may need a little pruning before it is planted. If its roots are more than a foot (30 cm) long or frayed, trim them back with clean, sharp pruning shears. If the tree is branched, choose three or four healthy branches to become its permanent limbs. The lowest of these should be about two feet (.6 m) above ground level, and successively higher ones should be a few inches apart and arranged in a spiral around the trunk. Shorten these branches to just a few inches, making sure when you cut that each one ends in an outward-pointing bud. This pruning will induce vigorous, spreading growth.

Once you've prepared the main branches, cut away any other branches, and cut off the top of the trunk just above the upper-most branch. If the tree is not branched, simply cut the trunk back to three feet (.9 m) high.

2. PREPARING THE PLANTING SITE Peach trees thrive in well-drained soil with a pH of 6 to 8. If a soil test shows that your soil isn't in that range, add the necessary lime or sulfur. If the test also shows that your soil is deficient in phosphorus, add bonemeal or rock phosphate. Phosphorus and lime move down slowly through the soil, so now is an opportune time to get them close to the roots. Do not use synthetic fertilizers, for they can burn tender new roots.

Spread the amendments over an area as wide as the eventual spread of the tree's branches — approximately six feet (1.8 m) in all directions. In the center of the area, where you will dig the planting hole, mix the amendments into the top foot (30 cm) or so of soil with a shovel or garden fork. This is not necessary farther out from the hole, where the amendments can be allowed to work their way down into the soil gradually.

Next, dig your planting hole. Assuuming the site is well drained and the necessary amendments have been added, the hole need only be large enough to accommodate the tree's roots. After you've finished digging the hole, rough up the soil on the sides and bottom to help the roots penetrate the surrounding soil.

3. POSITIONING THE TREE Return some of the excavated soil to the bottom of the hole to make a mound on which to set the tree. To allow for settling, adjust the height of the mound so that your tree will stand roughly two inches (5 cm) higher than it previously stood in the nursery (the level is indicated by the old soil line on the trunk).

Place the tree atop the mound and spread out its roots evenly, taking care to neither bend nor crowd them. If the tree is branched, orient it with the lowest branch facing southwest. As this branch grows, it will shade the trunk and lessen the chance of sunscald. If the site is windy, lean the tree slightly into the wind.

4. FILLING IN Hold the tree steady with one hand, and push soil back into the hole around the roots with the other. As you fill the hole, bounce the tree up and down slightly to settle the soil among the roots. Once the tree is self-supporting, shovel in additional soil, tamping it gently with your fingers or a stick as you work.

After you've filled in the hole, construct a low dike of soil around the base of the tree to form a catch basin for water — two feet (.6 m) out from the trunk in all directions should be sufficient. Spread compost or manure over the bare soil in the catch basin to provide nutrients for the tree's shallow feeder roots. Top this layer with a straw or leaf mulch, which will suppress weeds and still allow water to penetrate the soil.

Slowly pour enough water into the catch basin to drench the soil thoroughly and to settle the tree into place. Water generously once a week through August. Be sure to weed the catch basin diligently, as weeds will compete with the tree for nutrients and water.

Hardening off Seedlings

Nancy Bubel

ONE BRIGHT DAY in May last year I received a call from some young friends who had carefully raised a batch of zinnia seedlings on a windowsill. All had gone well until they planted the thriving plants directly into the garden. The little zinnias were still alive, but they didn't look good — the leaves were pale, their edges dried out. The sudden exposure to the stronger sun and cooler air outside had traumatized them. The ultraviolet sun rays that had been blocked by the window glass now shone on them full force — a stress they could have become accustomed to with a more gradual exposure. Having learned the hard way, my friends are carefully preparing this year's crop of seedlings for the move to harsher outdoor conditions. This process, called hardening off, starts at least two weeks before planting-out day.

Seedlings should be prepared in advance for their move. Water them sparingly and withhold fertilizer for a week or so. You're aiming for a tougher, more fibrous plant that will be less vulnerable to outdoor conditions. If possible, move the plants to a cooler room so they can also grow accustomed to lower temperatures.

1. MOVE THE SEEDLINGS OUTSIDE The introduction to outside conditions should be gradual. Young plants need protection from wind, strong sun, and cold air. Strong spring winds can damage plants by drying them, breaking their stems, and tearing their roots while whipping them around. Spring rains can also harm them. All seed flats and other containers holding outdoor seedlings should have drainage holes in the bottom, or rain will soon flood and kill them.

Find a sheltered spot for their first week outdoors. I set my seedlings outside on a patio with an eastern exposure, where they receive several hours of morning sun but are shielded from the more intense midday and afternoon sun. Other good places include benches or picnic tables, or near trees or hedges. If you set them out in a cold frame, leave the top open during the day.

After the seedlings have spent about five to seven days in the more sheltered location, move them to a southern exposure where they will receive sun all day. The longer, stronger sun dries out soil more quickly, so water the seedlings more often — perhaps three or four times a week rather than twice.

2. SET PLANTS IN THE GROUND Zinnias, like many other tender annuals, should be planted in the ground on or after the frost-free date for your area. A cloudy, damp day that allows the seedlings a more gentle introduction to the garden bed is best.

Use a trowel to make a generous hole in soft soil. Pop the plants out of their pots by tapping on the bottom or knocking the pot rim on a piece of wood. Those in plastic cell packs must sometimes be pried or squeezed out. For those raised in a flat without divisions between them, use your fingers or the trowel to remove them while retaining a cushion of soil around their roots.

Settle each plant in its hole and press the soil gently but firmly around its base. If you wish, add a handful of compost to the hole before filling it.

3. WATER THE PLANTS If there is a soothing spring shower the day you plant your seedlings, so much the better — for the plants, if not for the gardener. Even if you can count on rain after planting, it is still wise to water them in. Watering revives roots and leaves that might have dried in transplanting, and helps to settle the seedlings into their new home. Those that were set out with bare or disturbed roots are especially vulnerable.

When dealing with a small number of seedlings — a dozen or two — pour one or two cups (250 or 500 ml) of water directly on the roots after settling the plant in its hole, and again before filling the hole completely. However, if you're planting so many seedlings that this procedure would be cumbersome, soak the bed or row with a sprinkler for several hours after planting. Give the plants a second good watering if several days go by without rain.

4. PROTECT THE PLANTS Frost, sun, and wind are the forces you need to guard against. Be prepared to cover the plants if frost threatens, if searing sun strikes soon after planting, or if a harsh wind whips them around. The new spunbonded row covers work well for large areas, or you can use whatever you have around the house: plastic food containers, bottomless plastic jugs, old sheets. Berry baskets are my favorites. They nest neatly for storage and can be left in place for days (the wood mesh ones for a few days, the plastic mesh kind for up to 10 days because they admit sun). If the protective covers are lightweight, perch a stone on the top of each so it won't blow away.

Planting and Training Wisteria

Oliver E. Allen

WITH ITS PROFUSION of springtime blooms, the wisteria is an elegant adornment for pergolas and arbors. Trained against the side of a house, it can turn an entire wall into one continuous bloom. However, this lusty vine can present two serious problems. First, it may stubbornly fail to bloom, and second, its vigorous tendrils may threaten gutters, shingles, and anything else they can grab. The solution to these dilemmas lies in supporting your plant properly and pruning it on a regular schedule.

Wisterias are not likely to put out flowers until they are at least five or six years old. So avoid buying seedling plants — the wait is too long. Instead, look for a plant that has been matured properly by a reputable nursery. It may well have been grafted or grown on from a cutting. A good nurseryman should be able to recommend a dependable variety.

Your wisteria must get at least six hours of direct sunlight daily. One planted in the shade will grow well enough but hardly bloom.

Finally, a full-grown wisteria can be heavy, so supports must be strong. A light, wooden trellis may well collapse under the weight of a mature plant. Some growers use three-quarter-inch (1.9 cm) lead pipe, but it is easier to install galvanized wire, attaching it to the wall with sturdy, metal L-shaped brackets. When your house needs painting, the brackets can be unscrewed and the entire wisteria dismounted.

1. CONSTRUCT THE SUPPORT SYSTEM AND PLANT Your wisteria needs good air circulation, so use brackets that will hold the wires at least four to six inches (10 to 15 cm) out from the wall. If you have no gutters, make sure the plant is not directly under the roof's drip line (runoff would water the plant unduly). Install the wires at two- to three-foot (.6 to .9 m) intervals, the topmost being at least two feet (.6 m) from any eave so that the plant will not invade that area.

Next, prepare a generous planting hole — a good foot (30 cm) or so deep. Check the quality of the soil you remove; the soil next to the foundation (particularly around new houses) may be second-rate fill. Your wisteria needs well-drained soil reasonably rich in organic matter. Before setting in the plant, scatter a well-balanced fertilizer (5-10-5, for example) in the hole. If your wisteria is grafted, set it deep enough so the graft union is below the surface. Water the plant well, and keep watering as it begins climbing. As the tendrils reach up, choose the strongest one (or more than one if your plant calls for multiple leaders) and attach it with string to your wire (it will readily twine around the wire). Remove any other tendrils.

2. ESTABLISH THE FRAMEWORK As the leader reaches out, it will
form side branches. These side branches will themselves produce shoots
that will carry the flower buds in their axils. Train the leader to the upper wires.
Similarly, train side branches as needed, aiming toward a framework that will
eventually allow at least a foot and a half (46 cm) between its principal
members. Pinch off the main leader when it reaches the desired height.

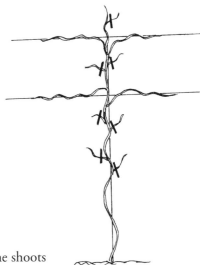

3. BEGIN PRUNING Each summer cut back the shoots
that form on your main branches by about half, or just
beyond the sixth or seventh leaf. If they in turn have formed side shoots, cut these back to
an inch or two (2.5 or 5 cm). In late winter cut your main branches back by at least a half
— the more drastically you prune them, the more energetically they will grow — and cut
all side shoots back to three or four flower buds. Flower buds appear at the base of the
previous year's wood. Each year while your wisteria is filling out its allotted space you may
want to feed it a well-balanced fertilizer to encourage vegetative growth. Be sure to work
the fertilizer down into the soil around the roots. Water as needed to keep the soil moist.

4. GROWTH COMPLETED, PRUNE FOR
BLOOM After your wisteria has attained its desired
size, prune each summer as before, but in winter prune all
shoots back to four or five buds. Remove any suckers that
appear at the base of the plant. Also stop fertilizing; from
now on you will want to discourage vegetative growth.

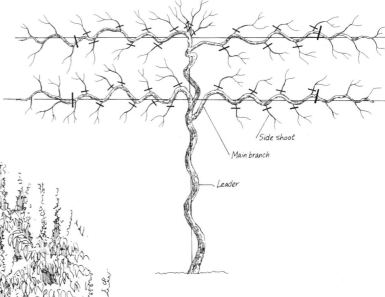

Side shoot

Main branch

Leader

An occasional feeding of
superphospate (half a pound (200
grams) per inch (2.5 cm) of main
trunk diameter) may spur flowering,
but if in doubt do not apply. Water
your wisteria only in a drought.
Given a starvation diet when fully
grown, the plant should reward you
annually with glorious bloom.

Staking Tomatoes

Lee Reich

TOMATOES SUITABLE FOR STAKING are the so-called indeterminate types. These varieties form fruit clusters at intervals along their ever-elongating stems. Determinate varieties, by contrast, fruit at the ends of their branches and thus are not suited to staking. The pruning required by staked tomatoes would reduce a determinate plant to a single short stem with little or no fruit. A tomato's habit is usually indicated in the seed catalog, on the seed packet, or on the label of a transplant, so check before buying.

There are several advantages to staking tomatoes. Since the plants grow upwards rather than outward, they are forced to provide more pounds of tomatoes from a given area of ground than will unstaked plants; this is especially important in small gardens, because the plants can be set as little as 18 inches (46 cm) apart. The fruits of a staked tomato plant ripen earlier and are larger (though fewer) than fruit of the same variety trained to a sprawling habit. Staked tomatoes also receive better air circulation around their leaves and fruits, which generally lessens disease. In addition, fruits held high above the ground are free from dirt and out of the reach of slugs.

There are also a couple of things to watch out for: A staked plant needs a healthy leaf cover or fruits will get sunscald. Fruits on staked plants are also vulnerable to blossom-end rot, so pay special attention to proper nourishment (particularly calcium), and see that the plants get an even supply of moisture.

1. **PLANTING THE STAKE** Do not be misled by the puniness of a tomato transplant. Each plant needs a sturdy support. Use rough-cut wooden stakes that are six to eight feet (2 to 2.5 m) long, no narrower than one by two inches (2.5 to 5 cm), and pointed at the bottom.

To avoid root damage later on, set stakes at the same time you set out transplants. Pound a stake into the ground about three inches (7.5 cm) from a plant on its north side so that the tiny plant will not be shaded. Sink the stake one to two feet (30 cm to .6 m) into the ground — you may need to start the hole with a crowbar. This depth provides enough stability to keep gusts of wind from toppling the plant when it is laden with fruit.

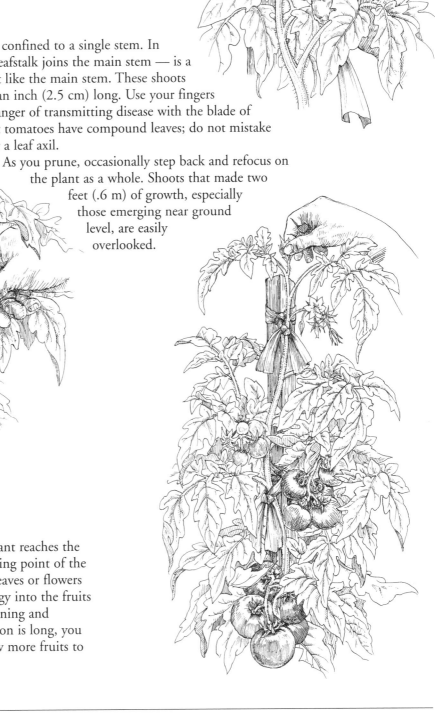

2. TYING THE PLANTS Tying is necessary because a tomato plant has no natural way to hold itself up. Material for ties should be strong enough to last the whole season and bulky enough not to cut into the stems. Coarse twine will do, but I prefer cotton rags torn into inch-wide (2.5 cm) strips, 18 inches (46 cm) long. These weaken enough by season's end so that I can simply pull spent plants off their stakes, and any ties left will decompose on the soil or compost pile.

First tie a square knot around the stake tight enough to prevent downward slippage, then use the free ends of the rag strip or twine to tie a square knot loosely around the tomato plant's stem. As the plant grows, anchor the stem to the stake every 12 to 18 inches (30 to 46 cm).

3. PRUNING A staked tomato is best confined to a single stem. In each leaf axil — the point where a leafstalk joins the main stem — is a lateral bud that can grow into a shoot just like the main stem. These shoots must be removed, ideally before they are an inch (2.5 cm) long. Use your fingers to snap off each one, thus avoiding the danger of transmitting disease with the blade of a knife or pruning shears. Remember that tomatoes have compound leaves; do not mistake the junction of a leaflet and a leafstalk for a leaf axil.

As you prune, occasionally step back and refocus on the plant as a whole. Shoots that made two feet (.6 m) of growth, especially those emerging near ground level, are easily overlooked.

4. PINCHING THE TOP Once a plant reaches the top of its stake, pinch out the growing point of the shoot and continue to remove any new leaves or flowers that form. Pinching directs a plant's energy into the fruits that have already set, hastening their ripening and increasing their size. If your growing season is long, you may wish to delay pinching so as to allow more fruits to set and ripen.

Planting a Window Box

Nancy Bubel

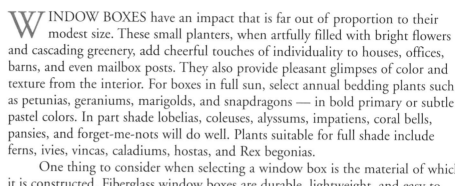

WINDOW BOXES have an impact that is far out of proportion to their modest size. These small planters, when artfully filled with bright flowers and cascading greenery, add cheerful touches of individuality to houses, offices, barns, and even mailbox posts. They also provide pleasant glimpses of color and texture from the interior. For boxes in full sun, select annual bedding plants such as petunias, geraniums, marigolds, and snapdragons — in bold primary or subtle pastel colors. In part shade lobelias, coleuses, alyssums, impatiens, coral bells, pansies, and forget-me-nots will do well. Plants suitable for full shade include ferns, ivies, vincas, caladiums, hostas, and Rex begonias.

One thing to consider when selecting a window box is the material of which it is constructed. Fiberglass window boxes are durable, lightweight, and easy to clean. Metal ones conduct heat readily, often causing plant roots to overheat. Wood boxes are heavy, insulate well, and may be custom-made — rot-resistant redwood, cedar, and cypress all make long-lasting boxes.

1. MOUNT THE WINDOW BOX

Any window box full of soil is heavy. To spare your back, mount the box before planting it. In most cases you'll be attaching the box to a windowsill. Use four 2-inch (5 cm) screws for a 36-inch-long (.9 m) box, more for a longer one. If the windowsill protrudes, as most do, nail cleats or short support boards to the back of the box to keep it level and prevent it from tipping forward. If you are attaching the box directly to siding, don't mount it flush against the house; protect the siding and provide for ventilation by attaching a one- by two-inch (2.5 by 5 cm) wood spacer between the box and the house.

When replanting a window box from a previous season, remove all the old soil. Whether the box is new or old, it should be empty as you start the planting process.

2. MAKE DRAINAGE HOLES AND PREPARE THE SOIL

Waterlogged plant roots soon die from lack of oxygen; a window box, therefore, should have drainage holes at each end, and a box longer than 36 inches (.9 m) should have a drainage opening in the bottom center as well. A metal liner tray inserted in a permanently mounted wood box should, of course, have matching drainage holes. It's a nice touch, though not a necessity, to line the bottom with a piece of screen to prevent soil from washing through. A one- or two-inch (2.5 or 5 cm) layer of torn or shredded sphagnum moss can serve the same purpose, while at the same time retaining water and providing air spaces to encourage healthy roots.

Use a balanced planting mix, because the confined plant roots can't range far in search of nutrients. Whether you buy a soil mix at the garden center or mix it yourself, a good formula is equal parts of compost, sharp sand (or perlite or vermiculite), and good loamy soil.

Avoid using garden soil alone. No matter how rich our ground may be, soil unmodified by a lightening agent will pack into a dense, air-excluding, root-suffocating mass when used for container plantings.

3. SET PLANTS ACCORDING TO A PLANNED DESIGN When planting young seedlings, fill the box with soil to within one inch (2.5 cm) of the top and use a fork handle or other slender tool to dibble holes for the small plants. For well-rooted transplants, put two to three inches (5 to 7.5 cm) of potting soil into the window box before adding the plants.

The most pleasing window-box arrangements include plants of compatible colors and varied heights, textures, and growing habits. Put upright plants such as dusty miller, geraniums, salvias, and dwarf nicotianas at the back of the box. In the foreground dot a few sprawling plants that will tumble over the edge of the box: lantanas, verbenas, lobelias, alyssums, nasturtiums, torenias, and schizanthuses. Vining plants such as *Euonymus,* myrtles, ivies, and strawberry begonias will also soften the edges of the box. Set plants four to six inches (10 to 15 cm) apart — somewhat closer than you would plant them in the garden — and water them in well.

4. WATER, FERTILIZE AND MAINTAIN Water every second or third day in summer (unless it rains) and as often as daily in extremely hot, sunny weather. If overhanging eaves block rainfall, you'll need to water even in rainy weather. There should be enough nourishment in the soil mix for the first two or three weeks. After that, feed every 10 to 14 days, using an all-purpose liquid fertilizer diluted according to package instructions. To encourage an abundant and long-lasting display of flowers, pick off faded blooms before they produce seeds.

You might also want to spread a half- to one-inch (1.25 to 2.5 cm) layer of fine mulch on the exposed soil to retain moisture; pinch back growing tips of certain bushy plants (impatiens, ornamental basil, and geraniums, for example) to promote more compact growth; thin out plants if they begin to crowd each other; and replant periodically for a continuous show of color from early spring through fall.

Pruning a Spring-Flowering Shrub

Janet H. Sanchez

MANY DECIDUOUS SHRUBS flower in spring, providing a beautiful and often fragrant backdrop for the early-season garden. Shrubs such as mock orange (shown here), barberry, deutzia, forsythia, honeysuckle, lilac, weigela, and spring-flowering forms of spirea are also easy to care for, requiring only basic watering, fertilizing, and pruning. It is important, however, to prune these shrubs soon after the flowers fade, since this is when they begin to develop the new growth that will mature over summer and fall and produce flowers next spring. If you wait to prune until winter, when the plant is dormant, you risk cutting off much of this mature wood and significantly reducing the amount of bloom.

REMOVE DEAD AND CROSSING BRANCHES

When pruning, aim to retain and enhance the shrub's naturally graceful habit, taking care not to cut it into a boxy or unnatural shape.

Before starting, it's a good idea to clear out fallen leaves and other debris from the plant's crown and the area beneath its branches so you can see the whole plant.

Using pruning shears or, if necessary, heavy-duty loppers, prune out any obviously dead branches, cutting them flush to the ground. Also remove any branches that seem diseased or abnormal, and those that cross each other awkwardly or rub together.

2. RENEWAL PRUNING

In time, the branches of old vigoruos-growing shrubs tend to become overcrowded, preventing the oldest stems from producing sturdy new side shoots. To give the shrub renewed strength, let light and air into the center of the plant, and provide growing space for new flowering stems, cut about one-fifth to one-third of the oldest canes back to the ground. Repeat the process next year if the shrub seems to need further thinning.

If some overly long stems remain, consider shortening them, but keep in mind that branches cut back partway often give rise to a dense profusion of new shoots, making the shrub appear even more overgrown. Cut these stems back to just above a side branch that is growing in the direction you want, usually away from the center of the plant. This way new growth will be concentrated in one side branch rather than in several new shoots.

3. DEADHEAD FLOWERING STEMS

You can begin this phase of the project while the plant is still blooming by cutting a few branches for fragrant bouquets. Then, immediately after the flowers have faded, selectively remove the dead blossoms, cutting each stem back to a pair of young laterals, or side shoots. These shoots will continue to grow over the summer, forming buds for next year's blossoms.

4. ROUTINE CARE

Besides proper pruning, some routine maintenance will keep your spring-flowering shrub healthy and blooming prolifically. If you haven't already fertilized this spring, do so after pruning. Use an all-purpose fertilizer, such as 5-10-10, spreading it lightly in a circle around the outer edges of the branches. Thoroughly water it into the soil. A mulch of aged compost, shredded leaves, or straw will benefit the shrub by conserving moisture and preventing most weed growth. Though an established shrub is able to endure considerable drought, it will flower more reliably if you help it through dry weather with a weekly watering.

Pruning Lilacs

Oliver E. Allen

ALTHOUGH LILACS are hearty, long-lived shrubs, without regular attention they become scraggly and overgrown, their fragrant blossoms appearing only toward the top of the plant and their interiors a tangle of unattractive shoots. They soon lose their elegant natural form. Such specimens may appear beyond redemption; in fact, they possess great vigor and can almost always be successfully renovated. Remember that any large shrub has an extensive root system, and if part or even most of its aboveground growth is removed, the roots will almost always respond with a burst of energy to replace the lost growth. So be bold. The plant will regain its former beauty.

You can tackle this job in early spring or early summer. Lilacs set their blossoms on the previous year's growth, so if you want this year's blossoms hold off pruning until after bloom is finished. Otherwise begin in early spring and take advantage of a full year's new growth.

1. REMOVE DEAD, DISEASED, OR UNSIGHTLY STEMS Using loppers or a small pruning saw, clear away any dead or diseased branches or stems. Then cut out crossed and otherwise unattractive branches.

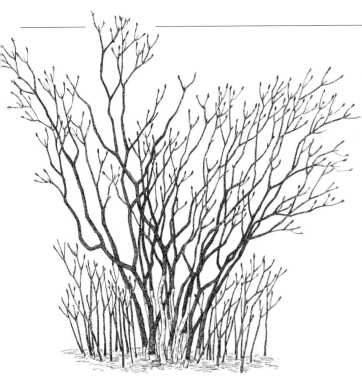

2. **REMOVE SUCKERS AND PRUNE BACK HARD** Lilacs have a tendency to produce suckers, stray shoots that spring directly from the root structure but are not true stems. As they detract from both the appearance and the vigor of the shrub, remove them by cutting under the soil level.

Of the stems that remain, choose about half that seem most pleasing aesthetically and prune these back until they are a foot or two (30 cm or .6 m) high, with no side growth (work toward an open, vase-shaped form). Then cut all the other stems back to within two to four inches (5 to 10 cm) of the ground. Apply an appropriate fertilizer, water the shrub well, and water it weekly during the rest of the growing season. Vigorous new growth should soon appear from both the taller stems and the other, severely pruned ones.

3. **THIN OUT NEW GROWTH** The chances are that more than one new stem will sprout from each cut you have made. The following spring, therefore, choose one from each group and prune away the others — or all but one other if you want the stem to divide. Remove any new suckers that have appeared around the base of the shrub. Fertilizer once again and water as needed, making sure the plant does not dry out during the summer. If the lilac produces blossoms this year, remove them once they are spent, as the energy the plant would normally put into seed development is better applied to additional vegetative growth.

4. **PRUNE ANNUALLY THEREAFTER** By the beginning of the third year your lilac should in most cases be fully restored. To prevent overgrowth in the future and to maintain the shrub's form, however, you should adopt an annual pruning program. Each year after blossoming, remove any dead or diseased stems, cut away a third of the remaining stems and excavate any new suckers as before. If you want to make the most of future bloom, remember to prune away the old blossoms. Under such vigilant care, your lilac will be a delight, a handsome, full-blooming example of a genus that has charmed gardeners, poets, and everyone else for centuries.

Roses from Cuttings

Janet H. Sanchez

Whether antique climber, modern miniature, or somewhere in between, roses are among the best-loved flowers. And growing them from softwood cuttings — those taken from the current season's growth — is an easy way to add to your collection, propagate a coveted variety from a friend's garden, or produce enough plants for a hedge. Unlike most nursery-grown roses, those you start yourself grow on their own roots, which often results in stronger plants. Exceptions include the Bourbon, hybrid perpetual, and Portland roses, which usually perform better as nursery-grafted plants.

You can use the same technique to reproduce certain other shrubs as well, including boxwood, cotoneaster, flowering currant, forsythia, mock orange, smoke tree, and weigela. Note that the mother plant should be healthy and growing vigorously — cuttings taken from stunted plants often fail. It is ideal to start the project in early summer, when it will be easy to find the necessary young stems.

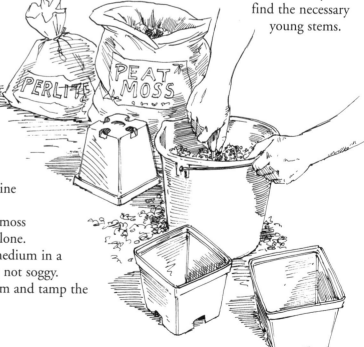

1. **PREPARE THE POTS** To prevent new cuttings from drying out, make as many advance preparations as possible. Start by gathering some pots or flats with drainage holes. I like to use six-inch (15 cm) plastic pots, which hold four or five cuttings comfortably. Scrub used containers and rinse them with a disinfecting solution of one part bleach to nine parts water.

For planting, use a light, half-and-half mix of peat moss and perlite or sharp sand, or even perlite or vermiculite alone. (Cuttings tend to rot in heavier soil.) Place the rooting medium in a clean bucket and add enough water to make it damp but not soggy. Then fill the pots to about an inch (2.5 cm) below the rim and tamp the mix lightly.

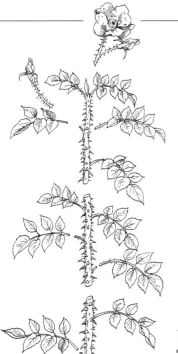

2. MAKE THE CUTTINGS Take softwood cuttings in the morning when the plants are fresh and full of moisture. Avoid soft, easily mashed stems and those that are abnormally thick or thin. The best candidates are those that are still green and flexible. When possible, remove stems a foot or two (30 cm or .6 m) long and take them back to your work area for further cuts. If you're more than a few minutes from home, wrap them in damp paper towels and place them in an unsealed plastic bag out of the sun.

Use a sharp knife to cut off any lateral, or side, shoots from each stem. (If the shoots are firm enough, use them to make more cuttings.) Remove and discard any flower buds or flowers, but leave any thorns. Then slice the remaining length of stem into three- to four-inch (7.5 to 10 cm) pieces, each with at least two nodes, or growing points. Make each cut just below a node, which is where new roots will form. Strip the lower leaves from each cutting, sparing the top leaves to continue photosynthesis and produce auxins, which aid in root formation.

3. POT THE CUTTINGS
Although roses often form roots without it, many gardeners dip the lower end of each cutting in rooting hormone, a powder that contains a synthetic form of auxin. Don't allow the powder to clump on the stem — a few gentle taps with your finger will shake loose any excess and assure a light, even coating.

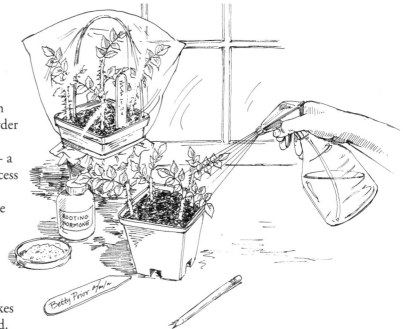

Using the eraser end of a pencil, make holes in the rooting medium near the edges of the pot. Insert each cutting up to half its length, and firm the medium around it. Water immediately with a fine spray, and label each pot with the variety name and date.

To prevent wilting, cover each pot with a clean plastic bag, supported above the foliage with plastic stakes or wire. Secure the plastic to the pot with a rubber band.

4. CARE Set the covered pots in a warm and shaded, but not dark, location. To prevent moisture from building up and causing the cuttings to rot, ventilate them daily by briefly unfastening the bags.

Once the cuttings have taken hold and are growing roots, they will send out new leaves, usually in five to eight weeks. To check, tug gently on a cutting. If it resists being pulled up, it has rooted. Then expose the cuttings to a drier atmosphere for a few days by slitting open the tops of the bags. If the plants begin to wilt, water them and reseal the bags for a day or two before trying again.

When the plants seem acclimated to open air, transplant each to its own pot, keeping them moist and shaded. They won't be strong enough to grow in the open garden until they're about a year old. To protect them over the winter, place the pots in a cold frame, surround them with leaves, and cover the frame securely.

Growing Corn

Janet H. Sanchez

THERE IS NOTHING quite so delicious as sweet corn, served on the cob, dripping with butter. Gardeners have the opportunity to enjoy this treat at its very best by harvesting the ears at the peak of ripeness and rushing them indoors to a pot of boiling water.

Deciding which variety to grow from among the many available today can be daunting. You can start by asking experienced local gardeners to recommend ones that do well in your area, and reading catalogs to discover new varieties. The catalogs will also give you information on days to maturity and any growing requirements — for example, the need to isolate some "supersweet" varieties to prevent unwanted cross-pollination, which makes the kernels starchy.

If you wish to get started early, sow the seeds indoors at least two weeks before your last frost date and plant them outside once they're several inches high. Because corn seedlings don't always transplant well, grow them in peat pots and set them out pot and all. For an extended harvest, plan to sow every two or three weeks during the summer, or plant varieties with different maturity dates simultaneously.

1. **PREPARE THE SOIL** Corn requires a highly fertile soil, which isn't surprising when you consider how quickly it grows into a six-foot (1.8 m) giant.

Work several inches of compost or aged manure into the soil in an area of the garden that receives full sun. Then add some cottonseed meal or bloodmeal at the rate of five pounds (2 kg) per 100 square feet (9.3 square m), or a chemical fertilizer such as 5-10-10 at the rate of two pounds (.9 kg) per 100 square feet (9.3 square m).

Wait until the soil has warmed up to at least 65°F (18°C) before planting — I use a soil thermometer to check. Seed sown in soil that is too cold tends to rot before it has a chance to sprout.

2. LAY OUT AND PLANT THE PATCH I have found that the best way to direct-sow corn is in blocks of three or four rows. Corn is wind-pollinated; for each kernel to form, pollen from the tassels must either fall or be blown onto each of the silks of the ear below. If you plant only one long row, a lot of the pollen will blow away, and many of the ears will have missing kernels.

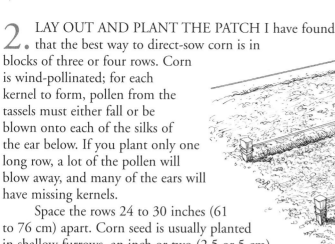

Space the rows 24 to 30 inches (61 to 76 cm) apart. Corn seed is usually planted in shallow furrows, an inch or two (2.5 or 5 cm) deep. If you are concerned about the tall stalks blowing over before harvest, plant the seeds in a deeper furrow and plan to fill it in gradually as the plants grow. In any case, sow the seeds every eight to 12 inches (20 to 30 cm) within the rows, in groups of three or four.

3. CARE Protect corn from crows by covering the patch with antibird netting. Elevate it slightly on short stakes so the birds can't stand on it. Leave it in place until the plants reach the safe height of about five inches (12.5 cm). When the plants are a few inches high, thin them, eliminating all but the strongest seedling in each group. As the season progresses, hoe gently or hand weed to prevent weeds from competing with the crop for moisture and nutrients, taking care not to injure the corn's shallow roots.

Be sure the plants receive at least an inch (2.5 cm) of water a week. When the tassels start to emerge from the top of the stalks, give the patch an especially deep soaking.

Corn earworms are a widespread pest, though early plantings often mature before the adult moth begins laying eggs. Protect later crops by treating each ear with mineral oil three to seven days after the silks appear. Use a medicine dropper to apply about 20 drops to the base of the silks. In some parts of the country, the European corn borer can severely damage the stalks. Control this pest by spraying with Bt (Bacillus thuringiensis).

4. HARVEST Corn is generally ready to pick about three weeks after the silks appear, although unusually warm or cool weather will affect the days to maturity. When the silks wither, check the ears to see if they feel plump. If they do, test for ripeness by peeling back a piece of husk and puncturing a kernel with your fingernail. If it squirts milky juice, the corn is just right. Watery juice means it isn't quite ready, while a doughy kernel indicates overripeness.

After harvest, remove, chop, and compost the stalks to prevent insects from overwintering in them. It's also a good idea to move next year's patch to a different part of the garden to avoid a buildup of pests and the depletion of nutrients in the soil.

Raising Pole Beans

Janet H. Sanchez

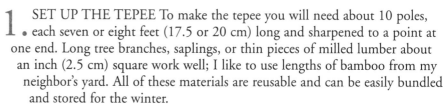

THE DELICIOUS, old-fashioned flavor of beans seems to develop fully only in pole bean varieties. Pole beans have other advantages as well. Unlike bush beans, which typically produce for only a few weeks and must be planted several times to ensure a steady supply, pole beans offer a long season of harvest from one sowing. And because they grow vertically, they take up less space in the garden.

When my son was younger, one of our favorite spring projects was constructing tepees for our pole beans. Having reached the advanced age of 14, Ramon's interest in tepees has diminished, but I don't mind setting up a tepee or two by myself, as it is a quick and easy way to provide the support pole beans require. If the five- to 10-foot-long (12.5 to 25 cm) vines are allowed to trail on the ground, they will not only become a tangled mass, but their pods and leaves will rot from contact with the damp soil.

As the leafy vines grow up the poles of the tepee, they create a shady enclave, a perfect hideout for a small boy, or, more prosaically, a cool spot for a summer sowing of lettuce. Two tepees should provide a family of four with plenty of fresh beans for the table, plus some extra for the freezer.

1. SET UP THE TEPEE To make the tepee you will need about 10 poles, each seven or eight feet (17.5 or 20 cm) long and sharpened to a point at one end. Long tree branches, saplings, or thin pieces of milled lumber about an inch (2.5 cm) square work well; I like to use lengths of bamboo from my neighbor's yard. All of these materials are reusable and can be easily bundled and stored for the winter.

It's best to set up the tepee before doing any soil preparation so as not to compact the soil as you work. Locate it north of the other vegetables in your garden to avoid shading them. Begin by making a circle on the ground about four feet (1.2 m) in diameter. Next, place the poles evenly around the circle. (If a hideout is desired, leave a two-foot (.6 m) opening for the door.) For maximum stability, push each pole about a foot (30 cm) into the soil. Finally, tie the tops of the poles together with strong twine or wire.

2. SOIL PREPARATION Beans require a well-drained soil amended with several inches of compost or rotted manure. Like other members of the legume family, beans "fix" nitrogen. Adding a fertilizer high in nitrogen is therefore unnecessary and may even prevent nitrogen fixation. However, the plants do benefit from additional

phosphorus and potassium, so you may want to work in a fertilizer that is higher in these elements, such as a 5-10-10. Dig the amendments into the soil around the perimeter of the tepee, making a bed a foot (30 cm) or so wide. Then rake the area smooth.

If rainfall has been sparse, irrigate the bed a few days before sowing. On planting day the soil should be moist but not soggy; overly wet soil can cause bean seeds to rot.

3. SOW SEEDS For fast and even germination, wait until the soil temperature is 65°F (18°C). Cool soil can also cause the seeds to rot.

Before planting, you might want to treat the seeds with a bacterial inoculant powder. Such a powder will encourage nitrogen fixation and may increase your harvest. Inoculants are available from garden centers and seed catalogs. Be sure to choose one that is formulated especially for green beans.

Sow four or five seeds about six inches (15 cm) away from each pole of the tepee, poking them an inch (2.5 cm) or so into the soil. Don't water the bed until the seeds germinate unless the weather is extremely hot and dry.

4. CARE AND HARVEST When the seedlings are up and growing, thin them out, leaving one or two strong plants per pole. As the vines start to elongate, they may need help climbing. Lead each one to its designated pole and gently twist it counterclockwise around the bottom.

As they flower and start to develop pods, beans are especially sensitive to moisture stress. Be sure the plants receive an inch (2.5 cm) or so of water each week from you or from rainfall. To prevent the spread of any diseases that may be present, don't work near the plants when the leaves are wet.

Most varieties of pole beans are ready to harvest 60 to 70 days after sowing. For maximum flavor and tenderness, pick the beans while they are young and while they still snap easily when bent. For a long season of harvest, be sure to pick them every three or four days. Otherwise the pods will mature and form seeds inside, and the vine will cease production.

New African Violets from Leaf Cuttings

Oliver E. Allen

AFRICAN VIOLETS and certain other fleshy-stemmed houseplants (streptocarpus, rex begonias, and gloxinias, for example) are difficult to propagate by conventional stem cuttings. But they are extraordinarily easy to propagate by so-called leaf cuttings. No rooting powder or other special substance is needed, and there is an added bonus: the method may well yield three or four new plantlets from each cutting instead of just one.

Leaf cuttings may be taken at any time of the year if you grow your African violets under lights. If you rely on sunlight, swifter results can be obtained during the spring and summer (the amount of light available to your plants is apt to be less during the winter, inducing slower growth).

One cautionary note needs to be sounded. The African violet's fleshy stems are particularly susceptible to rot and other ailments, so make sure all tools, soil, and equipment used are absolutely clean.

Cuttings can be rooted in any pot or shallow flat — plastic freezer containers are handy but must have holes punched in their bottoms for drainage. You will need a soil mix consisting of one part peat moss and one part vermiculite, perlite, or sharp sand; soak the mix with warm water before starting, but allow it to drain so that it is moist but not sopping. The only other items you'll need are a very sharp knife (or better yet a single-edged razor blade) and a plastic food-storage bag.

1. CUT A YOUNG LEAF Choose a healthy, young leaf that has nearly reached its full size — it will probably be among the plant's top leaves. Holding the tip of the leaf gently with one hand (do not bruise it by grasping too tightly), make a diagonal cut in the stem one and a half to two inches (3.75 to 5 cm) from the base of the leaf, severing it from the plant.

2. INSERT AT AN ANGLE Using a pencil or small screwdiver, poke a shallow hole in the soil mix at a low angle and insert the leaf stem; the leaf should be almost flat against the soil, and up to half an inch (1.25 cm) of its stem should be in the rooting soil. Firm the soil around the stem, put the container in the plastic bag to hold the moisture in (if necessary, use sticks or short lengths of wire to hold the plastic away from the leaf), close the bag, and set the container in a spot that is warm but not hot, light but not sunny.

3. WAIT FOR NEW SHOOTS In five to six weeks new shoots should appear at the point where the stem meets the soil mix. When these plantlets are about one-third the height of the leaf itself, open the bag and allow them to adjust to room conditions for a couple of days.

4. REPOT PLANTLETS After two or three days, water the soil mix lightly, then carefully knock the entire soil mix out of its container and gently separate the plantlets from the parent leaf and from each other. Pot them up in small pots in your usual African-violet soil mix. Water them thoroughly, and in the future move them on to larger pots as needed.

Summer

All that in this delightfull Gardin
*   growes,*
Should happie be, and have immortall
*   blis.*

— Edmund Spenser

Training Climbing Roses

Oliver E. Allen

IN TRUTH, there is no such thing as a "climbing rose," for no rose possesses tendrils or other contrivances enabling it to cling by itself to a vertical surface. But because certain roses grow canes that are extra-long due either to genetic mutation or to deliberate hybridizing (or both), and because such plants when tied to trellises, arbors, walls, fences, or other structures can be truly stunning with their myriad blossoms, most gardeners are happy to go along with the misnomer. Indeed climbers possess two assets not claimed by other roses: with their ample proportions they can be distinct features of a landscaping design, and with their luxuriant growth they offer the boon of shade in the hot summer.

Like other roses, climbers produce their best bloom on the youngest wood — canes (or stalks) that have appeared in the past year or so. New canes will, in fact, continue to sprout from the base of the plant at the rate of one or more a year, constantly renewing it. But because climbers become very large it is impractical, as well as unnecessary, to prune them as severely as you would a hybrid tea. Another guideline: you'll get better flowers on canes that grow horizontally rather than vertically. So the trick to managing a climber is to thin out the oldest wood from time to time (keeping the number of canes constant), to prune the newer canes with some restraint so as to keep young shoots appearing throughout the bush, and to guide canes to grow horizontally when possible.

1. ENSURE GOOD AIR CIRCULATION
Unlike vines, which can grow flat against a wall, roses need air space around them — especially in hot weather, when the heat of a wall can cook them. A freestanding trellis or fence provides such circulation, but if you want your climber to creep up a wall be sure to position its support at least three inches (7.5 cm) away from the surface. Guy wires held away from the wall on metal pegs can accomplish this handily. Hinges built into the trellis will enable you to get at the wall for maintenance.

2. TIE AS YOU GO
You will probably want to hold off any pruning for at least two years to enable a new plant to achieve some size. As a cane reaches a support or needs support to keep from drooping, tie it up. Use string or strips of cloth in lengths of eight to 10 inches (20 to 25 cm). First tie the string tightly around the support, then loop it around the cane and tie it very loosely to avoid binding or constricting the tissue.

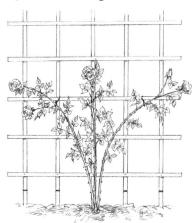

3. ENABLE CANES TO GROW UPWARD, THEN OUT
To start, guide the canes to form a fan-shaped pattern. As a cane approaches a desired height, begin training it sideways so that its tip will start growing more or less horizontally. Although at first, as the bush gains size, this will place much of the bloom (which occurs on the youngest wood) out toward the edges, you can fill in the lower and inner areas with the younger canes that will keep appearing from the base.

4. PRUNE LIGHTLY IN SPRING After your climber has achieved its full expanse you will want to do some pruning each spring — just after the bush begins to put out new growth — on the smaller stems that have grown out from the main canes. This will promote more vigorous flowering. Trim each stem back so as to leave three or four bud eyes (the bright-green buds in the leaf axils) on it. You may also want to trim the longest canes back by about a third to keep them in bounds. Use sharp shears or clippers (scissors-type rather than anvil-type, to make a clean cut with minimum damage to the stem), and cut on the diagonal.

5. REMOVE BLOOMS AS THEY FADE To encourage an everblooming climber to repeat during the season, cut the blossoms off after they have passed their prime. Cut back to a leaf (rose leaves consist of five, or sometimes three, small leaflets) in whose axil a good live bud appears, and make the cut just above the bud.

6. CUT AWAY OLD WOOD After four or five years some of the canes are likely to bear hard, treelike bark. In time this old bark tends to constrict the flow of sap within, and flowering suffers. Thick bark thus serves as a signal that the cane should be removed. A good time to do this is either at the end of the year, when flowering has passed, or better yet at the beginning of the next year, during the regular spring pruning. Trim away any diseased canes as well, plus canes that cross others in the center and make for congestion. Cut the canes close to the ground using long-handled loppers (sometimes a saw will be needed). You may want to cover the larger cuts with wound paint (available from garden centers), although rosarians disagree on the necessity of this step. After the old canes have been removed, new growth will soon appear to replace them.

From time to time suckers (unwanted growth arising not from the climber itself but from the rootstock on which the climbing plant was grafted) may shoot up next to the proper canes. Dig away the soil to be sure the new cane does indeed come from the rootstock, and if it does lop it off immediately.

Trellising Melons

Thomas Christopher

I KNOW OF two excellent reasons for growing melons: Doing so lets you experiment with interesting cultivars that never appear on the greengrocer's shelf, and commercially grown fruit, harvested while still green, never develops the sweet bouquet of a homegrown fruit "slipped" at the peak of ripeness. There is, however, a persuasive reason *not* to grow melons if your garden, like mine, is small: A single muskmelon plant (the least expansive of the melons) may spread its vines over 16 to 24 square feet (1.5 to 2 square m) of soil. The last time I set out melons the traditional way, two hills devoured a quarter of my garden, returning only six fruits.

Training melons to grow on a trellis, a technique Oriental gardeners use, is a good solution. Trellising encourages the vines to climb rather than sprawl, increasing the surface area available to other plants in a small garden. Growing melons on a trellis also simplifies harvesting. Also, the improved air circulation helps keep the vines healthier and free of that fungal scourge, powdery mildew. The system described here can be used to grow all sorts of vining crops — cucumbers, squashes, even pumpkins.

1. SITE THE TRELLIS An A-frame structure of wooden two-by-threes (5 cm by 7.6 cm) and concrete reinforcing mesh is sturdy, cheap, and easy to build. Make it about four feet (1.2 m) tall, and tailor its length to your garden. A 60-degree angle between legs and frame is optimum for exposure to sunlight and ease of harvesting. Treat the wood with the preservative Cuprinol before driving the legs a foot (30 cm) into the ground to anchor them firmly.

The more heat and light the vines receive, the better the harvest, so site the trellis as you would a solar collector. The trellis ought to face south, so run it from east to west along the northern end of your garden, where it won't block the sun from other crops. (The strip of shaded earth underneath the trellis is ideal for a summer crop of leaf lettuce, by the way.)

2. PLANTING The first week of June is melon-planting time in my area of New York (USDA Zone 6), though I start the seedlings in peat pots around the first of May. Since melons are greedy feeders, plant them out in a row of specially enriched soil. Dig a trench one foot (30 cm) deep and two feet (.6 m) wide along the front of the trellis. Line the bottom with six inches (15 cm) of well-rotted horse or cow manure and several handfuls of bonemeal; then replace the excavated soil.

Bear in mind that this southern crop sulks when set out in soils cooler than 80°F (27°C). Covering the mound with a piece of black-plastic mulch (it comes in three-foot-wide (.9 m) rolls) will warm the soil to the temperature that melons prefer.

Plant the seedlings at two-foot (.6 m) intervals. If you covered the bed with plastic, make slits with a knife to plant the seedlings through. Water them in (through the slits) with a soluble fertilizer high in root-promoting phosphorus. During their first weeks of growth, cover the young plants with a floating row cover to protect them from marauding cucumber beetles.

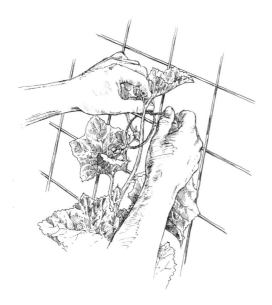

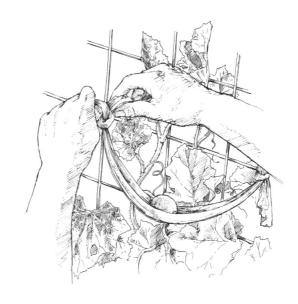

3. TRAINING Train the vines up the wire while they are young and soft, and keep an eye on them — the earlier you redirect runaway vines, the better. As they age, vines become more brittle and may snap if you try to move them. Fasten the new growth in place with ties of soft yarn or strips of old nylon stockings (plastic- or paper-coated wires will choke and cut the vines). To avoid compacting your carefully prepared soil, stand on a scrap of lumber while you work around the trellis.

4. SECURE THE FRUITS Because a melon stem will not support the weight of the maturing melons, you must give each fruit extra support. As the melons grow, they will hang down behind the trellis. When the melons are about the size of golf balls, cradle them in a strip of old nylon stocking (some vertical gardeners favor old onion sacks), and tie both ends of this improvised sling to the back of the trellis. The melons will grow into these pockets, and harvesting is simply a matter of releasing them when they are ripe.

Installing a Preformed Pool

Teri Dunn

A GREAT WAY to take the plunge into water gardening is by starting with a preformed pool, available from catalogs and some garden centers. This is less daunting than digging your own free-form hole and cutting a large piece of plastic sheeting to size. A person can install one of these alone in a single afternoon, although the work will go more smoothly with a helper.

Pools sold for this purpose come in a variety of shapes and sizes and are durable and puncture resistant. Those made of quarter-inch-thick (.6 cm) fiberglass will last up to 50 years. If you want to grow waterlilies in your pool, you must choose a form that is at least 18 inches (46 cm) deep. The four-by-six-foot (1.2 by 1.8 m) kidney-shaped pool shown here will hold about 150 gallons (68 kg) of water and can provide a home for one or two waterlilies, three or four marginal plants such as rushes or aquatic irises, some oxygenating plants to keep algae at bay, and perhaps a few goldfish or koi.

1. SITE THE POOL Waterlilies and many other aquatic plants do best when they receive at least six to eight hours of direct sunlight a day, so choose a spot out in the open or at least away from the shadow of overhanging trees and shrubs. This also ensures that you won't encounter tree roots when you begin to dig or have to clean the pool of fallen leaves later. A water garden tends to look more natural when sited in a low, level area. Avoid putting it in the lowest part of the yard, however, because it may overflow during rainy spells or be vulnerable to runoff that is contaminated by fertilizers, herbicides, or insecticides that you have used elsewhere in your garden. If possible, try to station the pool within reach of a hose as well. This will make it easier to fill the pool initially and to top off the water level when necessary.

Set the pool on the chosen spot. The sides are slightly angled to prevent them from caving in, so your hole will need to reflect this shape. Use a trowel, rope, or a couple of hoses to mark an outline of the pool's bottom and of its top edge. The result should be a circle-within-a-circle design.

2. DIG THE HOLE Make the hole an inch or two (2.5 or 5 cm) bigger than the pool, excavating from the outer boundary down to the inner one, and trying to match the angle of the pool. Remove all sod, rocks, and debris as you work.

It is critical that the bottom of the hole be level so that the surface of the water will be level when the pool is filled. Once the hole is deep enough, stomp on the bottom or tamp it down with the back of the shovel blade. Smooth it further with a piece of lumber.

The top of the hole should also be level. If the site is level to begin with, chances are this will not be a problem. To determine this, lay a board across the hole at various points and set a carpenter's level on the board. If the top isn't level, it's better to adjust the soil on the ground's surface than to change the depth of the hole.

3. SET IN THE POOL The pool will sit more easily in the hole and respond better to fine-tuning if you set it on a base of sand. The sand also forms a protective cushion and provides a smooth surface for the pool to rest on. Empty enough builder's sand into the hole to make a layer an inch (2.5 cm) or more deep. Then set in the pool and wiggle it into position. Remove it temporarily to see if it made a level impression. If not, add extra sand until it does. Add even more sand if you want the pool to be slightly elevated above the hole. This is a good idea if you're concerned about runoff entering the pool.

Return the pool to the hole and maneuver it into final position. Use the board and carpenter's level to make sure the pool is even all along the rim.

4. FILL THE POOL To equalize the pressure from the water and the soil and to prevent bulges, it is important to fill the pool with water and surround the liner with soil simultaneously.

Set the end of a hose in the bottom of the pool and start filling it slowly with water. Begin filling the gap between the ground and the pool with the excavated soil. Tamp the soil in with a trowel or board. Work your way around a few times until the gap is filled evenly on all sides.

To hide the pool's unattractive edge and give it a more natural look, lay bricks, rocks, or stone slabs around and slightly over the edges. Wedge them in well or set them in with mortar so that you and other kneeling admirers won't dislodge them.

Once the pool is finished, wait at least 24 hours before adding plants and fish to give the chlorine in the water a chance to evaporate. If your water also contains chloramine, treat the pool with the liquid-concentrate chemicals sold for this purpose by water-garden suppliers.

Planting a Water Lily

Teri Dunn

A TUB OR POOL of water lilies can bring all sorts of pleasures to a garden, among them constant, colorful blossoms, fragrance (if you choose the right kind of lily), and a parade of admirers ranging from your neighbors to bees and frogs. Once you have chosen a lily that suits your needs in terms of size and color, you'll find that it is easy to plant and care for. All it requires is a pot to put it in, a tub or pool that is at least a foot and a half (46 cm) deep, and a spot that receives at least five or six hours of sun a day.

There are two kinds of water lilies: those that are cold hardy and those that are not, called tropicals. The simplest way to tell them apart is to remember that the blossoms of hardy water lilies usually float on the surface of the water, while those of tropicals are raised several inches above.

Hardy water lilies grow from a rhizome and can be set in water as cool as 50°F (10°C). You therefore can plant them early in the season and enjoy their flowers well into the fall. Tropical water lilies, on the other hand, grow from tubers and require

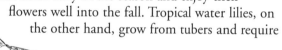

warmer temperatures. Plant a tropical lily when the water temperature has climbed to at least 65°F (18°C). Tropicals have a shorter bloom season than hardy water lilies but can better endure the heat of summer.

1. PREPARE THE RHIZOME OR TUBER Water lilies are sold bareroot, usually with a few leaves intact. It is important to keep the rhizome or tuber moist, so place it in a bowl of water as soon as you get it home. Keep it moist until you are ready to plant.

Carefully inspect the rhizome or tuber for viable roots, which are white and crisp. Use a small, sharp knife to trim off any brown, black, or limp ones. You may also notice some tiny lime-green or bronze leaves emerging from the plant's growing point.

2. GET READY TO POT In nature, water lilies grow in soil at the bottoms of ponds, but garden hybrids will do fine in containers. The size of the pot you use will depend upon the size of your tub or pool. The more room you give the roots, the more robust the plant will be. A four-quart (4 litre) pot is fine for a half barrel; for a pool, you may use a larger pot or even a small laundry tub. Either way, be sure the container has a drainage hole, even though plant and pot will be immersed in water. This prevents gases from building up inside the pot.

Fill the container one-third full with heavy topsoil or garden loam. This type of soil is closest to pond muck, plus it won't float away the way a peat-based soil mix will. In addition, heavy soil helps hold the rhizome or tuber firmly in place.

Once the container is one-third full, stop to insert a water lily fertilizing tablet (available from mail-order nurseries that sell water lilies and supplies) or a handful of a low-analysis granular fertilizer, such as 5-10-5 or 6-10-4. Some people crush the tablet or mix in the fertilizer to spread it evenly through the soil, though this is not mandatory. Then fill the container to the top with soil and drench it until water runs out the drainage hole at the bottom.

3. POT THE PLANT To pot the rhizome or tuber, remove a third of the saturated soil and set it aside. (You may want to wear rubber gloves, as this can be a muddy operation.) If you are planting a hardy water lily, set the rhizome roots-down in the pot at a 45-degree angle. Aim the rhizome so the plant has room to elongate across the pot and the crown is pointed upward. It's okay to place the opposite end flush against the pot if necessary. If you are planting a tropical water lily, look for a white line on the tuber. This indicates where the soil level should be once you fill the pot. Set the tuber lengthwise in the center of the pot, roots down.

Gently top off the pot with the reserved soil, filling it to within an inch or two of the rim. Be sure to leave the growing point of the rhizome or tuber free of soil. To avoid air pockets, firm the soil with your thumbs as you work. Water the pot once more, taking care not to wash soil away from the root. Then top off the pot with pea gravel (again, making sure to leave the growing point exposed) to prevent soil from washing away once it is in the tub or pool.

4. SET THE POT IN WATER Most water lilies prefer to be a foot (30 cm) or so beneath the water's surface. If your pool is deeper than that, place some bricks or an empty, overturned pot on the bottom to elevate the plant to the correct height. Lower the pot in slowly at an angle to allow any air bubbles to escape, then set the pot on its base. If the plant has a few leaves, gently position them so they float on the surface of the water.

Within a few weeks, your water lily will have adjusted to its new home. New leaves will soon begin to appear, and shortly thereafter the first blossoms should make their debut.

Brewing Manure Tea

Thomas Christopher

ANURE IS MY STANDBY IN THE GARDEN. Horse, cow, chicken, rabbit, goat — I'll take whatever I can get. If composted and dug into the soil in late fall, the excreta of herbivorous animals replenishes the three major plant nutrients (nitrogen, phosphorus, and potassium) as well as the trace minerals essential to healthy growth. It also furnishes organic material, which soil microorganisms turn into humus. And in springtime, manure provides the makings of a nutritious tea.

This beverage, I hasten to add, is not for me but for my plants. It makes a good spring tonic for hardy shrubs and is an excellent liquid feed for container-grown plants. Manure tea instantly replaces the nutrients that are leached out of soil by winter snow and rain. For that reason, I also recommend it for use in greenhouses and cold frames and even for the summer-time baskets of foliage and flowers with which we adorn decks and patios.

The place where I apply manure tea most liberally, however, is the vegetable garden. I use it first to get the seedlings off to a good start at transplanting time. And because the tea is rich in nitrogen, I use it again later to nourish leafy crops, such as lettuce, spinach, and chard, and cole crops, such as Brussels sprouts and kale.

1. BLENDING THE INGREDIENTS I brew manure tea in quantity, since it will keep the better part of a season (though as it ages it diminishes somewhat in nutritional value). I use a 55-gallon (208 litres) drum as the kettle, but by reducing the ingredients proportionaly you can easily make it by the bucketful.

However big a batch you brew, use the freshest manure you can find, as manure that has decomposed in an uncovered barnyard heap has lost most of its nutrients. Rainwater washes away the phosphorus, potassium, and minerals, while much of the nitrogen escapes as gaseous ammonia.

Fresh manure is also full of weed seeds. To avoid sowing these problems in your garden every time you fertilize, seal the manure in a burlap feed sack, making a sort of a barnyard tea bag, before dropping it into the barrel.

The amount of manure you'll need for a barrel of tea depends on the type you use. If it's horse, cow, sheep, or goat manure, you'll need about five gallons (19 litres) per barrel of tea; if you are using poultry manure, reduce that quantity by half, as poultry manure is considerably richer in nutrients.

After shoveling the manure into its sack, tie it shut with one end of a three-foot (.9 m) length of quarter-inch (.6 cm) rope. Tie the other end of the rope to a stout garden stake, and prop the stake across the barrel's mouth so that the sack dangles inside. Then fill the barrel with water and cover it with a scrap of plywood. Covering presents both water and nutrients from evaporating, keeps out flies, and contains the odor.

2. BREWING THE TEA Let the manure soak for at least a week, jerking the bag up and down by its rope once a day to mix the barrel's contents. Be sure to replace the cover after every inspection.

By the end of the week, the water should have turned a dark, murky brown. Remove the manure bag and empty it into the compost heap. Then top off the barrel with water and cover it again.

3. USING THE TEA AS A STARTER SOLUTION Even if you enriched the soil generously the previous fall, a gentle feeding with a fast-acting fertilizer will benefit a young vegetable garden. If administered right at transplanting time, the extra nutrients will help seedlings weather the trauma of transition and speed their return to normal growth.

Manure tea is ideal for a starter solution, as it soaks right into the soil around the roots. But the brew in the barrel is too concentrated, so dip it out a half-bucketful at a time and dilute it with fresh water until the blend is light amber.

As you plant each seedling, form the soil around it into a shallow dish, and pour in a pint (475 ml) of the solution. Sprinkle some tea over the seedlings' leaves too, since plants also absorb nutrients through their foliage.

4. SIDE-DRESSING WITH MANURE TEA Because nitrogen fosters foliar growth, manure tea makes a very effective side-dressing for all leafy crops, helping to keep them strong yet tender.

For best results, make the first application about three weeks after transplanting or thinning the seedlings. Once again, dilute the tea until it is a light-amber color. Sprinkle it over the plants at a rate of about one gallon (4 litres) to five square feet (.5 square m) of bed. Reapply at intervals of three or four weeks throughout the plants' season of growth. But resist the temptation to give your plants an extra snack between meals; too much fertilizer can be as harmful as too little.

Propagating Lilies

Oliver E. Allen

LILIES ARE particularly adept at multiplying themselves. Many (*Lilium tigrinum* and *umbellatum* hybrids, for example) double each year and must be divided to maintain optimum flowering ability. A few species (*Lilium tigrinum* and *L. bulbiferum* among others) develop tiny bulbils, or proto-bulbs, in their leaf axils that may simply be picked off and planted. Others develop bulblets underground that may also be separated for planting. Still other lilies can be propagated via stem cuttings. All of them set seed. But the easiest way to reproduce exact clones of your favorite lilies is to make use of the scales they produce. Each of these, if properly severed from the parent bulb and immersed in a soilless mix, will produce three to five (or even more) bulblets that can in due course become full-fledged lily bulbs.

Unlike other bulbs such as tulips and onions, which have successive layers of scales completely enclosing each other and an outer skin that seals the whole affair, lily bulbs are constructed somewhat like artichokes, with overlapping scales that may be picked off in moderation without injuring the bulb itself or lessening its flowering capacity. The best time to collect scales is when the lily is in flower, or immediately thereafter, but no later than midsummer if you want to be sure of having usable new bulbs the following spring.

To convert the scales into bulblets, all you need is a moderately large plastic bag (foot-square [77 square cm] food-storage bags are good); enough peat moss, vermiculite, or sphagnum moss to fill the bag (a suitable mix is half peat and half vermiculite); and a fungicide such as captan or ferbam. Your mix should be damp but not wet: immerse it in water and then drain it thoroughly, so that it feels barely moist to the back of your hand.

1. COLLECT THE SCALES If you want many clones of a lily, you will probably need to lift the entire plant from the soil and break off the scales; if you're looking for only a few new bulbs, you may prefer to dig down and carefully clear the soil from around the bulb, then reach down and take off the scales. Whichever method you use, be sure to break off the scales as close to the base of the bulb as possible, for the new bulblets will appear on the callus made by the break, and the callus forms more readily on the lower portions of the scale. Up to half a bulb's scales may be removed without harming it; you may get several dozen to work with. Discard any partly decayed or withered scales. Dust the others with fungicide and set them aside temporarily on a damp cloth or paper towel to prevent their drying out. Give the parent bulb a good dusting with fungicide too, and return it to the soil (or replace the soil around it that you dug away).

2. IMMERSE IN THE MIX

Put an inch or two (2.5 or 5 cm) of the soilless mix into the plastic bag. Plant the scales in the mix so that they will be visible through the plastic; this will allow you to check their progress over the ensuing weeks. To do this, you might insert a few of them around the edges of the mix already in the bag, then add more mix, plant a few more, and so on, until you have planted all your scales or filled the bag. Seal the bag tightly, but punch a small hole in the plastic near the top to let some air in. Then place the bag in a protected spot where the temperature remains around 68° to 80°F (20° to 27°C), and leave it there for six to eight weeks.

After about six weeks, begin checking the bag to see how bulblets are forming at the base of each scale. When most of them have attained the size of a pea (some may have acquired roots), transfer the bag to a cool cellar, cold frame, or refrigerator in which the temperature is 35° to 46°F (2° to 8°C), and leave it there for two or three months. This will enable the bulblets — tiny as they are — to break dormancy.

3. POT UP THE SCALES

Although it is permissible after the cooling period to separate the bulblets and plant them in the garden, a safer course at this stage is to plant the scales — with bulblets still attached — in a good potting mix (either in small pots or in a flat) and hold them there until the end of winter. The scales will have retained some food reserves, and the new bulblets will benefit, becoming larger and healthier.

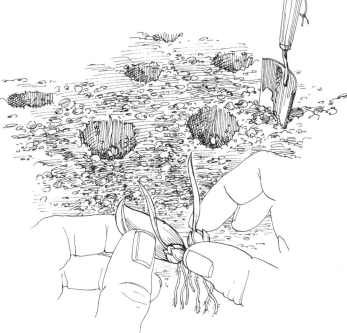

4. PLANT OUT IN SPRING

After the ground thaws, retrieve the bulblets from their pots or flats, separate them from the scales (take special pains to protect the fledgling roots), and plant them out as you would a conventional lily bulb. They are now on their own.

Rooting Buddleias

Thomas Christopher

IN MY UNPAID (and generally uninvited) role of garden adviser to my friends, I always urge them to plant more buddleias. These excellent shrubs bloom all summer, bridging the gap between spring prodigies — azaleas, rhododendrons, and the like — and fall foliage. What's more, buddleias really earn their nickname, butterfly bush, by attracting a steady stream of Lepidoptera, and I can think of no more pleasant occupation for a summer's day than butterfly watching. Besides planting buddleias myself, I have been known to give them away. Luckily, I get the bushes for free, by propagating them.

Buddleias are easily grown from semihardwood cuttings, which should be taken now, at midsummer, from partially matured stems. A woman in Texas taught me how to root these cuttings with no more equipment than a sharp knife, a few square feet of sandy soil, and a couple of one-quart (1 litre) canning jars. She uses the technique to increase her rose collection, but it works equally well for many other deciduous shrubs: forsythias, kerrias, philadelphus, viburnums, and, of course, buddleias. My success rate is at least 50 percent. This doesn't approach the results one would get with a proper rooting bench and mist system, but it's certainly sufficient for my needs.

1. MAKING THE BED Before setting knife to bush, prepare the bed in which you'll set the cuttings to root. Exposure is crucial. Cuttings need bright light to root but will wither in direct sunlight, so find a sheltered spot — the foot of a north-facing wall is ideal. The size of the plot will vary with the number of cuttings you take, but make sure to allow an area four inches (10 cm) square for each (enough space, that is, to accommodate a canning jar).

Turn the soil one spade-length deep, adding one part peat moss and one part sharp builder's sand for each part soil. These amendments will raise the bed, providing the perfect drainage that the cuttings require and a moist yet well-aerated medium that encourages root growth. Rake the bed smooth, then tamp it down firmly with a brick to eliminate any air pockets. These measures will keep water from puddling and keep the bed uniformly moist.

2. TAKING A CUTTING Early morning is the best time to take cuttings, since the buddleia's shoots and foliage will be most crisp and turgid with water then. Search the new growth for a pencil-thin shoot just beginning to harden into mature wood. To see if it is suitable, grasp the shoot near its tip and bend it; it should flex easily but snap back when you release it.

Inspect the shoot. A cutting should have at least two lateral (axillary) buds; these are the buds that form on the main stem just above the union with a leaf stem.

With a razor-sharp knife (I use a Swiss pocketknife made for horticultural work, but an inexpensive artist's razor knife works just as well), cut off the topmost four to six inches (10 to 15 cm) of your chosen shoot just below the lowest set of leaves. Then slice off any side shoots and carefully strip away the foliage from the lower half, leaving one or two leaves at the top.

—Axillary Bud

—Main Stem

3. STICKING A CUTTING Dust the bottom inch (2.5 cm) or so of the cutting with rooting hormone, removing any excess by taping the stem sharply with your forefinger. With a dibble (a pointed piece of half-inch (1.25 cm) dowel), push a hole into the rooting bed. It is important to make the hole wider than the cutting so that the rooting hormone isn't rubbed off and the cutting isn't injured when it is thrust into the soil. The hole should be deep enough to accommodate at least half of the cutting's length.

Lower the cutting into the hole. Make sure there is at least one lateral bud (two or three is even better) below the soil's surface, and only one bud above. Roots will develop from the buried buds or, sometimes, from the cutting's base.

Firm the soil around the stem with your dibble. When you have finished sticking all your cuttings, moisten the bed thoroughly with a gentle spray of water. Finally, cover each cutting with a wide-mouthed one-quart (1 litre) jar.

4. AFTERCARE Never let the bed go dry. Conscientious watering through dry spells is essential if the cuttings are to root (though if you are lucky a rainy season may make this kind of care unnecessary). But be careful not to drown the cuttings. If moisture condenses inside the jar, slip a pebble under its lip to let air circulate around the cutting. Replace the jar immediately, however, if the cutting starts to flag.

Four to six weeks should see the cuttings rooted, but this will vary with soil temperature and the type of buddleia. Test for roots toward the end of this interval by gently tugging at one of the cutting's leaves. If the cutting begins to pull free of the soil, it hasn't rooted yet.

Drying Herbs

Nancy Bubel

GATHERING HERBS for drying is one of midsummer's most pleasant tasks. Using the heat of the season to preserve some of this bounty always makes me feel in tune with my garden. When sheared in midsummer, most herb plants respond by growing bushier and more attractive; plants from which you take cuttings now will produce another harvest before frost. Drying herbs is not hard work, and you don't need special equipment. A pinch of dried herbs can make a significant difference in stews, sauces, salads, and soups. You might also want to dry some mint or lemon verbena for teas, or prepare jars of dried herbs for thoughtful, personalized gifts.

1. CUT THE STALKS For best flavor, pick herbs when blossoms first begin to form, but before they open; this is when their volatile-oil content is highest. Wait until late morning on a sunny day, after the dew has dried. The leaves should be dry when you gather cuttings.

Use scissors or pruning shears to clip off the herb stalks. It's better to cut than to break the stems, because breaking them leaves a harder-to-heal ragged edge on the remaining stem, and tugging on the plant may disturb its roots. In most cases it's best to remove up to two-thirds of an herb plant's top growth. (In the fall, as frost approaches, perennial herbs such as sage should be trimmed more conservatively — perhaps by one-third to one-half — because they may not survive winter if pruned too severely late in the season.)

2. RINSE THE HERBS Now's the time to remove any grit, dust, or other residues; you won't want to wash the herbs after they've dried. Long-stemmed herbs are usually fairly clean, but creeping plants like thyme may have sand or mud clinging to their leaves. Hold muddy leaves under running water for a minute or two. If they're just dusty, you can plunge them briefly into a bucket of clean water. Then shake off the excess water thoroughly and pat dry with paper towels, or whirl the cuttings in a mesh basket to spin off the water.

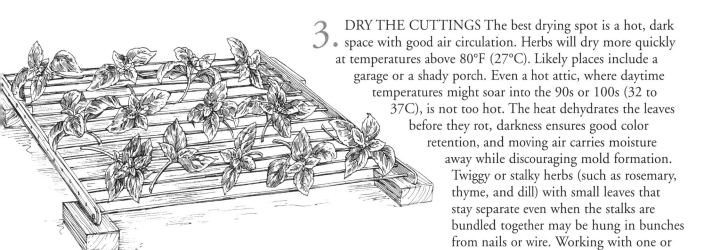

3. DRY THE CUTTINGS The best drying spot is a hot, dark space with good air circulation. Herbs will dry more quickly at temperatures above 80°F (27°C). Likely places include a garage or a shady porch. Even a hot attic, where daytime temperatures might soar into the 90s or 100s (32 to 37C), is not too hot. The heat dehydrates the leaves before they rot, darkness ensures good color retention, and moving air carries moisture away while discouraging mold formation. Twiggy or stalky herbs (such as rosemary, thyme, and dill) with small leaves that stay separate even when the stalks are bundled together may be hung in bunches from nails or wire. Working with one or

two dozen stalks at a time, tie the stems tightly together with string or fasten them together with rubber bands. String may need to be tightened periodically as the stems shrink in drying, while rubber bands will continue to hold as the bundles lose bulk. If possible, hang the bunches of herbs where air reaches them from all sides — from a rafter or ceiling hook, for example, rather than on a wall.

If you don't have a shaded place in which to hang your herbs, pop a brown paper bag over them. Cut small slits in the bag to admit air. Large-leaved herbs (such as basil or mint) may rot before they dry if they are bundled tightly together. Such herbs will dry more quickly and retain color better if their stems are grouped in small bunches or spread in a single layer on racks or screens, propped so that air can circulate under them. (Avoid using galvanized-metal screens; plant acids may react with the metal to form toxic compounds.)

4. STRIP THE DRY LEAVES To determine whether your herbs are dry enough to pack away, roll a leaf in your fingers. It should crumble readily. If it bends but does not break when folded, or if it feels leathery, it is not yet dry enough. In very hot weather, small-leaved herbs like parsley and thyme should dry within a week, provided they get good air circulation. Those with larger and fleshier leaves — basil, comfrey, and the like — may take two weeks or more to dry thoroughly.

Leaf stripping is a relaxing task after a day of gardening; just run your hands down the stalk and stems, rubbing the leaves off into a bowl on your lap. If you're aiming for that country-herb ambience in your kitchen, save several whole herb bundles to festoon the ceiling beams. Although hanging herbs look homey and inviting, a kitchen's warmth and occasional damp air will cause the herbs' flavor to fade as their volatile oils evaporate. You'll want to keep your cooking herbs under cover. Store the stripped dried leaves in tightly closed containers.

Making Cut Flowers Last Longer

Oliver E. Allen

THERE IS AN IMAGE FAMILIAR to all of us, solemnized in storybooks and romantically portrayed in many an advertisement: a lovely woman is gathering flowers from her garden, or perhaps from a sunny meadow, and dreamily laying them in a shallow wicker basket carried in the crook of her arm. The picture is fine except for that basket. By the time the woman gets back to the house the flowers in all likelihood will have wilted, done in by the hot, dry wicker. Experienced flower pickers know better: the young lady should have been carrying an unromantic pail of water.

True, some flowers can survive a lack of moisture for a time, but the tissues of many will dry out alarmingly in just a few minutes after picking if they are not plunged into water. Indeed, the act of cutting compounds the problem, as it causes a callus (much like a scab) to form over the cut and an air bubble to be trapped behind the callus; both impede the intake of badly needed water and ultimately result in shorter vase life. So it is that knowledgeable flower gatherers take some simple steps that, by assuring a continued flow of water into the stems of the picked blossoms, minimize or even eliminate the stress of the transit from garden to living-room bouquet. Then, by properly conditioning (or hardening) the flowers to life in a vase, they further extend the longevity of their displays, making a bouquet last more than a week instead of days.

Good cutting starts with the proper tools. A pair of sharp scissors, like butterfly-handled Japanese shears, is best. Avoid blade-and-anvil clippers, which crush the stems unnecessarily. A sharp kitchen or garden knife will also be needed. Plus the humble pail, one-third filled with water — that's all you need, and it's no chore to carry. Some plants prefer warm water, others cool; tepid is a safe compromise.

Timing is also important. Early morning before the dew has dried is ideal, but if you're slow to rise wait until evening. Although the flowers contain less water then, they have been producing food all day. During midday hours plants lose more moisture than they absorb and are much more prone to wilt. (On overcast or rainy days any time is permissible, however.) In choosing what to pick, you're generally better off taking flowers that have not quite reached their prime, although chrysanthemums are best picked when in full bloom. Blossoms that are beginning to fade will not last long after picking; another indicator of age is the presence of pollen in the flower's center. Also pass over flowers from plants suffering insect or fungus damage.

1. **CUT ON THE SLANT** Square-cut stems resting on the bottom of a pail or vase take in water poorly, so make an angular cut, and put the flower in the bucket immediately. (In cutting from either a perennial or an annual, by the way, be sure to leave enough leaves to ensure the plant's continued growth. Bulb leaves should never be cut as the plant depends on them to manufacture food for next year's growth.) The exception to the angle-cut rule is pithy- or woody-stemmed plants; a square cut will make splitting stems of these plants easier.

2. **RECUT STEMS UNDER WATER** Upon returning indoors, use the kitchen knife to strip

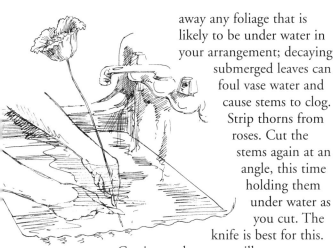

away any foliage that is likely to be under water in your arrangement; decaying submerged leaves can foul vase water and cause stems to clog. Strip thorns from roses. Cut the stems again at an angle, this time holding them under water as you cut. The knife is best for this. Cutting under water will remove calluses and air bubbles and will allow the stem's water-conducting cells to fill up. Some bulb flowers, like narcissus, should have the pale-green-to-white growth at the base of each stem removed, as it will not take up water. All woody-stemmed flowers such as roses, viburnum, and wisteria should be split an inch or so up from the bottom of the stem for better water intake. Hollow-stemmed flowers like delphiniums and large dahlias should be removed from the water, turned upside down, and their stems carefully filled with water as if you were filling a narrow test tube. Plug the stem end with cotton wool or wax and return it to the pail. Any plants whose stems exude a milky sap (poppies and heliotrope, for example) should have the ends of their stems singed with a match or candle flame, or dipped into boiling water for 30 seconds.

3. CONDITION FLOWERS Immediately after recutting or splitting the stems, transfer the flowers to a clean container of cool water reaching halfway up the stems. Mist the blossoms, then store the container in a cool, dark place (in the basement or in an extra refrigerator) for several hours or overnight. Flowers should be conditioned in darkness so that their stomata (minute pores in the stems and leaves) will close, reducing water loss. Two kinds of flowers require special treatment. Tulip stems are likely to arch or twist during conditioning. If you want some or all of them to remain straight, wrap them (blossoms included) in a few sheets of newspaper or waxed paper secured with rubber bands and set them in the water. The support of the paper will cause them to set straight. Violets, lilies of the valley, and hydrangeas absorb water through their blossoms as well as their stems and so should be completely immersed in water for an hour after picking, then allowed to rest with their stems only in water.

4. USE PRESERVATIVE IN VASE WATER Following their conditioning the flowers will be ready for arranging. Use only thoroughly clean vases. To extend flower life further add a preservative to the water. Commercial preparations such as Floralife, Oasis, and Petalife, available at florist shops and some garden centers, provide nutrients as well as a measure of protection against bacterial infection. While flowers vary in their responses to preservatives, such solutions can more than double vase life. Use preservatives only when you first make your arrangement. Thereafter top off the vase with fresh water daily. It is best not to use preservative in metal vases because the two can react, making the water toxic to plants. Some flowers (asters, snapdragons, dahlias, marigolds, calendulas, and stocks, for example) foul water remarkably quickly. Periodically change the water for these completely, replacing it with a fresh solution of preservative. It is also a good idea to mist the flowers each day, spraying the air above them rather than the blossoms directly so that the mist settles down gently among them. Remove blossoms or leaves as they fade or wilt.

Saving Squash Seeds

Janet H. Sanchez

SQUASH VINES BURGEONING in the garden give promise of a bountiful harvest soon to come. Why not go a step further and save seeds to plant next year? Saving seeds ensures a continuing supply even if your favorite variety becomes scarce or unavailable. And, by careful selection over several years, you may end up developing a strain that is better adapted to your taste, garden, and storage conditions.

All varieties of squash and pumpkins belong to the genus *Cucurbita*, which contains four species. Crosses occur easily among varieties within a species and sometimes between species, resulting in offspring that are unlike either parent. This happens because squash plants bear both male and female flowers, which are pollinated by insects (primarily bees) that rove from plant to plant. So to be sure the seeds you save reproduce true to type, you must isolate each variety of squash from the other varieties in your garden — and those in your neighbors' gardens — by at least 500 feet (152 m), or hand-pollinate the blossoms. Choose varieties that are not hybrids, since hybrids, like the accidental crosses, won't come true in the next generation.

1. PREPARE THE BUDS Wait until both male and female buds have appeared on your
. squash plants. The male buds usually appear first, growing on the ends of smooth, straight stems. Female buds appear several days later and have the beginnings of a tiny squash at the base of their petals.

Check your plants each afternoon for ripe buds — those with soft petals and a brighter orange color near the tips. Unripe buds are green and hard; wilted blossoms have already opened. When you spot ripe female and male buds, close several of each and seal them with twist-ties or masking tape to prevent insect pollination. Try to prepare an equal number of male and female buds so there will be enough pollen. It is wise to select flowers from more than one squash plant to avoid the possibility of inbreeding.

2. POLLINATE THE BLOSSOMS Early the next morning, pick one
. of the male blossoms you prepared the day before and take it to a prepared female blossom on a different plant. Once untied, the female blossom should open fully. If not, pinch off its very tip to help it expand. Remove the male blossom's petals and rub its pollen-covered anthers on the stigma of the female flower. Then tie or tape the female flower closed again, and mark the vine by loosely fastening a bright ribbon around its stem. You may need to repeat this process over a period of several days so that you have four or five hand-pollinated candidates.

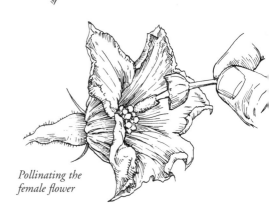

Removing petals from the male flower

Pollinating the female flower

Keep an eye on these female flowers as they develop into full-grown squashes. If any are growing on especially healthy vines, a quality you'll want in future crops, tie an extra ribbon on the stems. Other qualities you may wish to select for include fruit size, early ripening, and disease resistance. To keep the plants in good health, water them well if there is less than an inch (2.5 cm) of rainfall each week, and feed them monthly with diluted liquid fertilizer.

3. HARVEST THE SEEDS Allow your hand-pollinated squashes to ripen fully on the vine. If you pick them while they are still immature, their seeds will also be immature and will fail to grow properly.

Let summer squash mature until the fruits become large and hard-shelled; this will happen six to eight weeks *after* the usual harvesting time. But if frost threatens, bring the fully mature fruits inside.

Let winter squash and pumpkins remain on the vine until the outer shell cannot be pierced with a fingernail. These fruits will keep even better over the winter if they are cured outdoors. To do this, simply cut them from their vines and leave them in the garden for another 10 days. Cover them at night with a blanket if frost threatens. You may want to store the fruits (ideally at 50° to 60°F [10° to 16°C]) for several months to determine which ones keep longest in your storage conditions.

In any event, to extract the seeds from your best candidates, cut them in half, and place seeds and pulp in a bowl of water. Separate the pulp from the seeds with your fingers and spread the cleaned seeds on paper towels to dry for a week or so, turning them and replacing the towels daily.

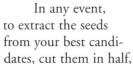

4. STORE THE SEEDS Seeds are living organisms and as such will deteriorate rapidly if stored damp or at high temperatures. When your seeds feel completely dry, place them in labeled envelopes in a jar that can be tightly sealed, such as a canning jar. A week later, check for signs of moisture and, if necessary, spread the seeds on paper towels again to dry further. Some seed savers place a small packet of silica gel desiccant (available from seed companies, as well as camera, florist, or craft-supply stores) in the jar with the seeds to help absorb excess moisture.

Store the jar of seeds in a cool, dry place; the refrigerator is best if you can spare the space. Properly dried and stored squash seeds will remain viable for up to five years.

Dividing Bearded Irises

Janet H. Sanchez

BEARDED IRISES are prized perennials that give us showy, fragrant flowers every spring. They usually bloom reliably for three or four years after initial planting but produce fewer and fewer blossoms in succeeding years. This is because their rhizomes (fleshy, thick underground stems that function as storage organs and give rise to both roots and leaves) increase each season until they eventually become overcrowded and starved for nutrients. Dividing the clump and replanting individual rhizomes in freshly prepared soil gives the plants a new lease on life, allowing them to gather the energy to produce abundant blossoms once again. And if borers are a problem in your area, your plants will gain renewed strength to resist their attacks.

In cold-winter areas, divide bearded irises in mid- to late summer, so the new plants will have plenty of time to become established before freezing weather arrives. Gardeners in milder climates can safely delay this project until September or even October, which will allow the divisions to settle in more comfortably after the heat of summer.

1. DIG UP THE CLUMP If the soil is dry, water the bed thoroughly a day or so before digging. When you have more than one variety scheduled for division, it is wise to deal with each in turn and to label each clump to avoid mix-ups.

Use a spading fork to loosen the soil around and under the clump, taking care not to cut into the rhizomes growing near the edge. Lift the entire clump out of the ground and shake off or wash away any soil clinging to the rhizomes and roots.

2. MAKE DIVISIONS The clump will consist of older, spongy rhizomes with lighter-colored young ones growing from their sides. Cut the young rhizomes away from the older segments with a sharp knife. Discard the older pieces and any parts that are undersize or diseased.

In some areas of the country, bearded irises may be infested with borers, pinkish-colored larvae (or grubs) with brown heads. These creatures tunnel into and devour rhizome tissues, leaving a wound open to infection by bacterial soft rot. Extract and kill any borers you find, and cut away all damaged tissue.

To reduce moisture loss, trim the leaves to about a third of their original height. Each division should consist of a vigorous, firm rhizome and a fan of healthy leaves.

To help prevent infection, soak the rhizomes for about half an hour in a 10 percent solution of household bleach, followed by a dusting of powdered sulfur. Then lay the trimmed plants in a shady place for several hours to allow the cut ends to dry and heal.

3. REPLANT THE DIVISIONS Always plant bearded irises in a sunny location with good drainage. If you are replanting in the same location as the old clump, first check for any inch-long (2.5 cm), shiny-brown borer pupae that may be hiding in the soil. Destroy them, or they will emerge in the fall as moths and lay eggs on or near the plants.

Bearded irises are heavy feeders. If possible, remove some of the old soil and add twice as much compost, or compost plus fresh soil. At the very least, work in an inch or two (2.5 or 5 cm) of compost or well-rotted manure. Also give the plants a light application of a 5-10-10 fertilizer (half the amount recommended on the label). As is the case with many perennials, it's best to avoid fertilizers with a high ratio of nitrogen, which can lead to excessive leafy growth that is susceptible to disease and damage from early frosts.

Space the divisions 12 to 18 inches (30 to 46 cm) apart. The plants will quickly form a natural-looking clump if grown in groups of three. Arrange them in a triangle with the fans of two of the divisions pointing outward, and the fan of the third pointed into the space between.

To plant, dig a shallow hole for each division, forming a low mound in the center on which to set the rhizome. Drape the roots down each side of the mound, and firm the soil around them. It's important to cover a freshly planted rhizome only lightly with soil. Those that are planted too deep are much more susceptible to borers and rot.

4. CARE Water the young plants at once to settle the soil around the roots. If the weather is hot and sunny, temporarily shade them by placing a shingle on their south side. If there is no rain, irrigate every 10 days or so throughout the summer. Don't overwater, however, as too much moisture makes the rhizomes vulnerable to rot.

In regions with cold winters, apply a mulch of evergreen boughs or salt hay in late autumn to prevent alternate freezing and thawing of the soil, which can heave the plants out of the ground. But be sure to remove the mulch in early spring, as a permanent mulch may cause too much moisture to remain around the rhizomes.

Preparing for a Soil Test

Lee Reich

EVERY FEW YEARS, and whenever I start a new vegetable garden, I have my soil tested to check its fertility and pH. Adequate fertility ensures that necessary nutrients are in the soil, and proper pH makes it possible for plants to use those nutrients. It also provides a friendly environment for beneficial soil microorganisms.

Late summer and autumn are good times to sample soil. Soil-testing laboratories are usually not as busy then as they are in late winter or spring, so you'll have the test results in hand in plenty of time to mix necessary amendments into the soil before spring planting.

I have my soil tested at my state university's soil-testing laboratory (via the Cooperative Extension Service), but private testing laboratories can perform the analysis as well. A good test takes your region's particular climate and soils into account.

1. DEFINING THE TEST AREA The area to be tested must have relatively uniform ground conditions. If your garden consists of two or perhaps more large areas where soil conditions obviously differ (if the soil changes from clay to sand, for example, or from well-drained loam to soggy muck), each of these areas will require a separate test.

As you look over the garden, make a mental note to avoid sampling where you previously had a compost pile or where you fill your fertilizer or lime spreader. Also avoid taking samples near boundaries.

Test your lawn soil separately. As with the garden soil, avoid taking samples from areas that aren't representative and keep in mind that more than one test might be needed if you have more than one type of soil.

2. TAKING SOIL SAMPLES

Because laboratories use only a small amount of soil for the actual test — one cup (250 ml), usually — the sample must be as representative as possible. To account for small differences in the test area, you will need to take at least a half-dozen samples from various spots within that area.

The roots of most vegetables feed in the top six inches (15 cm) of the soil, so each sample must be six inches (15 cm) deep. Brush aside any manure, compost, or plant residues on the surface of the soil, dig a hole with a trowel, then slice a uniformly thick section of soil along one side of the hole.

For lawn samples, remove the surface layer of sod first, then sample to a depth of two inches (5 cm).

3. MIXING THE SAMPLE

As you collect the samples, dump them into a clean plastic bucket. Mix them thoroughly to average out differences, and discard any large stones or debris. Then remove about a cup (250 ml) of soil for the test.

Spread the cupful of soil on a clean baking pan to air-dry for a day. Avoid contaminating the blended sample by touching it too much with your hands or with unclean utensils.

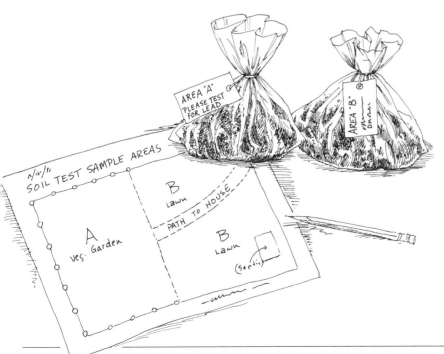

4. PREPARING THE SAMPLE FOR SHIPMENT

Carefully follow any packing instructions provided by the soil-testing laboratory. If you are having more than one area analyzed, label each sample before mailing it, and make a note to yourself of its location on your property.

The testing laboratory may request additional information, such as how you fertilized the garden in the past and what you intend to grow. Indicate whether you want any special tests, such as for micronutrients or toxic elements (lead, for example). In a few weeks' time you should receive test results and specific recommendations for fertilizing and for altering or maintaining the pH.

Raising Ferns from Spores

Thomas Christopher

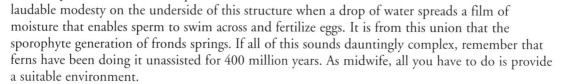

LATE SUMMER to early fall is the time when hardy ferns such as the Christmas fern bear spores. With just a pinch of these spores, you'll be able to grow all the ferns your garden can use. This is not a complicated process, and it succeeds with almost any hardy fern; however, it does differ from starting flower or vegetable seeds. A fern requires two distinct generations to complete its reproductive cycle. In the first the spore, a single cell encased in a thick, protective coat, germinates into a heart-shaped bit of greenery a quarter of an inch (.6 cm) across called a prothallium. Sexual reproduction then takes place with laudable modesty on the underside of this structure when a drop of water spreads a film of moisture that enables sperm to swim across and fertilize eggs. It is from this union that the sporophyte generation of fronds springs. If all of this sounds dauntingly complex, remember that ferns have been doing it unassisted for 400 million years. As midwife, all you have to do is provide a suitable environment.

1. HARVEST THE SPORES After locating a mature, vigorous Christmas fern, inspect its fronds to find a fertile one (in any fern, some fronds are sterile and do not bear spores). Look on the underside of the fronds for ripe, pimplelike sori, which are clusters of spore-bearing sacks (sporangia). Color is a reliable clue to ripeness: As the spores mature, the sori darken to a deep, rich brown. Cut the frond at its base and lay it spore-side down on a sheet of clean white paper (where the tiny spores show up clearly as they drop from the frond). Cover the frond with another sheet of paper and place a paperweight on top. Within a day or two the sporangia will open and release their spores.

2. PREPARE A STERILE NURSERY To germinate successfully, spores require 100 percent humidity and sterile conditions, because they cannot compete successfully with algae, fungi, or bacteria. I know of people who achieve good results using plastic pots covered with plastic bags, but I prefer a transparent plastic sweater box with a tightly fitting lid (available from the local

five and dime). I find that this setup combines ample humidity with the best security against infection. In any case, sterilize your container by scrubbing it with a 10 percent solution of bleach. Next, fill it with a one-inch-deep (2.5 cm) layer of perlite (for drainage), topped with a two-inch-deep (5 cm) layer of a commercial peat-lite mix (which, unlike homemade potting soils, will be sterile). Moisten the soil thoroughly with boiling water from a tea kettle, as ordinary tap water contains algae. Cover the container and set it aside to cool.

3. SOW THE SPORES A day or two after completing step 1, remove the paperweight, the top sheet of paper, and the drying frond. You should find the bottom sheet of paper covered with a fine dust of spores. Crease the paper down the center to form a channel into which the spores can settle. Open the nursery box, tip the paper over it, and tap the paper with your finger to gently sift the spores over the peat-lite mix inside. Spread the spores as evenly as possible, and replace the lid immediately.

4. GERMINATION The best place for the box is a north-facing window where it will receive bright but indirect sunlight (direct sunlight will cook the spores). Fluorescent light is also fine. Germination usually begins in two or three weeks, and a film of pale green should cover the growing medium within a month. Another month or two should see the appearance of recognizable prothallia. When these stop growing, little leaves should emerge. If they do not, it may be that conditions within the box are too dry for the sperm to make their swim to the eggs. Try misting the prothallia with distilled or boiled and cooled (i.e., sterile) water.

5. TRANSPLANTING As soon as fronds do appear, prepare another sterile box, this time covering the perlite drainage layer with a pasteurized commercial African-violet potting mix. Don't try to separate the plants; prick them out in little clumps (the tip of a butterknife makes a good lifting tool). Replant these plugs in rows at one-inch (2.5 cm) intervals. Water as necessary with sterile water — the growing medium should stay moist but not soaked. When the young Christmas ferns reach a height of two inches (5 cm) and all danger of frost has passed, dig them up, separate them, and transplant them to a shady bed outdoors.

Curing and Storing Onions

Nancy Bubel

THE FIRST YEAR I raised onion, I simply pulled them, braided their tops, and hung them in the garage. They looked wonderful hanging there while they lasted, but they didn't last long. A few made it into the stew, but most rotted. Because the onions had not had a chance to dry, fungi and bacteria were able to thrive in their damp necks and tops. I have since learned that there are a number of important steps to harvesting onions that, if correctly followed, will lengthen their keeping time. Now, with a plan of timely irrigation, harvesting, curing, and storing, I have onions from the garden year round.

For your storage crop, choose cultivars that are known to keep well. Good storage onions have traditionally been the more pungent cultivars like 'Copra', 'Early Yellow Globe', 'Stuttgarter', and 'Ebenezer', which contain more solid matter than the sweet Bermuda and Spanish types. Their higher sulfur content may also discourage the growth of fungi and bacteria. With the recent development of long-keeping sweet onions like 'Sweet Sandwich', this distinction is not as clear-cut as it once was. 'Spartan Sleeper', another recent introduction, is a hard, heavy-skinned storage onion that will resist sprouting for more than a year. And 'Walla Walla', although it's a Spanish type, has kept well into the new year for me.

1. KNOCK OVER THE TOPS Bending over onion tops promotes drying at the most critical point: the neck of the bulb. Soon after the bulbs have stopped developing, the tops start to flop over naturally. When the tops of about half the onions in a row have bent over, help things along by dragging a rake, teeth-up, along the row. This will flatten the remaining tops so that all the onions will be ready to harvest at the same time. As its top dries, the neck of the bulb shrivels, sealing off the bulb from invasion by organisms that thrive in damp places. Don't water onions after the tops have been bent over.

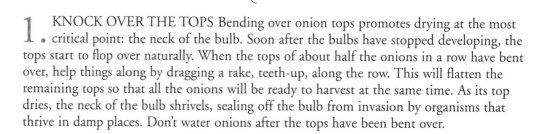

2. PULL UP THE ONIONS They will be ready to harvest when their bent-over tops have been exposed to drying sun for five to seven days. The joint between each bulb and its top will be limp, not stiff, and the tops themselves, although often still green, will have lost their succulence. Bulbs with bent-over tops may be left in the ground for as long as two weeks, but it's important to harvest them before the tops rot or weeds take over the row.

Grasp the bunch of wilted spears and gently ease each bulb out of the ground. If the ground is hard, you might need to use a digging fork to unearth a few stubborn onions. Dig from the side of the row to avoid puncturing bulbs.

3. CURE THE BULBS This vital step completes the drying of the necks and removes excess moisture, resulting in longer storage life. A well-cured bulb will have a thoroughly shriveled neck (which is not an inviting entry point for fungi and bacteria). To cure, spread the bulbs on a screen, net hammock, or slatted rack — any arrangement that will permit good ventilation. The combination of the sun's warmth and cirulating air will waft away excess moisture. I use old hardware-cloth screens set on top of a large garden cart, which I wheel into the sun each day and return to the shed when rain threatens. Many gardeners drape the limp green tops over the bulbs to prevent sunscald in strong sun. In hot, sunny weather, a week of curing is enough. Allow 10 to 12 days during cloudy periods.

4. CLIP OFF THE TOPS After the curing period, clip off the dried tops, leaving one- to two-inch (2.5 to 5 cm) stubs. Removing the tops allows the onion necks to continue drying in storage and makes for more compact storage — individual onions will be more accessible and less likely to be affected by any rotting tops that might be mixed in with them. If you want to make a decorative onion braid, leave the tops on some shapely bulbs that have thoroughly dried necks. Although well-cured, braided onions will last longer than my ill-fated uncured crop did, it has been my experience that topless onions keep best.

5. PACK CAREFULLY FOR STORAGE Onions will keep best in single layers spread in shallow cartons, which may be stacked. It's all right to arrange onions two deep, but avoid heaping them in large piles. Good air circulation helps to prevent spoilage.

For a long storage life, keep onions cold and dry (32° to 40°F [0° to 5°C], 60 to 70 percent humidity). Don't let them freeze. It is especially important to guard against dampness, which encourages decay. They are most likely to sprout at around 60°F (15.5°C). I've kept many a crop until spring in a dry, well-ventilated 50° to 60°F (10° to 15.5°C) room. If you haven't stored onions before, try keeping them in several different spots until you determine which works best for you.

Fall

A man does not plant a tree for himself,
he plants it for posterity.

— Alexander Smith

Seeding a New Lawn

Janet H. Sanchez

STARTING A NEW LAWN from seed is a satisfying project that rewards the gardener with an expanse of beautiful, soft, green grass in only a few weeks. Whether you are replacing an old lawn or starting from scratch, early fall is the ideal time to do so. Warm soil and fall rains help grass become established quickly. Also, fewer annual weeds germinate under these conditions, which reduces the competition for the grass seeds. Plan to plant at least six weeks before your first expected heavy frost.

When planning your lawn, think about its intended uses. If it will be mainly for show, or if it is in a shady or steep location where it is difficult to establish grass, consider planting a smaller area or using a groundcover to save on water and maintenance. In any event, choose a variety or mixture of grass seed that suits your climate and purposes. There are, for example, mixtures that are especially drought-tolerant and ones that produce lawns that are tough enough to withstand children's play. If you need help deciding what to buy, ask an experienced nursery person or cooperative extension agent.

1. REMOVE SOD AND WEEDS If you are replacing an old lawn, you should remove any existing sod, alive or dead, in order to prepare a smooth seedbed. (Working sod back into the soil results in a bed that is too rough.) Use a sharp spade or rented sod-stripper to slice away the old sod, which can then be composted. On a new lawn site, clear away any weeds, rocks, and other debris.

Use a heavy rake to level high spots and fill in hollows. Making the lawn area level now prevents a scalping by the mower or puddles of water later.

2. PREPARE A SEEDBED Like other plants, grass grows best and requires less maintenance and irrigation if planted in well-prepared soil. Spread a three-inch-thick (7.5 cm) layer of organic material (rotted manure, compost, well-rotted bark or sawdust, or dampened peat moss) over the soil. To promote good root growth, sprinkle a high-phosphorus fertilizer, such as 7-21-7, at the rate of two or three pounds (.9 or 1.4 kg) per 1,000 square feet (6,452 square cm). Thoroughly incorporate these materials into the top six inches (15 cm) of soil with a spade, or make several passes over the area

with a rotary tiller. Then smooth the seedbed with a rake, removing any stones or large clumps of soil that may have surfaced. Check again for hollows and hills. Use a roller (half filled with water) to firm the seedbed.

3. SOW SEED Choose a windless day to sow the seeds. Either by hand or using a mechanical seeder, scatter half the seeds as you walk back and forth across the seedbed. Spread the second half at right angles to the first. Rake the surface lightly to scratch the seeds into the soil, burying them an eighth to a quarter of an inch (.3 to .6 cm) deep. Next, add a sparse layer of mulch, such as chopped straw or aged sawdust, to help keep the soil moist and discourage hungry birds. Then go over the area with the roller to firm the soil and the mulch.

4. CARE After you finish rolling, water the bed thoroughly, soaking the soil to a depth of six inches (15 cm). Use a sprinkler that applies water slowly in fine droplets or you'll risk washing away your work.

It's important to keep the seedbed moist until the seeds have germinated and the new lawn has become established. Water by hand or turn on the sprinkler for five or 10 minutes two or three times a day; more frequent watering may be necessary during hot or windy weather. (An automatic timer is helpful if you are away during the day.) Once the grass is up and growing, usually between 14 and 21 days, gradually decrease the frequency of irrigation but increase the amount of water applied each time.

Setting up a temporary fence around the bed will keep the young grass safe until it's strong enough to take foot traffic (about six to 10 weeks after sowing). You can begin mowing when the grass is about two inches (5 cm) tall. Be sure the mower blades are sharp to avoid tearing the new grass.

Sowing a Cover Crop

Janet H. Sanchez

PUT YOUR VEGETABLE GARDEN to bed this fall with a cover crop. A planting of legumes or cereal gains on what would otherwise be bare ground will benefit your garden soil in several important ways. First, the crop will keep the soil from eroding over the winter. It will also ensure that important nutrients are not leached out. In addition, the humus a cover crop forms as it decays will improve the soil's structure and enhance its ability to retain moisture. This is especially important in vegetable gardens because organic matter and humus are constantly depleted as we cultivate and harvest.

Devoting your garden to a cover crop for the winter is therefore a good way to rejuvenate the soil. However, you needn't apply this valuable technique only in the fall — many types of cover crops can be sown in empty patches in the garden from early spring through summer.

Cover crops also have extensive root systems that bring up deeply buried nutrients. Legumes such as vetches, beans, and clovers add extra nitrogen because of their association with *Rhizobium* bacteria. These bacteria take nitrogen from the air and "fix" it in nodules on a legume's roots; this essential nutrient is then released into the soil as the plants decompose. Grass or cereal crops don't add nitrogen, but they do produce masses of organic matter. To give your garden the benefits of both types, plant a combination of legumes and grasses.

Sow fall cover crops early enough to give the plants four to six weeks to become established before the arrival of hard frosts. Hardy, quick-growing cereal grains such as winter rye and winter wheat are the best choices for short-season northern gardens; combine either one with hairy vetch to add nitrogen. Farther south, gardeners can also sow oats, several other vetch varieties, Austrian winter peas, annual clovers, and fava or bell beans. Whatever your climate, experiment with these and other cover crops to learn what works best for your garden. Seed for cover crops is available from farm-supply stores and many mail-order garden suppliers.

1. PREPARE THE PLANTING AREA Cover crops germinate and grow best in a well-prepared bed. Till in or remove and compost weeds and any plant residues, then rake the surface of the soil smooth.

You probably won't need to add fertilizer before sowing a cover crop. But if you are starting a new garden or if an existing garden has given disappointing results in the past, it is a good idea to have the soil tested and to follow the recommendations for amending it. If you plan to sow a grain crop in poor soil, first broadcast blood meal or another high-nitrogen fertilizer at the rate of three to five pounds (1.4 to 2.3 kg) per 100 square feet (9.3 square m). Legumes grown in poor soil certainly won't require extra nitrogen, but they will benefit from extra phosphorus and calcium, easily added in the form of bonemeal applied at the same rate.

2. SOW THE COVER CROP If you decide to plant a legume, treat the seeds with an inoculant powder to be certain that the *Rhizobium* bacteria needed to fix nitrogen in the soil are present. Packets of the proper strain of inoculant are available where the seeds are sold. Moisten the seeds and roll them in the powder, or sprinkle the powder on the prepared ground prior to sowing.

You can simply broadcast cover-crop seeds. If you sow the seeds in furrows, however, you will get a better stand of seedlings, because you can cover them more evenly with soil. Use a hoe to make the furrows, spacing them several inches apart.

Either way, for each 100 square feet (9.3 square m), sow about half a pound (200 grams) of winter rye, wheat, or oats; for the same size area sow only one-fourth of a pound (100 grams) of the vetches, clovers, fava beans, or Austrian winter peas. Rake soil over the seeds, firmly covering the smaller grain and clover seeds with half an inch (1.25 cm) of soil, and the larger seeds with an inch or two (2.5 or 5 cm).

3. EARLY CARE If there is no rain, water regularly until the seeds sprout and are growing well. Pull out any weeds that appear in the first few weeks. Usually only one weeding is necessary because cover crops grow quickly, shading out most weeds.

In some areas birds devour newly sprouted plants, especially in the fall. If this is a problem, cover the entire area with bird netting, supporting the netting several inches above the soil surface with wooden stakes or a framework of plastic pipe. Or spread a cover such as Reemay directly on top of the soil and anchor it with rocks or bricks. In either case, remove the cover once the seedlings are several inches tall, and leave the crop to grow for the ensuing months.

4. HARVEST Mow or chop your cover crop into smaller pieces before it becomes tough and woody, just before it begins to set seed. Then turn it into the soil, either by hand or with a rear-tined rotary tiller. If the crop is thick and impenetrable, harvest the leaves and stems for the compost pile, then dig in the remaining stubble and roots.

Keep in mind that a large mass of green manure worked into the soil all at once takes several weeks to break down. This is because soil microbes temporarily tie up much of the nitrogen already present in the soil while they are busy digesting the cover-crop remains. As the process is completed, the nitrogen is returned to the soil. Legumes break down more quickly simply because they themselves contribute nitrogen, which speeds decomposition. Your new, improved garden will be ready for planting when most of the stems and leaves of the cover crop are no longer recognizable, having become a part of the soil.

Dividing Daylilies

Janet H. Sanchez

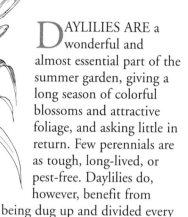

DAYLILIES ARE a wonderful and almost essential part of the summer garden, giving a long season of colorful blossoms and attractive foliage, and asking little in return. Few perennials are as tough, long-lived, or pest-free. Daylilies do, however, benefit from being dug up and divided every few years, a process their natural toughness allows them to endure with aplomb.

A clump of daylilies is formed of one or more fans — small plants made up of fibrous roots, a growing point (crown), and foliage. Each fan can reproduce itself each year, and before long a clump can increase into a sizeable mass of plants. After five or six years, this mass becomes overgrown, producing fewer flowers each season. Dividing the clump and replanting newly separated fans rejuvenates the plants and rewards your efforts with a renewed flush of flowers the following summer.

Of course, you can divide your daylilies before they become overcrowded. You may want to do so to increase your supply of plants, for example, or to slow down those clumps that are threatening to overpower less robust neighbors in the garden. A large clump of daylilies will yield enough new plants to repopulate the original site,

start a new bed, and provide extras to give away to friends.

The best time to divide and replant daylilies is after they have finished blooming, in late summer or really fall. This way the transplants will have time to become established before the first hard frost. In areas with short growing seasons, it is safer to wait until spring to divide daylilies; gardeners in mild climates can divide through the winter.

1. PREPARE A NEW DAYLILY BED Preparing the soil for a new daylily bed *before* digging the old clump allows you to get the divisions into the ground without delay, before their roots become dried and damaged from exposure to the open air. Remove any weeds from the chosen spot and work the soil to a depth of a foot (30 cm) or so, incorporating several inches of compost, well-rotted manure, or damp peat moss to make the soil more friable and moisture-retentive. Daylily divisions planted in well-prepared soil will begin to grow quickly and become established before the onset of winter.

$2.$ DIG THE CLUMP Cut back the clump's long outer leaves to about six inches (15 cm) to make it easier to handle. Try not to damage the new inner leaves growing in the center of each fan.

With a spading fork, loosen the soil all around the clump. Work around the perimeter several times to free as many of the roots from the soil as possible. Because daylilies develop extensive root systems, it may be necessary to dig down 10 to 12 inches (25 to 30 cm). Don't worry if you accidentally break a few of the longer roots — new ones will grow when the divisions are replanted. Next, use the fork to pry the entire clump out of the ground. Shake or wash excess soil off the roots so you can see the individual fans.

$3.$ MAKE DIVISIONS Once out of the ground, a large, solid clump of daylilies can look pretty daunting. Begin by separating it into two sections; use two spading forks placed back to back in the center of the root mass to pry the halves apart. Then pull each section apart or, if necessary, use a sharp knife to cut the clump into smaller and smaller chunks.

The pieces from around the outside of the original mass are the youngest and generally the best candidates for replanting. The final divisions should be made up of one to four healthy-looking fans with strong roots. Larger three- or four-fan divisions will reestablish quickly in the garden, soon growing to sizable new clumps. Smaller divisions take longer to make a display in the landscape but won't require further division for a few more years. You can compost older, woody, or broken shoots, leaves, and other debris.

$4.$ PLANT THE DIVISIONS If you can't plant immediately, protect the divisions from drying out by wrapping them in a damp cloth or a piece of burlap, by burying their roots in moist soil, or by temporarily planting them in pots of good garden soil.

Dig planting holes 18 inches to two feet (46 cm to .6 m) apart and wider than the root masses. Then make a small mound of soil in the center of each hole, set the crown of the division on it, and spread the roots evenly around it. If some roots are too long, trim them back to eight inches or so rather than cramming them into the hole. Firm the soil over the roots, covering the crown with no more than an inch (2.5 cm) of soil. A plant buried under too much soil may rot.

Water the plants well and tuck a light mulch in around their bases (but not over the crowns) to help the soil retain moisture. During hot spells, shade the new plants with a shingle or shade cloth supported on stakes. When freezing weather approaches, cover them with a mulch of straw or evergreen boughs. The covering protects the young plants from being heaved out of the ground by alternate freezing and thawing of the soil.

Balling and Burlapping a Crape Myrtle

Thomas Christopher

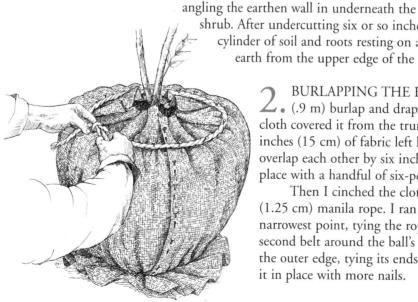

AFTER I DECIDED to transplant the crape myrtles that were growing alongside my driveway, I prepared them for the move by pruning their roots (an endeavor described in the following article). Autumn is an excellent season for transplanting trees and shrubs, as its cool, moist weather reduces a plant's need for water and so places less stress on the roots. By early fall, one year after I began the root-pruning, it was time to dig the root balls and wrap them in burlap and rope. Balling and burlapping, as nurserymen call this, is a laborious procedure, but it offers the surest way to move any tree or shrub with a trunk diameter of more than an inch and a half (3.75 cm) without bruising its roots or exposing it to dehydration.

1. DIGGING AND UNDERCUTTING The formula for calculating the appropriate size root ball for a given tree or shrub is discussed at length on page **104**; briefly, I added 10 inches (25 cm) to the diameter of the root ball for each inch (2.5 cm) of trunk diameter. After establishing the perimeter of each shrub's ball, I dug a trench around it. I made the trench about two feet (.6 m) wide, so that I would have ample room in which to maneuver my spade while shaping the root ball.

I cut the wall of the trench nearest the shrub in a vertical plane, working with the back of the spade facing the shrub to achieve a smoother finish. Since I had root-pruned the shrubs, I didn't have to sever any major lateral roots, but I did encounter many fine feeder roots. These I simply cut with the spade (which I had sharpened before digging in).

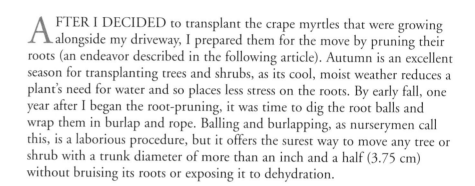

When I reached root-free soil, I began to undercut the ball, angling the earthen wall in underneath the shrub. After undercutting six or so inches (15 cm) all around, I stopped, leaving a cylinder of soil and roots resting on a pedestal of earth. Finally, I shaved a bit of earth from the upper edge of the root ball to give it a gently rounded shoulder.

2. BURLAPPING THE BALL Next I unrolled a bolt of three-foot-wide (.9 m) burlap and draped it loosely around the root ball so that the cloth covered it from the trunk all the way to its base, with an extra six inches (15 cm) of fabric left lying at the bottom. Allowing the ends to overlap each other by six inches (15 cm), I cut the cloth and pinned it in place with a handful of six-penny nails.

Then I cinched the cloth to the ball with two belts of half-inch (1.25 cm) manila rope. I ran one belt around the bottom of the ball at its narrowest point, tying the rope's ends together with a square knot. I ran the second belt around the ball's top, four to six inches (10 to 15 cm) in from the outer edge, tying its ends together in another square knot and pinning it in place with more nails.

3. DRUM LACING With larger transplants, such as my crape myrtles, a simple style of roping called "drum lacing" does the best job of securing the burlap to the root ball. The lacing should be done with lighter, more flexible line, so I began by tying one end of a length of quarter-inch (.6 cm) manila rope to the belt I had run around the bottom of the ball. I slipped the free end under the upper belt at a spot about six inches (15 cm) to the right of where I had just knotted the line to the lower belt. After pulling the line through to take up slack, I slipped it under the bottom belt, six inches (15 cm) farther to the right. Zigzagging up and down, I worked the lighter line all the way around the ball, producing something that looked like the lacing around the side of a drum.

Then I worked my way around the ball, tugging at the loops of lacing to take up any remaining slack. One final pass made sure the lacing was really taut before I tied off the rope at the bottom belt, right beside the knot that secured its other end. I cut off the extra line with my pocketknife.

4. FREEING THE BALL Once the root ball was securely encased in its skin of burlap and ropes, I finished undercutting it, then used the spade's blade as a lever to push it onto its side. I cut the taproot with pruning shears and shaved the excess soil off the bottom of the root ball with the spade until I began seeing feeder roots again. At last I pulled the flaps of extra burlap over the bare bottom and pinned them in place with a couple more nails.

A root ball that has been well and tightly laced will be so firm that it won't need any further reinforcement, although when you move it, you should carry it away on a piece of plywood or a garden cart. And be warned: You'll need a couple of sturdy helpers, for in the case of my crape myrtles, the finished balls weighed an average of 300 pounds (136 kg) apiece.

Root-Pruning a Crape Myrtle

Thomas Christopher

THE FILE OF CRAPE MYRTLES that stood guard along our Texas driveway — a relic of the garden's previous owner — irritated me. It made me feel as if I should salute every time I stepped out of the car. Yet when I threatened to cut the shrubs down my wife, Suzanne, objected, pointing out that they were fine, strapping specimens. So we agreed to move them, which is how I found myself root-pruning crape myrtles.

If I had transplanted the shrubs without any preparation, I would have had to sever virtually all of their roots, a trauma that would have likely killed the plants. By cutting the roots back in two steps over a period of a year, however, I persuaded the shrubs to form dense, compact root balls. (In fact, this is a technique commercial nurserymen apply to field-grown trees and shrubs.) Preparing the shrubs for transplanting in this fashion took time, but the labor was justified by the results. Every one of those crape myrtles survived the move, even though the first summer in their new homes was marked by a six-month drought.

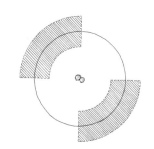

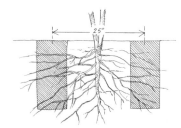

1. DESIGNING THE ROOT BALL Early fall or spring is the time for root-pruning, since plants respond best to this operation when their roots are actively growing. Ideally, the weather should be warm but not hot or dry, or the roots will suffer from water stress.

Begin by determining the size of the root ball you will allow the shrub. Soil weighs about 110 pounds (50 kg) per cubic foot ((197 cubic cm), so for your back's sake keep the ball as compact as possible. Yet beware of confining the roots within *too* small an area, as that leaves the plant vulnerable to drought. A good rule of thumb is 10 inches (25 cm) of root-ball diameter for each inch (2.5 cm) of trunk diameter. If one plant has several trunks, make your calculations using the combined diameter. For example, the combined diameter of one two-trunked crape myrtle was two and a half inches (6.25 cm); I multiplied this figure by 10, then drew a circle 25 inches (63.5 cm) across around the plant.

2. DIGGING THE FIRST SET OF TRENCHES Next I divided each shrub's circle into quadrants. Selecting two opposite quadrants of each root-ball-to-be, I cut a narrow, 18-inch-deep (46 cm) trench along the quadrants' outer arcs. The spade, of course, severed any roots it encountered. I trimmed the stumps with a cheap pair of pruning shears (don't use your good shears for this, as the soil that clings to the roots damages the cutting edge). Heading back roots this way will encourage them to make new growth within the area outlined for the root ball.

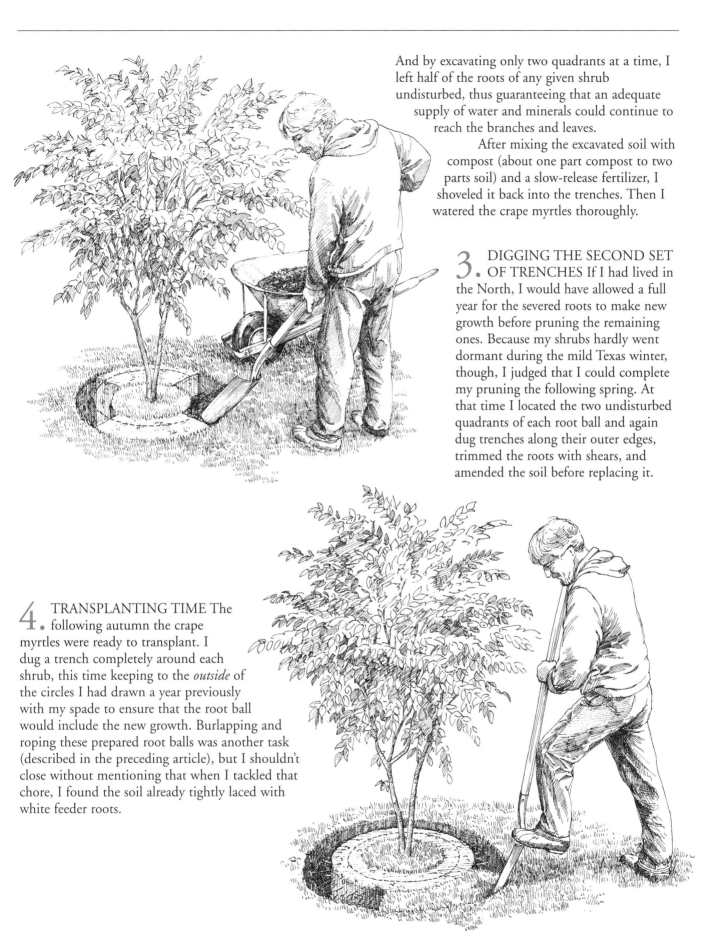

And by excavating only two quadrants at a time, I left half of the roots of any given shrub undisturbed, thus guaranteeing that an adequate supply of water and minerals could continue to reach the branches and leaves.

After mixing the excavated soil with compost (about one part compost to two parts soil) and a slow-release fertilizer, I shoveled it back into the trenches. Then I watered the crape myrtles thoroughly.

3. DIGGING THE SECOND SET OF TRENCHES If I had lived in the North, I would have allowed a full year for the severed roots to make new growth before pruning the remaining ones. Because my shrubs hardly went dormant during the mild Texas winter, though, I judged that I could complete my pruning the following spring. At that time I located the two undisturbed quadrants of each root ball and again dug trenches along their outer edges, trimmed the roots with shears, and amended the soil before replacing it.

4. TRANSPLANTING TIME The following autumn the crape myrtles were ready to transplant. I dug a trench completely around each shrub, this time keeping to the *outside* of the circles I had drawn a year previously with my spade to ensure that the root ball would include the new growth. Burlapping and roping these prepared root balls was another task (described in the preceding article), but I shouldn't close without mentioning that when I tackled that chore, I found the soil already tightly laced with white feeder roots.

Saving Tomato Seeds

Nancy Bubel

IMAGINE MY DISMAY when I discovered that 'Moira', one of my favorite tomato cultivars, was no longer offered by the seed company from which I was accustomed to ordering it. That sinking feeling didn't last long, though; I remembered that I had saved seeds from 'Moira' the previous season. I planted the seeds that spring and saved more again in the fall, grateful for this and all the other durable but fragile old strains that still have a chance to continue if gardeners will take care of them.

Saving seeds is a satisfying skill, and it is easy to learn. The seed saver not only has the advantage of preserving fast-vanishing flower and vegetable cultivars, but also the opportunity to encourage valuable qualities such as early bearing, disease resistance, good flavor, and uniform color. The tomato is a good choice for your first efforts because you needn't worry about cross-pollination; the blossoms are self-pollinating, so they rarely cross. Thus, you can be confident that the plants grown from tomato seed will produce fruit resembling that of the parent plant. If you save seed every year, selecting for the qualities that are important to you, you may be able to gradually improve the fruit (or any other vegetable or flower from which you save seed).

Unless you're experimenting, be sure to save seeds only from *nonhybrid* (open-pollinated) plants. Seeds from hybrids produce plants that are unlike the parent plant.

1. MARK THE BEST PLANTS Use a stake or bright strip of cloth to identify those plants that produced early, yielded well, or bore especially large or tasty fruits. If you're after early fruits, don't pick the first tomato; let it stay on the plant to ripen. It is generally recommended, though not mandatory, that you allow your seed tomato to remain on the stalk until it's a bit overripe — just past

eating condition, but not yet decaying — so the seeds will be fully mature.

For a representative sampling, save seeds from more than one of your choicest plant's fruits. If you're saving seed from more than one kind of tomato, be sure to label each fruit as you pick it.

2. REMOVE THE SEEDS Cut the tomato in half and, using a spoon, scrape out the seeds. Sometimes a sharp pointed knife is helpful in extricating seeds from paste tomatoes and other kinds that have particularly solid flesh.

3. FERMENT THE SEEDS Fermentation improves chances of future germination by dissolving the gelatinous membrane surrounding each seed, which in many plants contains germination inhibitors. Another advantage is that this process seems to control some seed-borne tomato diseases.

Put the seeds, along with any pulp that might be clinging to them, into a half-pint (238 ml) jar, then pour in a quarter of a cup (50 ml) of water. Put the lid on the jar (but don't screw it on tightly) and store at approximately 70° to 75°F (21° to 24°C); the gradual fermentation encouraged by this recommended temperature should provide just the right amount of treatment for most seeds. The mixture will soon start to smell a bit "ripe."

Keep the jar on the kitchen counter so you'll notice it and remember to remove the seeds at the right time. The brew will turn murky, and mold may form on the surface, so stir it each day. The good seeds will sink to the bottom, and the infertile ones will rise to the top along with the fermented pulp. After the seeds have spent two to three days (but no more than five) in the jar, pour the scum and liquid out of the jar, then dump the good seeds out into a strainer and rinse them off.

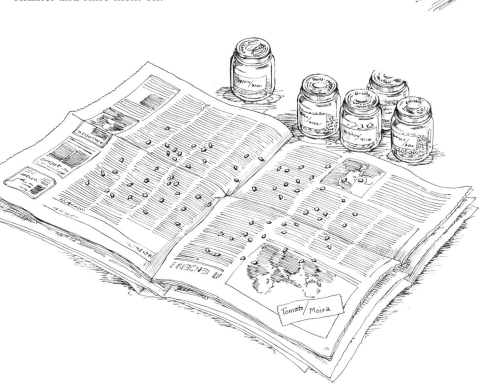

4. DRY AND PACKAGE THE SEEDS Spread the rinsed seeds on several sheets of newspaper to dry for a week. Change all but the top layer of paper after two days and again a few days later. When dry, the seeds will not stick to the paper. Package them in an airtight container (such as a small baby-food jar), label them, and store them in a dry, cold place — a refrigerator, freezer, or cold pantry.

Laying Sod

Lee Reich

The quickest way to convert a piece of bare ground into a lush lawn is to lay down sod. These pregrown rolls of grass are not only easy to install, they also look good instantly and protect the soil from being washed away by rain. Autumn is an excellent time to lay sod, since the grass will have a month or so to take hold before winter's cold halts growth for the season.

Sod is sold in strips two to 10 feet long (.6 to 3 m) and one to two feet (30 cm to .6 m) wide. Because these strips dry out quickly, you should pick them up or arrange for delivery as near as possible to the day you are going to lay them. In hot weather you'll have to get them down within a day, in cool weather within two or three days. Keep any stored sod strips damp but not saturated.

The strips will be less likely to dry out as you work if you tackle the project on a cool, cloudy day. Before you begin, however, check the moisture level of the site. The soil should be just moist enough to crumble in your hand with slight pressure. If it is too wet, wait for it to dry a bit; if it is too dry, sprinkle it thoroughly and start the job the next day.

1. PREPARING THE GROUND Do not expect sod strips simply dropped on top of the ground to grow; you have to prepare the site first. If the soil is covered with heavy weed growth or existing lawn, strip it off with either a shovel or a sod stripper to make subsequent rototilling easier.

Before tilling, broadcast any lime or sulfur needed to adjust the soil pH, then spread a three-inch (7.5 cm) layer of organic material such as rotted manure, compost, dampened peat moss, or spent mushroom soil. Organic matter will help make a clay soil porous and will help sandy soil retain water.

Rototill the patch first lengthwise and then crosswise to loosen the soil to a depth of six inches (15 cm). Do not overtill. Your objective is to turn the soil into pea-size granules, not dust.

Next, spread fertilizer on top of the ground at the rate of 25 pounds (11 kg) per 1,000 square feet (93 square m). Use a high-phosphorus fertilizer such as 10-20-20 or 5-15-15 to promote root growth. Then rototill once more to incorporate the fertilizer into the top three inches (7.5 cm) of soil.

Finally, rake the surface smooth, discarding rocks and other debris, and firm the soil by running an empty lawn roller over the surface.

2. LAYING THE FIRST ROW The first row of sod should be placed along a straight line. If you can, use your driveway or a path as a guide. Otherwise use a string pulled taut between two stakes.

Unroll each sod strip, taking care to avoid tearing it, and press it firmly into position. Sod will shrink slightly after it has been laid, so don't stretch it as you put it down — especially where edges meet. Don't let it buckle, either. If you are worried about the strips drying out as you work, simply sprinkle each one with the hose once it's laid.

3. LAYING SUBSEQUENT ROWS Lay a plank on the first row to distribute your weight as you work on the adjacent row. Snug the next row tightly against the first row, once again allowing for shrinkage. To avoid concentrating breaks in the sod in one area, stagger the joints between the pieces so they do not align with those in the first row.

Continue other rows the same way, kneeling on the plank as you work, staggering the joints, and watering lightly if necessary. When you reach the edge of your new lawn, cut the sod to size with either a sharp spade or a serrated knife (a bread knife will do fine).

4. FINISHING TOUCHES When you have covered the ground with sod, go over it lightly with a partially weighted roller to get rid of air pockets and to ensure good contact between the sod and the underlying soil. A roller that is too heavy will damage the sod and ruin the soil structure. Roll first at a right angle to the direction of the strips, then in the same direction as the strips.

After rolling, fluff up the grass blades lightly with a bamboo rake. This raking will also clean up any debris from your work.

5. WATERING Do not be lulled into complacency by the sod's established look. The top inch must not dry out while its roots are knitting into the underlying soil.

As soon as you finish rolling and raking, set up a sprinkler and water to a depth of six inches (15 cm). Every sunny, warm day for the next few weeks, water lightly around midday; the developing lawn is most vulnerable to losing moisture then. Pay special attention to sod near pavement; it will dry out quickest here and may need heavier spot watering. As the sod's roots grow into the soil below, approach a normal watering schedule.

Keep off the sod as much as possible for the few weeks it takes to establish.

Storing Gladiolus Bulbs

Thomas Christopher

LAZY GARDENERS (I prefer to think of myself as easygoing) treat their gladioli as annuals. Glads arrive at garden centers in late spring or early summer as corms — short, fat, bulblike lengths of stem with a bud on top. Gardeners tend to plant them in rows across the cutting garden to ensure a summer-long supply of cut flowers or plug them into the gaps that early bloomers leave in perennial displays. Despite gladioli's faithful service, when fall comes we too often don't bother to lift and store them. Instead, we abandon these tender southern flowers to a chilly death in the frozen soils of winter.

This is ungrateful. Worse yet, it's extravagant. Corms of the newer All-American Selections can cost 70 or 80 cents apiece to replace. And for each one planted and not harvested, we may lose not just one corm but several. For if the garden soil has been properly enriched, each of the original corms will have given birth to two or three new ones.

1. DIGGING THE CORMS Gladiolus specialists recommend lifting a corm four to six weeks after it has ceased flowering. In fact, the only hard-and-fast deadline for lifting is when the soil freezes, since that event makes digging impossible. Because the gladiolus corms are sensitive to cold, it is best to evacuate them to a temperature-controlled storage place before the first frost.

Use a spading fork to lift the corms. Drive the tines into the soil a few inches to one side of the plant so that you don't pierce the rootstock, then pull back on the fork's handle to gently lift the soil and the plant together. Grasp the glad's swordlike leaves, and carefully pull the whole plant from the loosened soil

2. DRYING THE CORMS Shake the soil from the rootstock, and you'll find one or more plump new corms riding piggyback on the withered remains of each corm you planted. If you are lucky, there will also be an encrustation of cormels around the point of union between old corm and new. Cormels are pea-size offshoots that can be planted out in a nursery bed to mature within a couple of seasons into the next generation of blossoms.

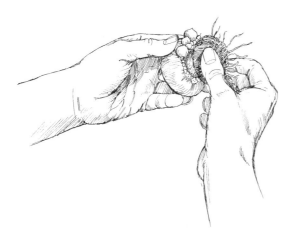

Twist the foliage off the corms, because cutting it off with a knife or shears, as many authorities recommend, may spread viral infections from one corm to another as you move down the row. Then set the corms out to dry in the sun — an old screen propped up on concrete blocks makes a fine rack. Spread the corms to allow the air to circulate around them, but be sure to segregate them by cultivar and keep them labeled (once mixed, there is no way to distinguish between cultivars). After a day or two in the sun, move the drying rack into an airy garage or shed to avoid excessive dehydration.

3. CLEANING THE CORMS After two or three weeks of drying, little will remain of the old corms but a husk. Pull the husk away from the new corms and the cormels (if any), but work carefully, since bruised or injured corms will rot in storage.

Discard the old material, and put all the corms and cormels of a single cultivar into a paper bag with a few tablespoons of an all-purpose rose or tomato dust, one that includes both fungicides and insecticides. Fold shut the mouth of the bag and tumble the corms around to coat them well; the powder will help protect them from decay and insects over the winter. Protect your hands with a pair of rubber gloves, then take the corms out one by one, shaking the excess powder back into the bag for the next batch. Pack the treated corms and cormels (again, segregating them by cultivar) into labeled paper bags, onion sacks, or sacks made from the legs of old pantyhose.

4. STORAGE Tie the bags shut and hang them up in a cool, dry place. An unheated cellar or frost-free garage are two possibilities — any place where the humidity remains low (otherwise, the bulbs may rot) and the temperature hovers between 40° and 50°F (4° and 10°C). Any colder and the gladioli — if they survive — may produce only foliage the following year; any warmer and the corms may break dormancy and begin growing prematurely.

Storing Tropical Water Lilies

Teri Dunn

TROPICAL WATER LILIES are a joy in the water garden. Their dramatic, sweetly fragrant blossoms are usually larger than those of hardy water lilies, and appear all summer and into fall. Given their spectacular performance — and their cost — it's a shame many gardeners north of USDA Zone 8 treat these lilies as annuals. With a little care, however, it is possible to overwinter the tubers indoors, and enjoy the flowers again next year.

In early fall stop fertilizing your lilies and watch for signs of dormancy. The plant will stop flowering and producing new leaves; older leaves will turn yellow and die.

Keep the plants in the pool until there has been a frost or two. The dying foliage will continue to feed the tubers, while the increasingly cool water will encourage the plants to go dormant. Once the water temperature drops to 50°F (10°C), bring the plants, pots and all, inside to a cool work area.

1. HARVEST THE TUBERS Gently tap each plant out of its pot and rinse off as much dirt as possible. Let it air dry a few days. Then snap or slice off the remaining leaves and flower stems.

Examine the area just below the crown for the smooth, black, grape-size tuber. (Pot-bound specimens may have produced additional tubers.) Gently separate the tubers from the crown and float them in tepid water for a day or so. Viable tubers will sink and spoiled ones will float. Discard the spoiled ones.

To ensure complete dormancy, some experts advise leaving the viable tubers in water for up to two weeks, rinsing them daily. Others suggest air-drying them for a few days in a cool room. Either technique works well.

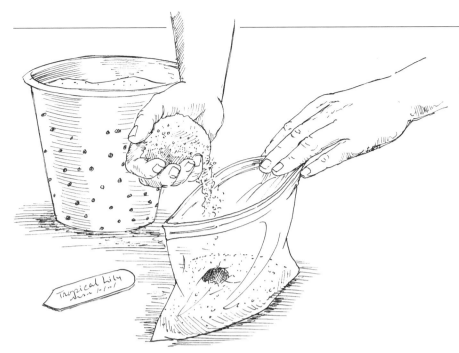

2. **STORE THE TUBERS** Keep the tubers in cool damp sand all winter. If the sand is too wet, the tubers will rot; too dry, and they will dehydrate. To get the right balance, fill a perforated container with sand, saturate it, and leave it to drain for a day. Then place some of the sand in a plastic bag, set in a tuber, top it with more sand, and seal and label the bag. Store the bag in a cool (55°F [13°C]) spot where the tubers will not freeze.

3. **POT UP THE TUBERS** About a month before your last expected frost date, check the tubers to see if sprouts have emerged. If they haven't, place the tubers in water on a sunny windowsill to get them going.

Pot sprouted tubers temporarily in five-inch (12.5 cm) pots, setting them ¼-inch (.6 cm) deep in heavy garden topsoil that won't float away once the pot is in water. Top the pot with pebbles or gravel and stick in a label.

To keep the plants moist, set them in an aquarium or large pail with about three inches (7.5 cm) of water over the rims of the pots. The water should be 70° to 80°F (21° to 27°C); use an aquarium heater if necessary. In two to six weeks, when new leaves make their debut, move the plants into bright light.

4. **TRANSPLANT THE TUBERS** Wait until the pool is at least 70°F (21°C) before moving the revived lilies outdoors. Overly cold water can shock them, delaying new leaves and blossoms for many weeks. Once the pool is ready, transplant each lily to a large pot, if possible one that holds up to three cubic feet (591 cubic cm) of soil. Take care not to cover the crown. Then tuck in a water-lily fertilizer tablet or two and submerge the plants in the pool for another summer of blossoms.

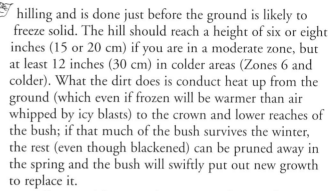

Winterizing Roses

Oliver E. Allen

hilling and is done just before the ground is likely to freeze solid. The hill should reach a height of six or eight inches (15 or 20 cm) if you are in a moderate zone, but at least 12 inches (30 cm) in colder areas (Zones 6 and colder). What the dirt does is conduct heat up from the ground (which even if frozen will be warmer than air whipped by icy blasts) to the crown and lower reaches of the bush; if that much of the bush survives the winter, the rest (even though blackened) can be pruned away in the spring and the bush will swiftly put out new growth to replace it.

One provision must be mentioned. As with most plants, the best guarantee of a rosebush's survival through the winter is good care in the summer, particularly pest control. A vigorous bush will withstand cold's rigors far more readily than a weakened one. On the other hand, take care not to stimulate your roses unduly as autumn approaches lest they put out new growth that will not be tough enough: cease fertilizing by summer's end, and stop deadheading spent blossoms at about the same time.

WHILE WILD ROSES and other native species are assuredly programmed to endure the wide temperature swings of their areas, hybrid teas are for the most part descended from plants of frost-free or moderate regions and are thus naturally vulnerable to the onslaught of cold. Deep freezing breaks their cell walls and dries out their canes; overnight they turn black and are gone. So the prudent gardener must protect them.

The amount of protection a hybrid tea rose needs depends on the climate. In general, roses grown in USDA Zones 8 to 10 need no special precautions, while those in Zones 6 and 7 will probably require covering and those in 5 and below most surely will. Another guideline: If your temperatures stay below 20°F (7°C) for considerable periods of time without a predictable snow blanket to shield plants, protect your roses. Still another: If the ground freezes solid for most of the winter and temperatures are likely to drop below 10°F (-12°C), again without consistent snow cover, your hybrid teas will need covering. But if very low temperatures are infrequent and heavy rains keep the ground wet, the bushes are better left uncovered, as wetness encourages fungus diseases and other ills.

Although specially made plastic coverings can be purchased, the time-honored (and perhaps simplest) method of protecting hybrid tea bushes is to pile up dirt around the base of the bush. The process is known as

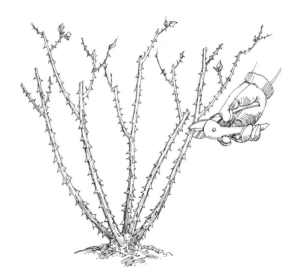

1. PRUNE BACK A couple of weeks after the first frost in your area, but before deep freezing sets in, prune your rosebushes roughly to eliminate any dead or weak shoots or any that show signs of disease. Trim long canes by half and shorter ones by about a third. The aim is to reduce each bush's overall bulk so that it can be protected most efficiently. Don't worry about such fine

points as the location of buds; that can be addressed in the spring when you do precise pruning.

At the same time, to help keep your bushes from drying out in the winter wind (dryness is if anything more of a threat to them than cold), spray them with an antidesiccant not long after you have pruned them. By sealing in moisture, the antidesiccant minimizes the damage that can come from cycles of freezing, thawing, and refreezing in midwinter.

2. BRING DIRT FROM ELSEWHERE In late November or early December, or whenever you sense that the ground is about to freeze, bring dirt from elsewhere in the garden and pile it around the base of your plants to the desired height. Lean, sandy soil is better than a humusy mix. Do not obtain it from between the plants, as that risks exposing roots and crowns to freezing and so defeats the purpose of hilling. Pat the mound firmly to make sure it encloses the canes snugly.

3. ADD A MULCH Especially if you are in one of the colder zones, you will want to add some kind of mulch — salt hay, bark chips, pine needles, leaves — as extra protection, holding it in place perhaps with evergreen boughs or other branches. The mulch further minimizes the possible damage that can come from abrupt temperature swings in midwinter.

4. BE CAUTIOUS ABOUT REMOVAL In the spring, wait until the ground has thawed for good before removing the dirt. But then remove it promptly so that new growth is not damaged. Be sure to keep some extra mulch on hand to pile temporarily around the base of your plants in the event of a sudden late frost.

Naturalizing Bulbs

Janet H. Sanchez

BULBS PLANTED IN large informal drifts create a lovely, natural-looking springtime scene. And with only a little attention on your part, a planting of bulbs will multiply, increasing the display year after year. You can naturalize bulbs in a grassy meadow, under fruit or other deciduous trees, at the edge of a woodland, or on a steep bank. Choose a semiwild area so that the foliage can wither away undistrubed after the plants are finished blooming. Naturalized plantings are usually deemed too untidy for beds or borders close to the house.

Daffodils are excellent candidates for naturalizing because they have a relaxed appearance, multiply readily, and will not be attacked by gophers, mice, or squirrels. Like most bulbs, they do best in sunny or partially shaded sites, and prefer a well-drained area. (Perpetually wet soil causes bulbs to rot.) Other reliable choices include crocuses, grape hyacinths, and snowdrops.

1. SELECT BULBS Naturalized plantings involve anywhere from several dozen to hundreds of bulbs. While it's not necessary to buy expensive, extra-large, double-nose bulbs, it is important to choose good-quality, healthy ones. If you buy bulbs from a local nursery, look for firm, plump ones, and inspect them carefully. Avoid any that are lightweight, soft, or moldy, as well as those that show injury to the basal plate (the flat, bottom side of the bulb that will eventually produce the roots). If you order from a mail-order company, choose one with a reputation for quality stock.

Bulbs are generally offered for sale at the best time for planting — in the case of daffodils, early to mid-fall. Buy and plant them as soon as they become available. They will begin to deteriorate if they sit on the shelf too long, whether at the nursery or in your garage.

2. **PLANT** In nature, bulbs spread outward from dense clusters, gradually colonizing large, open areas. To replicate this effect, gently toss handfuls of bulbs over the planting area, varying the density so that some are in groups and others are a bit farther away from their fellows.

Plant the bulbs where they fall. Use a trowel or special bulb planter to make a hole twice as deep as the bulb's height. Then loosen the bottom inch (2.5 cm) or so of soil in the hole, and mix in a teaspoon of 5-10-5 fertilizer formulated for bulbs. Place each bulb in its hole, pointed end up, and firm the soil over it.

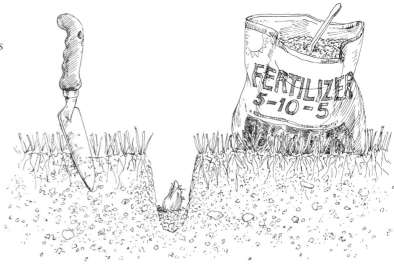

3. **WATER** When you have finished planting, water the area to encourage root growth. Keep in mind that the roots will grow into the soil beneath the bulb, so apply enough water to penetrate a foot (30 cm) or so into the ground. A light sprinkling won't do the job.

In areas where fall rains are plentiful, this initial irrigation will be enough to get the daffodils started. If you garden in an arid climate, or if the weather is unexpectedly dry, occasionally give the area a deep watering during the winter months to keep the root zone moist but not soggy.

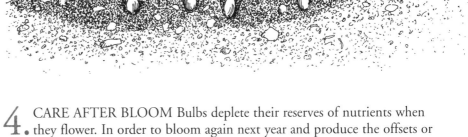

4. **CARE AFTER BLOOM** Bulbs deplete their reserves of nutrients when they flower. In order to bloom again next year and produce the offsets or new bulbs that will increase the overall size of the planting, the nutrients must be replenished. For this reason, it is vital to allow the leaves to remain after the bulbs have flowered, so that they can carry on the process of photosynthesis and manufacture the food they need.

You can enhance this process by fertilizing as soon as flowering is finished. Use the same bulb fertilizer as before, scattering about one tablespoon per square foot over the area. Water it in well.

If rains are scarce, continue to water the planting every week or so until the leaves turn yellow. (This usually takes five or six weeks.) Then stop watering and let the foliage wither on its own; once it does, you can mow or cut off the dead leaves. The bulbs will finish their yearly cycle by resting in a dormant state for several months until fall, when the roots will begin to grow once again.

Planting Tulip Bulbs

Nancy Bubel

WHEN I FIRST planted tulip bulbs in the front yard, I thought I had done the job once and for all. So I was surprised to see our neighbor, who has been gardening for 40 years, replanting his tulip bed. "Tulip bulbs don't last as long as daffodils; they tend to lose vitality as they age," he explained. To be sure of having a nice display, he replants his tulip bed every five or six years, or whenever he notices that the tulips are declining.

Well-prepared plantings tend to have a longer productive life than spot-plantings. The soil will be loose and the drainage better, and the bulbs will be less likely to be surrounded by air pockets, which discourage growth. If you've been tucking tulip bulbs in here and there, using a dibber or trowel, you might want to try this planting method. Wait until the soil is cool before putting the bulbs in the ground. For most gardens, that's sometime between mid-Ocober and mid-November. Pick a site with excellent drainage; never plant tulips in a waterlogged spot. Although many cultivars will bloom in light filtered shade, most perform best in full sun. (Bulbs that receive too little sun are not able to store enough energy to bloom a second year.) The blooms will last longer if the planting is sheltered from wind.

1. **PREPARE A HOLE** It need not be rectangular — a circular or free-form bed might be preferable for your site. Dig to a depth of 10 to 12 inches (25 to 30 cm), then thrust your digging fork into the bottom of the hole to aerate the bed a bit more. Next return a couple of inches of the soil you removed to the bottom of the hole so that the bulbs will rest on loose, free-draining soil with no air pockets. Smooth the bottom surface to make it level.

If the neighborhood wildlife has gobbled up many of your flower bulbs in the past, consider encircling the hole with a barrier of small-gauge chicken wire or hardware cloth. If the hole is particularly large, you could encircle groups of bulbs within it. Some gardeners line the entire thing, bottom and sides up to soil level, with an open box of half-inch (1.25 cm) mesh hardware cloth. These wire barriers should be smoothed into place before the first few inches of loose soil is shoveled back into the hole.

2. **FIRM THE BULBS INTO PLACE** If the bulbs are all planted at the same depth, they'll bloom together. Keep the pointed growing tip of the bulb on top and press the rounded bottom into the loose earth. Use a slight twisting motion to ensure that each bulb is in good contact with the soil.

Set tulip bulbs six to eight inches (15 to 20 cm) deep — that is, they should rest on a surface six to eight inches (15 to 20 cm) below ground level. If planted too deeply, they waste energy working their way up to the light. Bulbs that are too close to the surface, on the other

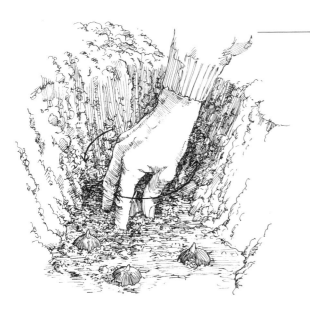

hand, are more likely to be damaged by soil heaving or eaten by rodents, who consider them a delicacy. Also, shallowly planted bulbs tend to divide into many small bulbs, none large enough to bloom, and they may be more vulnerable to Botrytis blight.

Space the bulbs about eight inches (20 cm) apart. The planting will be showier if bulbs are grouped rather than strung out in a single line. When planting many bulbs at one time, protect them from prolonged exposure to sunlight, which may induce surface cracks (entry spots for fungi and bacteria).

3. FILL IN THE HOLE Use a nice sandy loam if you have it, and if you have some finished compost, mix it with the soil you use to fill the hole. Tulips have recently been found to require a good supply of nitrogen, so if you don't add compost, you might mix in dehydrated or thoroughly rotted manure. (Avoid using fresh manure; it may burn the bulbs.) Gardeners also have tradtionally added bonemeal — an excellent source of phosphorus — to the soil when planting bulbs. If you use a chemical fertilzer, that, too, should be mixed with the soil that you put back into the hole.

Shovel the soil in gently at first, so the bulbs don't get jostled out of position. Fill the entire hole with soil, making sure it is in contact with every bulb surface. Finish off by mounding the soil slightly above ground level (it will sink as it settles).

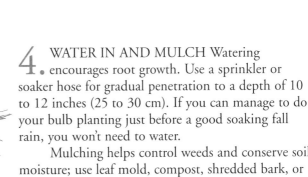

4. WATER IN AND MULCH Watering encourages root growth. Use a sprinkler or soaker hose for gradual penetration to a depth of 10 to 12 inches (25 to 30 cm). If you can manage to do your bulb planting just before a good soaking fall rain, you won't need to water.

Mulching helps control weeds and conserve soil moisture; use leaf mold, compost, shredded bark, or other attractive organic materials. One or two inches (2.5 or 5 cm) should be enough. Don't pile much more than that over your bulbs, or next spring the stems will have to travel too far to reach the light.

Planting an Acid-Loving Shrub

Lee Reich

I F YOU ARE LIKE MOST GARDENERS, you sometimes long to grow a shrub that does not naturally thrive in the conditions found in your yard. Azaleas, rhododendrons, mountain laurels, blue-berries, heathers, and heaths all belong to a group of plants native to soils that have the unique combination of being humusy yet infertile, moist yet well aerated, and very acidic. Provided you pay attention to their rather exacting soil requirements, you need not deny yourself these ericaceous plants. The instructions that follow are for planting a heath (*Erica* species), but they apply equally well to its relatives.

Autumn is the best time to plant a heath. Soil is generally crumbly and moist then, whereas in spring it is often too soden to plant in. With the help of a little mulch, the roots of a heath planted in autumn will grow until the soil freezes, giving the plant a head start for spring.

1. ADJUSTING THE SOIL'S PH Take a soil sample from the area in which you intend to plant the heath, and send it to a lab for a pH test. Remember to tell the lab that you are planting an acid-loving plant in the spot, and ask for specific instructions for altering the soil's pH to the appropriate level. Even acidic garden soils are often not acidic enough; heath and its relatives require soil that has a pH between 4.5 and 5.5.

The lab will most likely instruct you to increase soil acidity by adding a couple of teaspoonfuls of powdered sulfur per square foot. The heath's roots will grow at least as wide as its branches, so treat an area as wide as the eventual spread of the plant. Broadcast the sulfur over the ground, then mix it thoroughly into the top six inches of soil with a spading fork or shovel.

If your soil is not at all acidic, lowering the pH and keeping it there may not be feasible. In that case, prepare a mix of equal parts sand and dampened peat moss and use it to fill a raised bed or to replace soil excavated from the planting site.

2. ADDING ORGANIC MATTER Heaths also require soil that is especially rich in organic matter. This helps soil retain moisture and furnishes reserve acidity years after the effect of the sulfur wears off. Organic matter also lightens the soil, providing oxygen and an easy root run for a heath's fibrous roots.

Mix a bucketful of peat moss or composted sawdust into the soil right where you are going to plant. Since dry peat moss does not readily absorb water, moisten it with hot water before you begin.

3. PLANTING Next, dig a hole wide and deep enough to accommodate the plant's root ball. Slide the plant out of its container and position it on a small mound of soil in the planting hole. Make sure that the crown of the plant is at the same level that it was in the pot. Gently loosen the roots around the outside of the root ball with a stick to encourage them to grow out into the surrouding soil.

As you backfill the hole, tamp the soil with your fingers to eliminate air pockets, then give the ground a thorough soaking. Fall and winter rains will take care of further watering until late spring.

4. MULCHING Mulch delays freezing of the soil in autumn, giving the roots more time to develop. And during the winter months, it lessens the soil's alternate cycles of freezing and thawing, protecting a young plant — as yet poorly anchored — from being heaved.

An organic mulch is best, because it provides the cool, moist conditions enjoyed by heath roots, the bulk of which occupy the top six inches (15 cm) of the soil. Over time, the decomposing mulch will enrich the soil and help maintain its acidity.

Sawdust, fresh or decomposed, is an ideal mulch. Other good materials include leaves (except those that tend to mat down, like maple leaves), pine needles, wood chips, and bark chips.

Avoid using manure, which is too concentrated in nutrients for the heath's delicate roots. Lay the mulch to a depth of three to six inches (7.5 to 15 cm) around the base of the plant. As with the sulfur, apply the mulch to an area as wide as the eventual spread of the plant.

Growing and Harvesting Garlic

Janet H. Sanchez

GARLIC GROWN IN YOUR OWN GARDEN and properly stored has a fresh pungency quite unlike the musty odor and bitter flavor too often present in cloves that have been sitting on a grocery shelf. Fortunately for those who enjoy cooking with it, this bulbous herb is easy to grow and requires very little space in the garden.

You can plant store-bought garlic cloves, but it is more fun to experiment with varieties available from mail-order sources. This allows you to find the variety that is best suited to both your garden and your storage conditions.

The secret to a harvest of large garlic bulbs is fall planting — generally four to six weeks before the soil freezes, or as late as the beginning of December in mild-winter regions. This way the roots can become established before winter sets in and will be ready to support vigorous leafy growth come early spring. It also makes for larger plants and therefore larger bulbs. The plants will begin to produce bulbs once the long days of June arrive.

1. PREPARE THE PLANTING BED

It's wise to plant garlic in a spot not recently used for garlic or other plants in the onion family. As is the case with most vegetables, rotating crops prevents the buildup of disease organisms in the soil.

Garlic requires a reasonably fertile, well-drained soil. Avoid planting in areas where water can collect around the roots, causing them to rot or become diseased. Planting in a raised bed works well. A raised bed lined with chicken wire will also exclude gophers, which are fond of garlic. Work several inches of compost or well-rotted manure into the bed, plus a complete fertilizer such as 10-10-10. Then smooth the soil with a rake.

2. PLANT AND MULCH Garlic reproduces vegetatively — that is, it grows from individual cloves broken off from a whole bulb. Each clove multiplies in the ground, forming a new bulb that consists of 10 to 20 cloves.

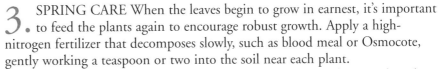

Break a bulb apart into individual cloves, keeping only the largest, firmest ones for planting. Space the cloves four to six inches (10 to 15 cm) apart and allow about a foot (30 cm) between rows. Be sure to set the cloves in with the pointed end up and the flat, basal plate down. Push each one an inch (2.5 cm) or so into the ground, firm the soil around it, and water the bed if it is dry.

After planting, lay down a protective mulch of chopped leaves, straw, or grass clippings. In cold-winter regions the mulch should be four to six inches (10 to 15 cm) thick to prevent the roots from being heaved out of the soil by alternate freezing and thawing. A lighter mulch is useful in milder climates, where it slows the growth of winter weeds. Don't worry if a few garlic leaves sprout; most of the plant's aboveground growth will occur in spring.

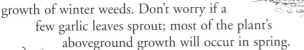

3. SPRING CARE When the leaves begin to grow in earnest, it's important to feed the plants again to encourage robust growth. Apply a high-nitrogen fertilizer that decomposes slowly, such as blood meal or Osmocote, gently working a teaspoon or two into the soil near each plant.

If the mulch has decomposed, apply another layer to reduce weeds and to help retain moisture. Pull any weeds that do appear, or they will rob moisture and nutrients from the garlic. And be sure to keep the garlic patch watered during dry spells.

In late spring some varieties send up flower stalks that will eventually produce small bulbils. Cut these stalks off (you can add them to salads and vegetable dishes if you wish) to help direct the plant's energy into forming a large bulb.

As the summer solstice approaches, garlic plants stop producing new leaves and begin to form bulbs. Remove any remaining mulch and stop watering. Allowing the soil to dry out around the maturing bulbs will help the garlic store better.

4. HARVEST AND STORAGE When most of the leaves have turned brown (in mid-July to early August, depending on your climate), gently pull or dig up the bulbs, being careful not to bruise them. Don't leave them in the ground too long, or they may begin to separate and will not store well.

Now lay the plants, leaves and all, out to dry for two or three weeks in a shady spot with good air circulation. An old window screen set on sawhorses under a tree works well. Be sure to bring the plants inside if rain threatens. When the roots feel dry and brittle, rub them off, along with any loose dirt. Don't wash the bulbs or break them apart, though, or the plants won't last as long.

Either braid the garlic, tie it in bunches, or cut off the stems a few inches above the bulbs. Hang the braids, or store the loose bulbs on slatted shelves or screens in an airy, cool (but not freezing) location. Set aside the largest bulbs to replant later in the fall. During the winter check your harvest often, and promptly use any bulbs that show signs of sprouting.

Winterizing a Tub-Grown Tree

Janet H. Sanchez

A DECIDUOUS TREE GROWN IN A LARGE TUB gives a feeling of permanence, grace, and beauty to a terrace or patio. But as many cold-climate gardeners have discovered, such a tree is often more vulnerable to injury from winter cold than it would be if it were growing in the ground. During the coldest weather, the roots of a container-grown tree are exposed to below-freezing temperatures on all sides, which can seriously damage them. In addition, soil in a container thaws and refreezes quickly when temperatures fluctuate, which can cause the tree to heave out of the soil and tear its roots or expose them to drying winds. Sudden temperature changes also may damage the container itself. Finally, an exposed tree's branches can break off as winter winds whip around the corners of buildings.

How do you avoid the heartbreak of losing a prized tub-grown specimen? Although smaller plants can be moved to a sheltered spot, it is virtually impossible to shift larger ones. Fortunately, you can protect larger trees and their containers by moderating winter's effects with wire fencing and some insulation. Bear in mind, however, that if the tree is too tender for your climate, or if the weather is unusually harsh, these measures will not be adequate to bring it through the winter.

1. PREPARE THE TREE Your tree needs to go into winter in a healthy state. While you should continue watering it through autumn, you do not want to fertilize after the first signs of fall. In particular, you must not feed the plant any nitrogen, which would encourage it to continue producing tender new stems and leaves rather than gradually ceasing to grow and hardening its tissues in preparation for the winter ahead. After the first hard frost, when the tree has lost most or all of its leaves and become fully dormant, you can get it ready for its winter "nest." Trim back any extra long shoots and prune out any dead branches. Gently tie together those branches that are wide-spreading or trailing so that they will not be injured when you pack stuffing around them. Water the tree well, then mulch the top of the soil with several inches of straw or leaves.

2. GATHER MATERIALS For the next steps, you will need a piece of wire fencing long enough to make a cage about a foot (30 cm) wider than the diameter of the tree's canopy. Two-inch-mesh (5 cm) chicken wire (poultry netting) is inexpensive and available in heights up to six feet (1.8 m). It can be cut to whatever length you need. Any other field or garden fencing will serve as well, including the type sold to support tomato plants. If the tree and container are tall, you'll need extra fencing to fashion a taller cage.

You'll also need a sturdy wooden slat or stake that is as long as the proposed cage is tall, baling wire or a staple

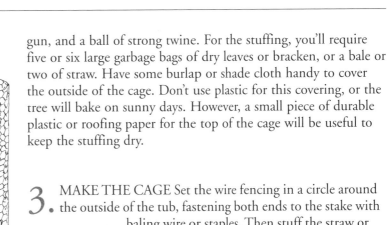

gun, and a ball of strong twine. For the stuffing, you'll require five or six large garbage bags of dry leaves or bracken, or a bale or two of straw. Have some burlap or shade cloth handy to cover the outside of the cage. Don't use plastic for this covering, or the tree will bake on sunny days. However, a small piece of durable plastic or roofing paper for the top of the cage will be useful to keep the stuffing dry.

3. MAKE THE CAGE Set the wire fencing in a circle around the outside of the tub, fastening both ends to the stake with baling wire or staples. Then stuff the straw or leaves around both container and plant, taking care not to break any branches as you work.

For a tall tree, work in two stages. Fill as much as you can of the initial cage, then add a second tier of wire. This may require a stepladder and a helper. Overlap the two tiers by at least six inches (15 cm), wiring them to each other and attaching the sides to the stake as before. Then finish stuffing with the leaves or straw.

Next, wrap the burlap or shade cloth around the outside of the cage and secure it with twine. This will prevent the stuffing from blowing away. Finally, cover the cage with plastic or roofing paper. Cut a piece about a foot (30 cm) larger than the top of the cage, then tuck the edges down firmly inside. Tie a couple of lengths of twine over the cover to ensure that it stays in place.

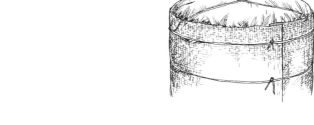

4. UNCOVER THE TREE As spring approaches, unwrap the tree gradually — taking off all the coverings at once would expose the tender bark to sunburn and windburn. Furthermore, a sudden late freeze could damage new buds. Remove the cap first and gently pull out the leaves or straw around the tree's branches. You can reuse the stuffing as garden mulch. Leave the fencing and the outside wrap in place for now. If the soil is dry, water the tree.

When you are sure spring has truly arrived, remove the cage. If possible, choose a cloudy day to do this so that the tree can slowly become acclimatized to daylight. Finally, store the fencing and burlap. You'll need to use them again next winter.

Making Hardwood Cuttings

Janet H. Sanchez

TAKING CUTTINGS of deciduous shrubs is a relatively easy and economical way to make new plants for a hedge, shrub border, or large-scale screening project. This technique can be used with privets as well as with crape myrtles, deutzias, euonymuses, forsythias, hydrangeas, mock oranges, spireas, and many roses. Certain edible plants, including currants, figs, gooseberries, grapes, and quinces, can also be increased by hardwood cuttings.

In most cases, it's best to take cuttings in autumn, soon after the shrub's leaves drop and the plant goes dormant. Given proper preparation and safe storage through the winter, the cuttings should produce roots the following spring.

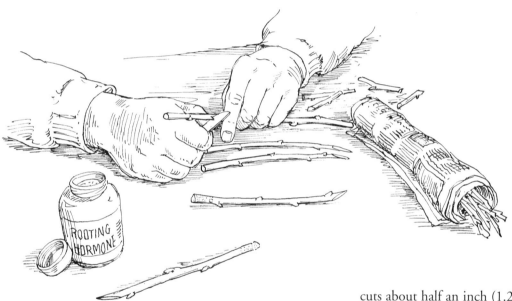

1. TAKE CUTTINGS Choose a mother plant that is healthy and vigorous. Then look for one-year-old wood, which is often lighter in color than older wood. The stems' thickness will vary depending on the type of shrub; year-old privet wood is usually a quarter-inch (.6 cm) in diameter.

Use a sharp knife to cut suitable stems a foot or two (30 cm or .6 m) long. If you cannot work on them within a few minutes, wrap them in damp paper towels or newspaper to prevent drying. Begin by discarding the top inch or two of each stem, since this unripened wood doesn't have enough stored nutrients to survive. Then cut the stems into six- to nine-inch (15 to 22.5 cm) pieces, each with three or more modes (leaf buds). Make the cuts about half an inch (1.25 cm) above or below a node. Because a cutting won't grow if planted upside down, make the top cut at a slant, so you can keep track of it. Then dip the bottom ends in rooting hormone and tap off any excess.

If you live in a place where the ground doesn't freeze more than two or three inches (5 or 7.5 cm) deep, you may plant the cuttings directly into a nursery row, as described in step 3.

2. STORE THE CUTTINGS Those who need to protect their cuttings through the winter should bundle them with rubber bands or string, making sure the top ends all face the same direction. If you are making cuttings of different types of shrubs, label each bundle. Then place the bundles in boxes filled with slightly moist vermiculite, sawdust, or sand, and store them in an unheated (but not freezing) room, garage, or root cellar.

If you prefer to store the bundles outdoors, you can dig a trench in well-drained soil, six to eight inches (15 to 20 cm) deep. Lay the bundles horizontally in the trench and cover them with soil. Water lightly if the soil is dry, but don't soak the area because too much moisture might cause the cuttings to rot. Then cover them with an insulating mulch of straw or leaves.

During the winter, each cutting should form a callus on its bottom (basal) end, where roots will eventually form. Retrieve the cuttings from storage in early spring, just before the leaves on dormant shrubs outdoors begin to unfurl.

3. PLANT THE CUTTINGS Prepare a nursery area in a spot protected from strong winds. I've set aside a corner of my vegetable garden for this purpose — the soil is reasonably friable, and a hose for irrigation is handy. Dig a narrow trench about as deep as your cuttings are tall, then place an inch or two (2.5 or 5 cm) of coarse sand in the bottom.

Set the cuttings in the trench about six inches (15 cm) apart, standing their bases in the sand and leaving only the top bud exposed above the rim of the trench. Backfill with some of the excavated soil, mixed half and half with well-rotted compost, sand, or perlite to make it lighter and more porous. Firm the cuttings into their temporary home and water well.

4. CARE It's a good idea to shade the cuttings from hot sun until they are growing well. Use either shade cloth or a lattice supported on stakes. Provide water as needed to keep the nursery bed moist but not soggy. Once the new plants develop leaves and increase in size, start feeding them monthly with a complete fertilizer.

By fall your new shrubs should be well established. In mild-winter climates, they will be ready to be moved to their permanent place in the landscape, but in colder areas, it's prudent to wait until spring before transplanting.

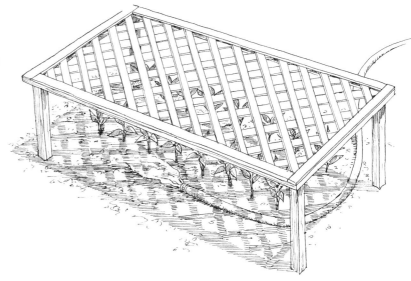

Making a Terrarium

Nancy Bubel

A TERRARIUM CAN provide a welcome spot of greenery all winter long, and fall is a good time to make one. There's a special satisfaction to be found in arranging this small, bounded green world to your liking. You can use almost any transparent, waterproof, easily-covered vessel, from a one- or two-quart (1 or 2 litres) candy jar to an old fish tank. Wash the container well to get rid of any debris or mold, and let it dry so the soil won't adhere to any damp spots that remain.

Most terrariums thrive in indirect light; strong sunlight can cook the glassed-in plants. In a dark room the terrarium will need several hours of artificial light a day (fluorescent light is the most economical).

For a pleasing effect, include plants with different forms and textures — some creeping, others bushy. Small rocks or gnarled pieces of wood make for interesting terrarium topography. In a woodland terrarium I once made, a tiny mushroom emerged from the clump of forest sod that I had tucked in. It didn't last long, but while it was in fruit it was a nice spontaneous addition.

A woodland terrarium might include wintergreen, bearberry, and pipsissewa; a houseplant terrarium might have peperomias, fittonia, and baby's tears. Other good terrarium plants include episcias, small ferns like ebony spleenwort and rusty woodsia, sedums, mosses, ground pine, and evergreen seedlings. Most herbs, especially rosemary, thyme, and other plants requiring excellent drainage, do not fare well in a terrarium.

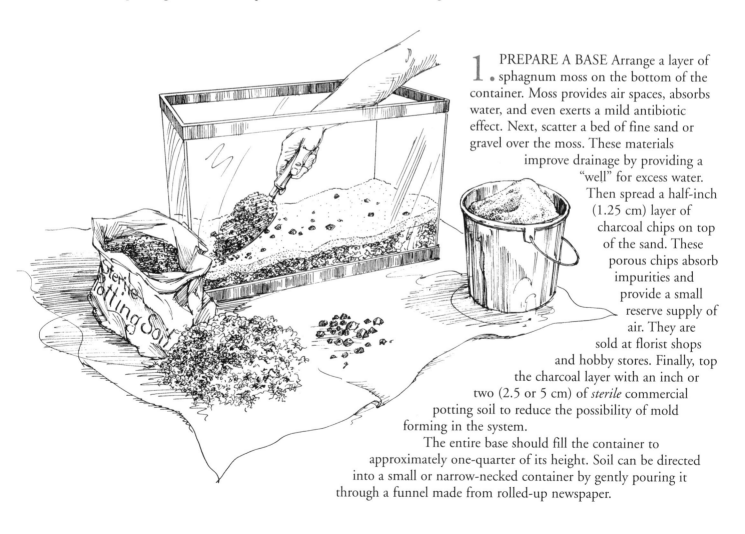

1. PREPARE A BASE Arrange a layer of sphagnum moss on the bottom of the container. Moss provides air spaces, absorbs water, and even exerts a mild antibiotic effect. Next, scatter a bed of fine sand or gravel over the moss. These materials improve drainage by providing a "well" for excess water. Then spread a half-inch (1.25 cm) layer of charcoal chips on top of the sand. These porous chips absorb impurities and provide a small reserve supply of air. They are sold at florist shops and hobby stores. Finally, top the charcoal layer with an inch or two (2.5 or 5 cm) of *sterile* commercial potting soil to reduce the possibility of mold forming in the system.

The entire base should fill the container to approximately one-quarter of its height. Soil can be directed into a small or narrow-necked container by gently pouring it through a funnel made from rolled-up newspaper.

2. SET THE PLANTS IN PLACE This is delicate work. If your fingers don't reach or if they get in the way, use long-handled tweezers or a staightened coat hanger with a loop on one end to maneuver each plant into its spot. An old spoon taped to a long stick makes a good miniature trowel. Once a plant is in position, firm a little additional potting soil around it. A good tamper for hard-to-reach areas is a cork or spool attached to a stick.

3. WATERING Add water sparingly after planting, just enough to settle the plants into place. You can always add more water if necessary, but flooding can't be undone. For a fish-tank-size container, a small watering can with a rose will do nicely; for smaller containers, add water by spoonfuls or with an eyedropper. Check the plants a few hours afterwards — if they still appear perky, there's enough water. Later, if the soil appears dry and the container feels light, add water carefully.

4. MAINTENANCE Cover the terrarium with a sheet of glass or clear plastic wrap. Plants need some air, though, so do not make the cover airtight. Once covered, the terrarium becomes a self-contained system with its own weather. Moisture that transpires from plant leaves will condense on the cover and sides and trickle down to keep the soil moist. If the glass looks misty, if water pools at the bottom, or if mold begins to form on the surface of the soil, the moisture level is too high. Ventilate by removing the cover for a day.

Terrarium-grown plants can become rangy, so pinch them back periodically to keep them short and bushy. Prevent mold by cutting off spent flowers and dead leaves. (Do not pull them off, as you may dislodge the plant.)

Once planted, a terrarium seldom needs watering. Because you don't want to encourage plants to outgrow their space, don't fertilize them either, at least for the first year. Close observation of the terrarium is both a pleasant diversion and a means to gather clues for needed changes.

Winterizing Broadleaved Evergreens

Oliver E. Allen

THE EFFECTS OF winterkill are often slow to appear. A plant will seem to come through the winter unscathed, but as spring develops the edges of leaves turn brown, the bark may split, and eventually a branch may be lost, sometimes the entire plant. The cause is a temperature imbalance. During prolonged cold spells a plant goes largely dormant, neither taking in moisture nor transpiring it (i.e., venting it through the leaves). But on warm, sunny days in midwinter, such as during the traditonal February thaw, the leaves may begin to transpire. The roots, however, buried in the still-frozen ground, are unable to replace the lost water. If there is a brisk wind the effects are accelerated. The plant becomes desiccated. All broadleaved evergreens are prone to this calamity, but rhododendrons are especially vulnerable, as their leaves tend to be bigger than those of other evergreens.

Luckily, there are ways to prevent, or at least to minimize, the effets of winterkill. Part of the remedy is to make sure your plants go into the winter in a healthy state. The other is to protect their exposed surfaces once cold weather sets in by coating them with an antidesiccant spray.

Experts like to say that a good way to get a plant though the winter is to take care of it the previous summer, and this is certainly true of rhododendrons. Summer droughts weaken plants, imperiling their defenses. So make sure they are adequately watered during the hot months, and into the fall. Be sure to maintain your vigilance during the autumn — a lovely dry Indian summer stretch can prove deceptively menacing. Replenish the mulch around plants, and take care of insect or disease problems.

1. WATER THOROUGHLY BEFORE THE GROUND FREEZES Even if there has been normal rainfall during November, the single most important thing you can do to protect rhododendrons is give them an adequate water supply before the ground freezes. Once every two weeks water the soil around your plants to a depth of 18 inches to two feet (46 cm to .6 m). Keep this up until the ground freezes. Not only does this provide an insurance supply of moisture that the plants may need later, it also slows the actual freezing of the soil, as water must give off heat in order to freeze. Check to see that your mulch is adequate: a two- to three-inch (5 to 7.5 cm) layer of shredded bark mulch will keep the soil from freezing too abruptly and minimize the effect of later temperature shifts.

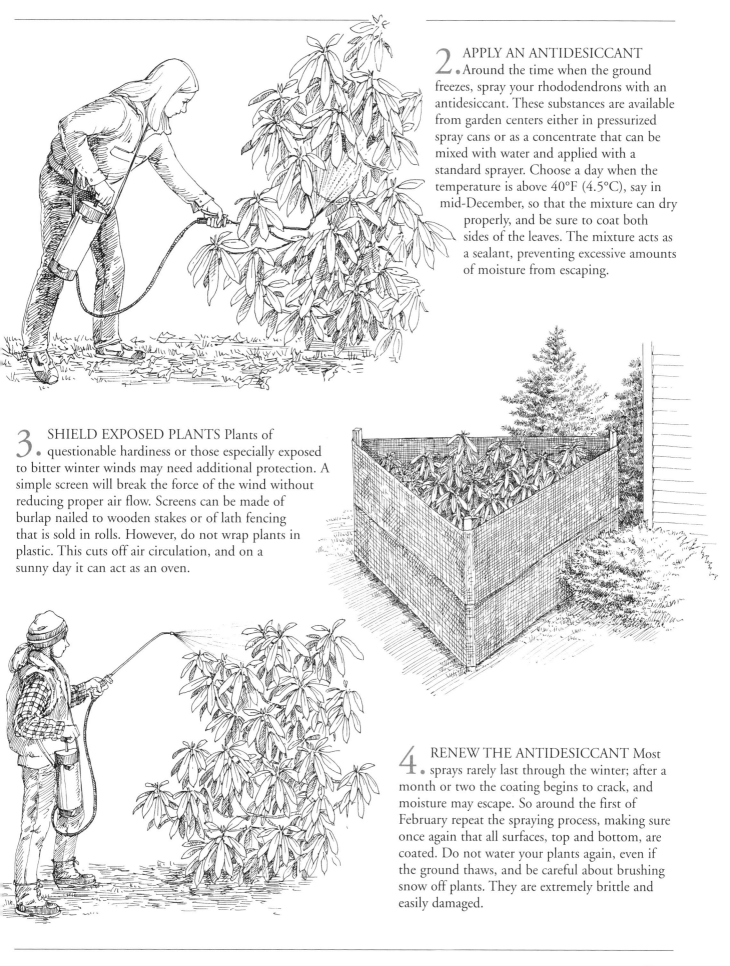

2. APPLY AN ANTIDESICCANT

Around the time when the ground freezes, spray your rhododendrons with an antidesiccant. These substances are available from garden centers either in pressurized spray cans or as a concentrate that can be mixed with water and applied with a standard sprayer. Choose a day when the temperature is above 40°F (4.5°C), say in mid-December, so that the mixture can dry properly, and be sure to coat both sides of the leaves. The mixture acts as a sealant, preventing excessive amounts of moisture from escaping.

3. SHIELD EXPOSED PLANTS

Plants of questionable hardiness or those especially exposed to bitter winter winds may need additional protection. A simple screen will break the force of the wind without reducing proper air flow. Screens can be made of burlap nailed to wooden stakes or of lath fencing that is sold in rolls. However, do not wrap plants in plastic. This cuts off air circulation, and on a sunny day it can act as an oven.

4. RENEW THE ANTIDESICCANT

Most sprays rarely last through the winter; after a month or two the coating begins to crack, and moisture may escape. So around the first of February repeat the spraying process, making sure once again that all surfaces, top and bottom, are coated. Do not water your plants again, even if the ground thaws, and be careful about brushing snow off plants. They are extremely brittle and easily damaged.

Freesias Indoors

Lee Reich

MOST GARDENERS do not live in areas of the country where it is warm enough to grow freesias outdoors, but anyone can grow these tender fragrant plants indoors. Unlike tulips, which are bulbs and already contain dormant flower buds, freesias are corms that form their flower buds as they grow. Freesias are therefore more of a challenge to force, but not if you understand their needs and give them proper care. The reward will be a potful of luxuriant, colorful blossoms.

1. POTTING UP Freesias need a well-drained soil, so your potting mix should be at least one-third vermiculite or perlite. It should also have a neutral pH. Fill the pot to within two inches of its rim, then set the freesia corms on top of the mix two inches (5 cm) apart with their pointed ends up. Do not overcrowd the corms for their roots will need sufficient space in order to provide adequate nourishment as the plants grow. Once the corms are in place, cover them with an inch (2.5 cm) of soil, then water thoroughly.

2. SITING THE POTS To become compact flowering plants, freesias require a cool period — 55°F (13°C) for about 45 days. Light is not needed until the first leaves show, so a good place to store the pot at this stage is an unheated garage or basement or a well-insulated cold frame. (Avoid keeping the plants at this cool temperature for too long a period, however, or they'll divert their energy into forming small corms above ground on their stems.)

   Once green leaf tips emerge, move the plants to a slightly warmer (65° to 70° [18° to 21°C]), brightly lit location. Light is all-important at this stage — the plants need it to manufacture enough food to form flowers.

An unheated sun-room or a south-facing basement window ought to provide the combination of brightness and coolness that freesias now need.

Do not be daunted by these rather exacting requirements. As long as your freesias receive sufficient light, they wil manage to bloom. Warmer temperatures, however, delay flowering and increase bud drop.

3. SUPPORTING THE STEMS Your pot of freesias will soon be filled with an abundance of lush, straplike foliage. The plants need some sort of support to keep the leaves from flopping over the sides of the pot and to hold up the long flower stems for best display. You can buy wire supports for this purpose. Twigs pushed into the soil will also do the job, or you can form a cage around the rim of the pot by inserting bamboo stakes and looping string from one stake to the next.

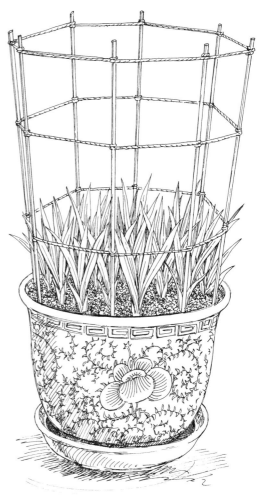

4. FERTILIZER AND WATER Fertilize the plants weekly with a neutral (nonacid) fertilizer. Throughout the plants' growth, keep the soil moist but not sodden. Fluoridated municipal water has been known to injure freesias, but this should not be a problem if you use a neutral fertilizer and potting mix.

Depending on the growing conditions and the cultivar, the first blossoms will appear between two and four months after planting. They will probably greet you with their sweet aroma even before their soft, cheery purple, red, yellow, or white petals catch your eye. Continue fertilizing and watering as long as the plants are in bloom, which should be a few weeks.

Winter

The Night is mother of the Day,
The Winter of the Spring,
And ever upon old Decay
The greenest mosses cling.

— John Greenleaf Whittier

Houseplants from Offsets

Janet H. Sanchez

CERTAIN HOUSEPLANTS have the helpful habit of reproducing themslves by forming offsets — small plants that cluster around their parent. Look for these offsets, or "pups," around the base of plants such as succulents, clivias, screwpines, and bromeliads. Pictured here is the succulent *Aloe vera,* an easy-to-grow plant whose sap is used as a home remedy for everything from burns to insect bites. After a few years an aloe tends to crowd its pot with clusters of offsets. The young plants are easily detached and replanted, which relieves overcrowded conditions and provides extras to keep or give away.

Most succulent offsets can be removed whenever it is convenient. To operate on other kinds of houseplants, it is best to wait until late winter, just before active growth resumes. You shouldn't intervene too early, however; offsets that have formed root systems are much easier to establish as independent plants. Aloe pups whose leaves are about three inches (7.5 cm) long ought to have sufficiently developed roots.

1. PREPARE POTS AND POTTING MIX The tender roots of offsets dry out quickly, so have your containers and potting mix ready in advance. Plan on one pot per offset, although small plants can be grouped in threes in a single pot. In the case of aloes, shallow four-inch (10 cm) pots work well for pups that are four or more inches (10 cm) long. Always use pots that have drainage holes, as trapped water causes root rot, which will kill the plants.

Scrub used pots with a stiff brush and rinse them with a disinfecting solution of one part bleach to nine parts water. This will prevent carry-over of disease from previous inhabitants. Then place a piece of screen or broken pot (rounded side up) over each drainage hole so soil won't wash out when you water.

While prepared soilless potting mix is fine for many houseplants, aloes and other succulents require a looser, more freely draining mix, so combine one part perlite or sharp sand to two or three parts potting mix in a bucket. Stir in just enough water to dampen the mix, but don't make it too soggy. Spread newspaper over your work surface to make cleanup easier, then put two inches (5 cm) of mix into each pot.

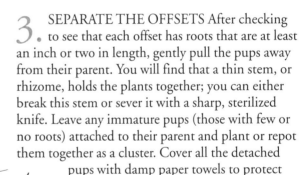

2. UNPOT PARENT AND PUPS Although it is possible to carefully cut off and pry out a few offshoots from around a parent plant, it's best to remove the entire mass from the pot. This makes it easier to see what you're getting and to determine how well rooted the individual pups are. To do so, simply lay the pot on its side, and slide an old table knife around the inside to loosen the roots. Tip the plants out, and gently disengage the soil from the roots.

3. SEPARATE THE OFFSETS After checking to see that each offset has roots that are at least an inch or two in length, gently pull the pups away from their parent. You will find that a thin stem, or rhizome, holds the plants together; you can either break this stem or sever it with a sharp, sterilized knife. Leave any immature pups (those with few or no roots) attached to their parent and plant or repot them together as a cluster. Cover all the detached pups with damp paper towels to protect them from drying out.

4. REPOT Place each plant in a prepared pot and cover the roots with potting mix. As you work, occasionally tap the pot on a hard surface to settle the soil. When you are finished, the crown should be about a half-inch below the rim of the pot to allow space for water. Be careful not to bury the fleshy parts of the plant, as this could lead to rot.

Water the new plants thoroughly (until excess water runs out of the drainage holes), then set the plants in a sunny window. Wait until the top of the soil feels dry before watering your collection of *Aloe vera* again.

Fighting Houseplant Pests

Janet H. Sanchez

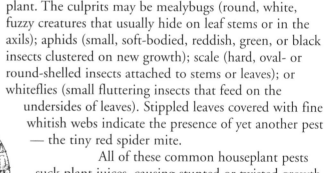

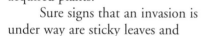

Houseplants bring a touch of the outdoors into our homes — an especially welcome addition in the depths of winter. Assuming we water and feed them correctly and place them in a suitable location, they should be free of insects and healthy most of the time. However, even the best-cared-for houseplants are sometimes attacked by pests that fly inside on their own or hitchhike in on newly acquired plants.

Sure signs that an invasion is under way are sticky leaves and activity that can be detected by peering closely at the plant. The culprits may be mealybugs (round, white, fuzzy creatures that usually hide on leaf stems or in the axils); aphids (small, soft-bodied, reddish, green, or black insects clustered on new growth); scale (hard, oval- or round-shelled insects attached to stems or leaves); or whiteflies (small fluttering insects that feed on the undersides of leaves). Stippled leaves covered with fine whitish webs indicate the presence of yet another pest — the tiny red spider mite.

All of these common houseplant pests suck plant juices, causing stunted or twisted growth. If you don't take action to stop the damage, the plant will eventuallly die. Shown here is the treatment of a grape ivy (*Cissus* species) afflicted with mealybugs; the same process will also eradicate aphids, scale, whiteflies, and red spider mites.

1. ISOLATE THE INFESTED PLANT Make a habit of regularly inspecting your plants so that you can spot insects and mites before their population has had time to increase drastically. You have a much better chance of controlling a small infestation than a major one. If you notice any pests, move the infested plant well away from other plants to keep the insects from traveling from one to the next. But don't shock the quarantined plant by putting it in a place that is much colder or sunnier than its previous location.

After moving the plant, wash your hands so that you don't help to disperse the pests, then inspect the rest of your collection. If you see signs that the insects have already begun to spread, you'll want to repeat the following steps for each infested plant.

2. WASH THE PLANT Dislodge as many insects as possible with a strong stream of water from a flexible hose hooked to the sink, bathtub, or laundry tub. Or, weather permitting, take the plant outdoors and spray it lightly with your garden hose. In the case of clinging scale insects, you might have to use a soapy cloth or toothbrush to wipe the plant clean.

If the plant is small enough, it is even more effective to submerge the foliage in water. To do so, fill a bucket or sink with lukewarm water. Then place foil, a rag, or a piece of paper over the top of the pot to hold the soil in place. Next, with your fingers spread around the plant's stem, turn the plant upside down, and swish the leaves in the water for two or three minutes. Finally, set the plant in indirect sunlight, where it can dry without getting burned.

3. SPRAY THE PLANT I prefer to spray with an insecticidal soap. These soaps contain fatty acids that help eliminate any pests that may remain on the plant after washing. And because they are of low toxicity to humans and pets, insecticidal soaps can be safely used indoors in a well-ventilated area. As with any pesticide, it's important to read the label carefully before applying. Never increase the recommended dosage, or you may harm or kill the plant.

When spraying, be sure to cover the entire plant, wetting both sides of the leaves so the soap comes in direct contact with its quarry. Don't spray in sunlight, and again, be sure to let the plant dry in a shaded location. Mealybugs and spider mites may require a second spraying two days later. Check the product label for the spray schedule for other pests.

The leaves of a few houseplants — ferns, jade plants, and palms — may be damaged by insecticidal soaps. Test-spray a small portion of the plant first; if it is sensitive, burned leaf tips or scorched leaf edges will appear within 48 hours. For these delicate plants, try dabbing the pests with a cotton swab dipped in rubbing alcohol, which will kill the insects by dehydrating their tiny bodies. Rinse the plant with water afterward.

4. REMAIN VIGILANT Keep the treated plant in isolation for a few weeks, checking frequently for a renewed buildup of the pest population. As new generations hatch, you may need to repeat the steps outlined here. Persistence should eventually result in a healthy plant that is ready to return to its decorative role in your home. To prevent future infestations, remember to quarantine all new plants for a month or so.

Air-Layering a Rubber Plant

Thomas Christopher

SAY WHAT YOU WILL about the rubber tree *(Ficus elastica),* you must admit that it's a supremely reliable houseplant. It seems as happy in an apartment window as it would be in its native East Asian jungle, thriving even in the arid atmosphere of a centrally heated North American winter. To my knowledge, the rubber tree has just one bad habit. Overwatering or the onset of old age causes the plant to shed its lower leaves, until all that remains is a tall, skinny stem topped with an anticlimatic tuft of foliage.

But there is a cure for that: air layering. this is a treatment that involves girdling the tree partway up its stem and packing the wound in damp sphagnum moss. In time, new roots emerge from the tissue above the wound so that after you severe the supporting stem, you can pot up a new, shorter plant in its own container. Often, air layering also stimulates branching in the lower part of the parent plant's stem, with the result that where once you had an eyesore, you now have two compact, mannerly houseplants.

1. PLOTTING THE CUTS Since success in air layering depends largely on timing, you must wait until the plant is in a period of active growth and then identify the wood that has reached the proper stage of maturity. New leaves are the obvious clue to growth, but you can also coax a plant into activity by setting it in a bright, warm spot and feeding it a complete houseplant fertilizer.

Girdling the rubber tree at the right point along the stem is essential. If you make the cut too close to the stem's growing tip, the wood will be so green and soft that it will rot rather than take root; if you cut too far down the stem, the wood will be so old and hard that it no longer sprouts roots readily. A point six to 12 inches (15 to 30 cm) below the growing tip is best; you shouldn't venture much farther than two feet (.6 m) down the stem.

2. GIRDLING THE STEM Having chosen your girdling spot, take a sharp knife and cut a ring all the way around the stem. Make sure to cut through the bark down to the stem's hard, wooly core. Then, at a point a half-inch (1.25 cm) farther down, ring the stem again. With the knife blade, carefully scrape off the bark between the two cuts, leaving a band of bare wood.

By removing the bark and underlying phloem tissue, you trap the nutrients and growth hormones flowing from the leaves and buds downward to the roots. As these accumulate above the wound, they will stimulate root growth. Since water and minerals travel upward through the stem's core, girdling won't deprive the foliage of these essentials. The technique is ideal for a number of other slow-rooting tropicals such as aralias, fatsias, dracaenas, crotons, and scheffleras — all plants that, like the rubber tree, often wither before striking root when propagated as regular stem cuttings.

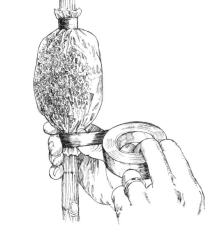

3. BANDAGING THE WOUND To encourage root growth, pack the girdled stretch of stem in a moist but well-aerated medium — dampened sphagnum moss works well. (Soak the sphagnum for an hour or two before setting knife to stem so that you don't leave the wound open to the air.) Then grab a double handful of moss and squeeze the water from it until it remains just slightly damp. Next, dust the wound with a root-promoting hormone and pack the damp moss around the girdled area of stem.

Wrap the resulting ball with clear polyethylene film; a piece eight inches (20 cm) square should be ample. Transparent film is best for this purpose because it allows you to keep a watchful eye on the progress of root growth. Strap the plastic in place with waterproof electrician's tape, sealing both the ends and the seam that runs the length of the bandage.

4. POTTING THE ROOTED LAYER If you've sealed the plastic carefully, the moss should stay moist while roots form. Watch the water droplets that condense on the inside of the bandage. If they dry up, open the bandage and sprinkle the moss with a little water.

The length of time your air layer will take to root depends on the vigor of the plant, the warmth of its environment, and the amount of light it receives (bright but not direct sunlight is best). Generally, though, the process is complete within eight to 10 weeks — at which time you'll see roots poking out of the sphagnum. Cut the stem just below the air layer with a knife or pruning shears, remove the tape and polyethylene, and pot the root-filled ball in a container of light, sandy potting soil. As always, pot the plant into a container only slightly larger than the root ball so that the roots will infiltrate the soil promptly.

Keeping a Poinsettia

Janet H. Sanchez

AFTER MARVELING at tree-size poinsettias near Victoria Falls in Zimbabwe, I've come to a great appreciation of our traditional holiday plant. Although it's unlikely that our potted poinsettias will ever achieve the grandeur of those grown outdoors in the subtropics, with a little care they can become long-lasting and attractive houseplants, living to bloom again during future holiday seasons.

As with any houseplant, choosing a healthy specimen makes subsequent care much easier. Look for a well-proportioned, compact plant with dense, vigorous, dark-green foliage on strong, stiff stems. The bracts, or colored, petallike leaves that surround the small, yellowish true flowers, should be well developed and fully colored to assure lasting color for the holiday season.

Chilly winds or temperatures below 50°F (10°C) will severely shock a poinsettia, causing it to drop its leaves, so protect your plant on the way home by placing it in a large shopping bag or a sleeve of paper or plastic.

1. CARE DURING THE HOLIDAYS Place your poinsettia near a sunny window where it will receive about six hours of bright light each day. Avoid cold, drafty spots and those with hot afternoon sun and temperatures much above 70°F (21°C), since too much heat makes the bracts fade. Also keep the plant away from the drying heat of a furnace or fireplace.

Like most other houseplants, poinsettias do best in moist but not soggy soil. When the soil surface feels dry, water until moisture begins to seep through the drain holes. Discard any excess water that collects in the saucer, because a plant left sitting in water may develop root rot, which can be fatal.

To keep your plant colorful until spring, feed it with a balanced, all-purpose houseplant fertilizer every two to three weeks, following the directions on the label.

2. PRUNE When the bracts begin to fade, usually in late March or April, cut back the stem (or stems) so that the plant is about eight inches (20 cm) tall. This pruning helps keep the plant from becoming overly tall and leggy. You might want to wear rubber gloves during this process, since the milky sap that oozes from the cut stems can irritate sensitive skin.

Before your plant resumes active growth, it needs to rest for a few weeks. You should keep it in a brightly lit place, but delay watering it until the soil dries to about an inch (2.5 cm) below the surface.

3. SUMMER CARE In early June, when new growth is well underway, gently transplant the poinsettia into a pot an inch or two (2.5 or 5 cm) larger than the original one. Water the plant thoroughly and return it to its sunny window, or move it outside to a warm, sunny spot sheltered from drying winds.

Continue to water and fertilize regularly over the summer. It's a good idea to pinch the new growth back by an inch or two (2.5 or 5 cm) in July to keep the plant compact. Pinch again in late August if growth is vigorous. If the plant spends the summer outdoors, be sure to bring it back inside before the cool nights of autumn arrive.

Sometimes a poinsettia attracts insect pests — whiteflies are a particular threat. Spray with an insecticidal soap as soon as you spot any signs of trouble, repeating the treatment as needed.

4. REFLOWERING Poinsettias are photoperiod plants, setting flower buds as the nights become longer. But the artificial lights in our homes upset this natural cycle. So, starting in mid- to late September, you will have to intervene to make sure your poinsettia gets around 14 continuous hours of darkness each night. This can be accomplished either by covering the plant with a cardboard box or a black plastic garbage bag, or by placing it in a dark closet. Take care that the poinsettia doesn't get too cold during these long nights — temperatures should stay between 60° and 70°F (15.5° and 21°C).

Uncover or retrieve the plant each morning and return it to a sunny window. Water every few days as needed, and fertilize as before. Continue to provide this long-night, short-day regimen for eight to ten weeks, or until small bracts begin to appear. At that point, you can bring the plant back into normal household lighting fulltime. The bracts will mature and develop, providing a colorful holiday decoration once again.

Keeping an Amaryllis

Janet H. Sanchez

BRIGHT, ALMOST AUDACIOUS COLORS and enormous flowers make amaryllis plants (*Hippeastrum* hybrids) an exuberant antidote to gloomy winter days. These large bulbs send forth one or two hollow stems that elongate quickly before unfurling three or four lilylike blossoms in vivid tropical shades of red, pink, salmon, orange, white, or various bicolors.

Usually we acquire our first amaryllis as a holiday gift, enjoy its blossoms that winter, then discard the plant, not realizing that amaryllis (like many gift plants) can live to brighten winter days again. True, the bulb uses up its reserves of energy in putting forth the first round of flowers, but with faithful care through the year, you can coax it to renew its strength so it will bloom again.

1. INITIAL PLANTING An amaryllis blooms best when somewhat pot-bound, so choose a pot that is about seven inches (17.8 cm) deep but no more than an inch or two (2.5 or 5 cm) wider than the diameter of the bulb. A clay pot is preferable to a plastic one, because its weight will provide stability when the plant becomes top-heavy.

Be sure the pot has one or more drainage holes; the roots of an amaryllis will die if the soil around them is constantly soggy. Cover the holes with pieces of broken clay pots or fine-mesh screen to keep the soil from washing out.

Fill the pot about halfway with commercial potting soil, packing it in fairly firmly. Then set the bulb in place and pack more potting soil around it, leaving an inch of space between the soil line and the pot's rim. The top third of the bulb should protrude above the soil line so that water won't accumulate around its neck and cause it to rot. When the bulb is packed in, water it well once. Don't water again until the bulb shows active growth.

Place the pot in a bright, warm room (65° to 75°F [18° to 24°C] by day, 5 to 10 degrees cooler by night) while the roots are developing. Within a few weeks, the first signs of the bud stalk will appear. Leaves usually begin to appear later.

Water the plant whenever the top of the soil feels dry, and feed it twice a month with bulb food or a liquid fertilizer (5-10-5 is best). Rotate the pot daily to encourage even growth of the broad, strappy leaves. You may wish to support the heavy bloom stalk with a wire stake. When buds begin to open, move the plant into a cooler, shadier room. Heat and bright light will cause the flowers to fade and wither more quickly.

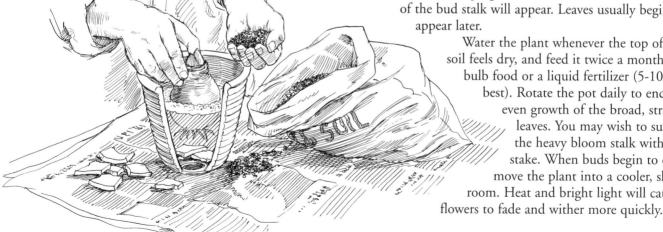

2. CARE AFTER BLOOM Your amaryllis bulb has just invested all its energy in producing flowers. It now needs plenty of water, fertilizer, and sunshine to allow its leaves to carry on the process of photosynthesis and replenish the bulb's food supply.

Pinch off spent blossoms so the plant doesn't waste energy forming seeds. Don't remove any foliage yet. Move the plant to a sunny window, continue to water as needed, and fertilize twice a month to promote healthy leaves. The more leaves the plant grows in summer, the more flower stalks it will be able to produce the following winter. If you wish, move the pot outside once spring has truly arrived, or put it in a greenhouse or on an indoor windowsill. Try to find a spot where it will receive at least four hours of sunshine each day.

3. DORMANCY AND STORAGE To some extent, each amaryllis bulb seems to set its own timetable for going dormant and then reblooming. Usually, however, the foliage begins to turn yellow and die back by late August (sometimes later, sometimes earlier), signaling the beginning of the plant's dormant stage. When this happens, stop watering and fertilizing. If you had set the pot outside over spring and summer, lay it on its side so that rain won't moisten the soil, and bring it in before the first hard frost. Cut off the dead foliage and store the bulb, still in its pot, in a dark, cool (about 55°F [13°C]) spot such as a basement for about two months.

4. REVIVAL Begin awakening your amaryllis bulb from its rest six to eight weeks before you want it to bloom again. Gently remove the top inch of soil with a spoon and replace it with fresh potting soil. Then water the plant well and fertilize. Follow the same schedule of care as last year to bring the plant into bloom and through the summer again.

An amaryllis may refuse to bloom again if its roots have been disturbed too often, so don't repot unless the bulb looks really crowded (once every three or four years is usually enough). You'll disrupt the plant least if you repot it at the start of the revival, or new-growth, period.

Occasionally, miniature plants (called "pups") appear around the mother bulb. If you want a clump of amaryllis in one pot, leave them be. If not, you can remove them and pot them separately at the beginning of the new-growth stage. Pups develop slowly but should bloom once they are three years old.

Sometimes despite your best efforts a revived amaryllis bulb sends up new leaves but no flowers. Don't despair! If the plant seems healthy and strong, give it another chance by carrying it through another growing season — it may just need more time to gather the strength to rebloom.

Training a Standard Lantana

Oliver E. Allen

AMONG THE MANY shapes and forms that house plants can be coaxed into assuming, one of the most elegant is the so-called standard. Designed to make an otherwise shrublike plant grow to resemble a small tree, with a straight, clear stem holding aloft a tight, rounded mass of foliage, the technique is most often practiced outdoors and has contributed to the classic look of many a formal garden. But in truth any plant with a woody stem can be trained in this fashion, and the result indoors is likely to be highly arresting. A standard can range in height all the way from eight or 10 inches (20 or 25 cm) to three or four feet (.9 or 1.2 m), depending on the species as well as our ingenuity and patience; popular houseplants considered fair game include herbs (rosemary, lavender), citrus ('Calamondin' orange, 'Meyer' lemon), and such diverse genera as gardenias, ficuses, geraniums, fuchsias, heliotropes, wisterias, and abutlions. The favorite candidates generally are plants with smallish leaves, which heighten the illusion of a miniature, stylized replica of a much bigger plant or tree. A likely choice for any indoor location that gets five or six hours of sun daily is one of the lantanas, for they not only bear attractive small leaves but bloom copiously for much of the year.

1. CHOOSE A STRONG, STRAIGHT SHOOT Standards are not made from mature plants. They must properly be started from mere shoots, fledgling plants, or cuttings so that the stem will develop properly. If you happen to have a young lantana only four or five inches (10 or 12.5 cm) high with a straight stem, you might try it. Otherwise buy a small, healthy new plant with a strong central leader, or, better yet, start with a well-rooted cutting that similarly has a good stem.

2. TRAIN THE LEADER Insert a narrow stake about 10 inches (25 cm) long next to the plant stem and tie the stem to it using a twist tie or soft cord (tie it firmly around the stake, loosely around the stem). Make sure the stem is held vertical.

Remove all branches or side shoots, and as the lantana gains height rub off any buds that represent potential side branches. Leaves growing along the stem may be retained temporarily, however, as they nourish the plant, helping it to grow rapidly; in time, they will fall off or can be removed. Add new ties every two or three inches (5 or 7.5 cm) to keep the stem growing straight, fertilize the soil regularly, and move the lantana to a bigger pot whenever its roots become crowded.

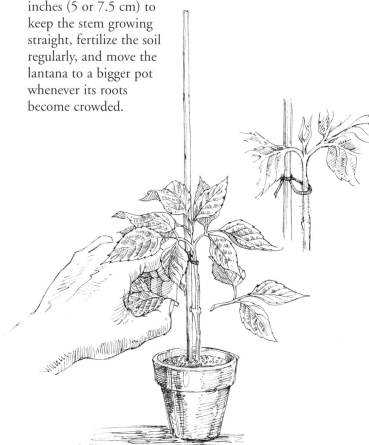

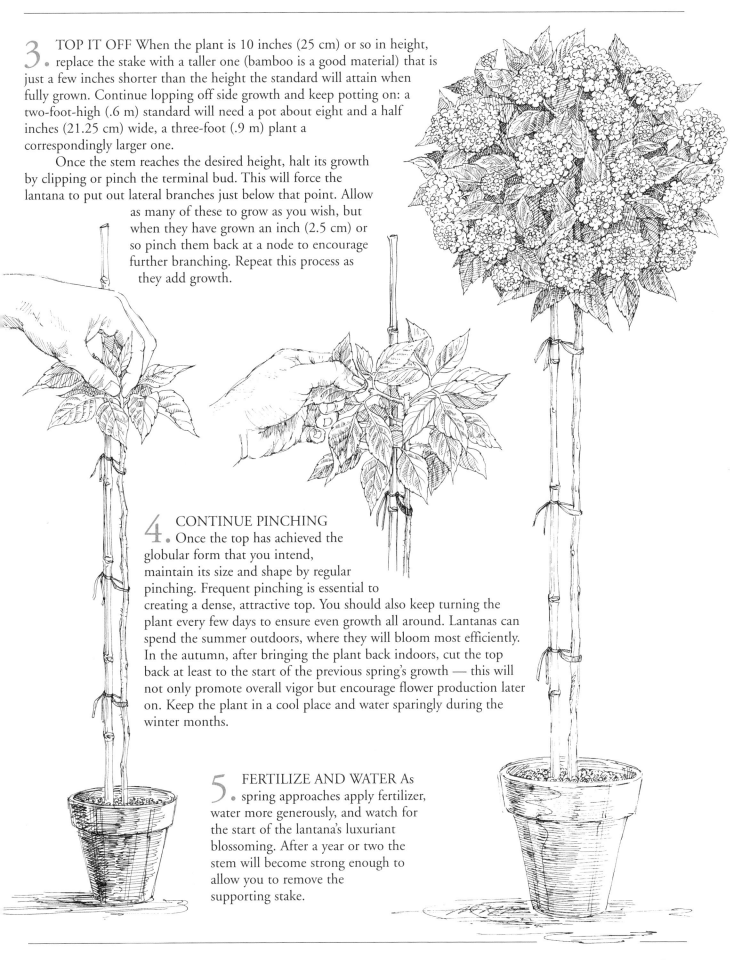

3. TOP IT OFF When the plant is 10 inches (25 cm) or so in height, replace the stake with a taller one (bamboo is a good material) that is just a few inches shorter than the height the standard will attain when fully grown. Continue lopping off side growth and keep potting on: a two-foot-high (.6 m) standard will need a pot about eight and a half inches (21.25 cm) wide, a three-foot (.9 m) plant a correspondingly larger one.

Once the stem reaches the desired height, halt its growth by clipping or pinch the terminal bud. This will force the lantana to put out lateral branches just below that point. Allow as many of these to grow as you wish, but when they have grown an inch (2.5 cm) or so pinch them back at a node to encourage further branching. Repeat this process as they add growth.

4. CONTINUE PINCHING Once the top has achieved the globular form that you intend, maintain its size and shape by regular pinching. Frequent pinching is essential to creating a dense, attractive top. You should also keep turning the plant every few days to ensure even growth all around. Lantanas can spend the summer outdoors, where they will bloom most efficiently. In the autumn, after bringing the plant back indoors, cut the top back at least to the start of the previous spring's growth — this will not only promote overall vigor but encourage flower production later on. Keep the plant in a cool place and water sparingly during the winter months.

5. FERTILIZE AND WATER As spring approaches apply fertilizer, water more generously, and watch for the start of the lantana's luxuriant blossoming. After a year or two the stem will become strong enough to allow you to remove the supporting stake.

Mixing Your Own Potting Soil

Oliver E. Allen

BECAUSE MOST houseplants tend to outgrow their pots and must be moved to larger ones, or their soil becomes worn out, indoor gardeners regularly need new potting soil. The temptation is to step outdoors and dig some topsoil from the garden, but that's a bad idea. Soil from the garden may be infested with weed seeds and disease spores as well as other unwanted substances, and sterilizing it is a nasty chore. More important, in the constricted environment of a pot ordinary garden soil is likely to become compacted, preventing sufficient air from reaching the plant's roots. Although you can compensate for these problems, the easiest approach is to buy packaged potting soil (which will have been pasteurized) from a garden center and amend it to your particular needs.

Good potting soil must be absorbent enough to retain moisture but loose enough to allow for good drainage and air circulation; its physical composition is actually far more important that its chemical content. In practical terms, potting soil should contain (1) loam, the equivalent of purified topsoil; (2) peat moss or leaf mold, for roughage and water retention; and (3) sharp sand or perlite (a substance made from volcanic rock), for drainage. Sand from the seashore is no good; not only is it likely to be salty, which is harmful to plants, but each grain is rounded — not "sharp" — from all that tumbling in the water and thus will pack too tightly and hinder good drainage.

In theory, packaged potting soil contains all the necessary elements in proper proportions. Many gardeners have found, however, that it tends to be too finely textured and not gritty enough, so they like to add more peat moss and perlite. A good formula for general purposes, in fact, is one-third packaged soil, one-third peat and one-third perlite. The formula, sometimes referred to as "houseplant thirds," can be adjusted for special situations.

Certain plants demand an entirely different mix. Orchids, for example, require a mix that contains tree bark or some similar porous substances, while cacti thrive on very sandy soil. Garden centers sell such special formulations, which rarely need further adjusting. But the houseplant thirds will do for most other indoor plants, from ficuses to geraniums.

1. CHECK INGREDIENTS After purchasing packaged soil, peat moss (not to be confused with sphagnum moss, which is used to line hanging baskets), and perlite or sand, make sure the soil and peat moss are slightly moist; if they are not, they will probably not absorb moisture effectively after mixing. If the peat is dry, empty it into a pail of warm water and squeeze handfuls under the water until no dry flakes float on top. Then remove the saturated peat, squeeze out the water until the peat is merely moist, and return it to the bag. If the bag is kept sealed thereafter, the peat will stay moist.

2. MIX SMALL BATCHES Pour small helpings of each ingredient into a pail or basin in roughly equal amounts (absolute exactness is not essential) and mix thoroughly with a trowel. Then add more of the ingredients in small, equal batches, increasing the total amount until you have what you need for the job at hand.

3. ADJUST FOR SPECIAL REQUIREMENTS Add extra amounts of peat moss or perlite to suit plants with particular needs. If you are mixing soil for African violets, for example, you should add extra peat plus more perlite; for succulents double the perlite or sand. Some experts advise adding ground limestone if a more alkaline mix is needed, or extra peat moss for a very acid one. But most houseplants are happy enough with a mix that is just slightly acid, as is the houseplant thirds. To give plants an extra boost, some experts recommend adding a pinch or two of bonemeal. This is not necessary, however, as the packaged soil will almost certainly include some kind of nutritive substance. In any case, do not add any fertilizer to the mix — it is probably rich enough as it is.

4. LABEL ANY LEFTOVER MIX If you end up with soil mix left over, put it in a plastic bag, seal the bag tightly with a twist-tie, and label it explicitly so that you will know at a later date precisely what ingredients have gone into it. Larger quantities can be stored in small plastic garbage cans.

Dividing a Houseplant

Janet H. Sanchez

HOUSEPLANTS HAVE A HABIT of outgrowing their pots, some more quickly than others. The signs are familiar: the plant looks crowded or top-heavy, its roots protrude from the drainage hole, and it wilts soon after watering because its roots have filled the pot completely, leaving no space for moisture-holding soil. You can move houseplants into larger and larger containers each time they outgrow their homes, but eventually all those large pots and plants may crowd you.

Fortunately, many houseplants can be divided. Generally, plants that respond well are those that form multiple crowns, such as Boston ferns (shown here); those that form miniature plantlets around the mother plant, such as African violets; and those that form offsets, or "pups," such as clivias. Don't try to divide vines or other plants that grow from a single stem.

Late winter is the best time to divide a houseplant. It is just about to enter a period of active growth, so it will recover quickly. You can also make the division later, when the plant is actively growing (usually until early summer), but avoid undertaking the project at the end of a growing season.

1. ADVANCE PREPARATION Withhold water for a day or two before dividing to encourage the plant's top growth to harden slightly.

Most houseplants recover from division more quickly if divided into just two or three new plants. The new pots should be the same size or an inch or two smaller (2.5 to 5 cm) than the container the plant currently occupies and should have at least one drainage hole. If you choose a pot that is too large, most of the soil won't have any roots growing in it and so will stay permanently wet.

If the pots are new, soak them in water for several hours so that their porous walls won't rob moisture from the potting soil. If the pots have been used, scrub them with a stiff brush, and rinse them with a disinfecting mixture of one part bleach to nine parts water. Then place a piece of screen or a potsherd over each drainage hole to prevent soil from washing out.

Spread newspapers on your work surface to make cleanup easier. Dump a soilless potting mix into a bucket and stir in water a little at a time until it is damp but not soggy. (If you are dividing African violets, be sure to use a mix made especially for them.)

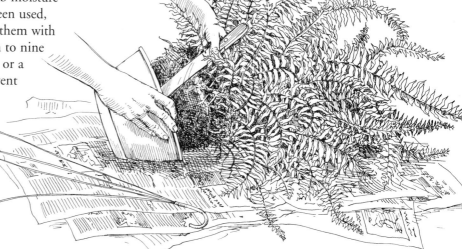

2. REMOVE THE PLANT FROM ITS POT To remove a fairly small plant from its pot, spread your fingers between the foliage and over the rim of the pot. Turn the pot upside down and either gently tap the edge against a hard surface or whack the bottom of the pot. If the plant doesn't slide out readily or if the pot is too large to turn upside down, lay it on its side and slide an old table knife or spatula around the inside of the pot to loosen the roots. Tip the plant out and shake the loose soil from its roots. Don't tug on the stems or foliage or you may damage the plant. Remove any potsherds that may be lurking in the roots.

3. MAKE DIVISIONS Examine the roots and foliage for places that seem to divide naturally. If possible, pull or tease the roots apart with your fingers, retaining a good chunk of roots for each clump of leaves. If a plant's roots form a dense mass (often the case with an overgrown Boston fern), it will probably be necessary to make clean, decisive cuts right through the root ball. Use a long, sharp knife.

Work quickly to keep the roots from being exposed to the air for too long. If you are interrupted before you can repot the divisions, cover the roots with damp paper towels to keep them from drying out.

4. REPOT THE DIVISIONS Put a shallow layer of the potting medium in the bottom of each container. Position each division so that the soil level is the same around the stem as it was in the original container. Gently push the mix in around the roots, tapping the pot occasionally to firm it in place and to eliminate air pockets. Leave about an inch (2.5 cm) between the top of the medium and the pot's rim to allow space for water.

Water each division thoroughly, adding a little more mix if watering causes it to settle. Don't water again until the top of the mix feels slightly dry. Let the plants recover from surgery in an airy but shaded location for a week or two before moving them back to brighter light. Resume fertilizing when they send out new growth.

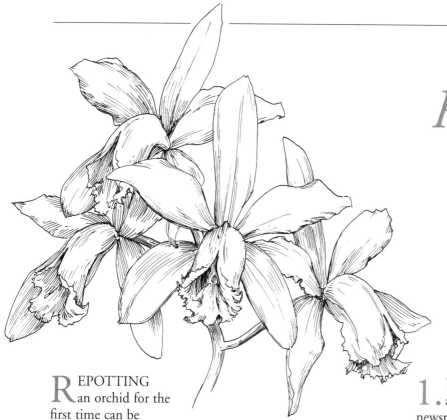

Repotting an Orchid

Thomas Fischer

REPOTTING an orchid for the first time can be daunting. Although it isn't a difficult task, it is sufficiently different from repotting other kinds of plants that you may be inclined to put it off. Don't. An orchid that is allowed to remain in the same pot too long will flower poorly and may even die. There are two ways to tell if your orchid needs repotting. First, your plant may simply have outgrown its pot. For example, if your orchid is one that produces pseudobulbs (bulblike, swollen stems that support the leaves), the new growths will extend beyond the edge of the pot, leaving brittle and easily damaged young roots dangling in the air. Second, the growing medium may have broken down. If it appears sodden and mushy and no longer drains freely, you must repot the plant in fresh medium to keep its roots from rotting.

Unless it is an emergency, the best time to repot an orchid with pseudobulbs, such as the cattelya shown here, is just after it has begun to produce a new growth but before the new roots have begun to elongate. As a potting medium, your best bet is a commercially prepared mix based on medium-size chunks of fir bark. If your orchid is the kind that lacks pseudobulbs, such as moth orchid (*Phalaenopsis*) or a slipper orchid (*Paphiopedilum*), you may repot at any time, although it is best to do so when the plant is not in flower.

1. **UNPOT THE ORCHID** Prepare your work area by spreading out several sheets of newspaper — repotting can be messy. Turn the plant upside down over the paper and thump the sides and bottom of the pot to dislodge it. Often the roots will stick to the pot, making removal difficult. If this happens, use a clean kitchen knife to loosen them. The plant will not be harmed if you inadvertently damage some of the old roots.

Once you have removed the plant, carefully pry the roots apart and shake off as much of the old potting mixture as possible. Don't worry if some still clings to the roots.

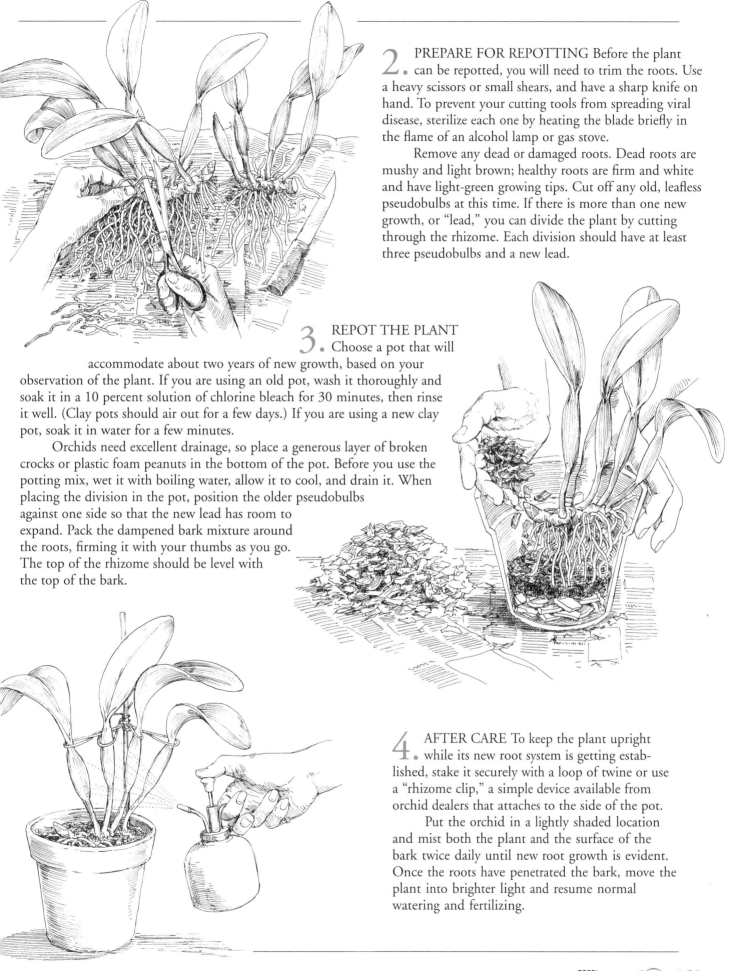

2. PREPARE FOR REPOTTING

PREPARE FOR REPOTTING Before the plant can be repotted, you will need to trim the roots. Use a heavy scissors or small shears, and have a sharp knife on hand. To prevent your cutting tools from spreading viral disease, sterilize each one by heating the blade briefly in the flame of an alcohol lamp or gas stove.

Remove any dead or damaged roots. Dead roots are mushy and light brown; healthy roots are firm and white and have light-green growing tips. Cut off any old, leafless pseudobulbs at this time. If there is more than one new growth, or "lead," you can divide the plant by cutting through the rhizome. Each division should have at least three pseudobulbs and a new lead.

3. REPOT THE PLANT

REPOT THE PLANT Choose a pot that will accommodate about two years of new growth, based on your observation of the plant. If you are using an old pot, wash it thoroughly and soak it in a 10 percent solution of chlorine bleach for 30 minutes, then rinse it well. (Clay pots should air out for a few days.) If you are using a new clay pot, soak it in water for a few minutes.

Orchids need excellent drainage, so place a generous layer of broken crocks or plastic foam peanuts in the bottom of the pot. Before you use the potting mix, wet it with boiling water, allow it to cool, and drain it. When placing the division in the pot, position the older pseudobulbs against one side so that the new lead has room to expand. Pack the dampened bark mixture around the roots, firming it with your thumbs as you go. The top of the rhizome should be level with the top of the bark.

4. AFTER CARE

AFTER CARE To keep the plant upright while its new root system is getting established, stake it securely with a loop of twine or use a "rhizome clip," a simple device available from orchid dealers that attaches to the side of the pot.

Put the orchid in a lightly shaded location and mist both the plant and the surface of the bark twice daily until new root growth is evident. Once the roots have penetrated the bark, move the plant into brighter light and resume normal watering and fertilizing.

Winter 153

Repotting a Ficus

Oliver E. Allen

ONE OF THE SIGNAL FACTS about most plants is that they persist in growing. And as their tops get bigger, so — hidden by the soil — do their roots. In the garden, plants need regular division. Indoors, they periodically need to be "potted on," or moved to a larger container, so that their roots will continue to enjoy enough room (but not too much) for proper nourishment. Otherwise the plants will be in danger of becoming potbound, or choked on their own root structure.

Any common houseplant like a Ficus benjamina will usually reveal its need to be potted on. It may droop only a few hours after watering: this means its roots have taken over so much space in the pot as to leave insufficient soil for holding moisture, and they are already thirsty again. (Water may indeed plummet right out the bottom, indicating almost no soil at all.) New leaves may be abnormally small, or the lower leaves may turn yellow: the ficus is adjusting to less than adequate nourishment. Roots may crawl above the surface of the soil, or, more likely, reach out the bottom of the pot: there is no place else for them to go. Most noticeably, the ficus may tip over easily or may just look top-heavy or ill-proportioned. The thing to do is to inspect the roots by knocking the plant out of its pot. (You will first have to snip off the roots that protrude from the hole in the bottom of the pot.)

Note the appearance of the roots. If you see only a few root ends here and there in the soil, there is no need to pot on just now — any troubles the ficus is experiencing are due to other causes. But if the roots cover the soil surface and even wrap around the root ball, the plant surely needs more growing room. Put it back in its pot and prepare for moving day. The ideal time to pot is just as a plant is starting new growth, but in most cases the job should be done without delay.

1. CHOOSE A NEW POT Pick a larger container, preferably of the same general shape as its predecessor (roots become accustomed to growing in a given direction) and the same material (if the ficus has been growing in a clay pot, another clay pot will be easier for it to adapt to). Make the pot no more than an inch or two (2.5 to 5 cm) larger in diameter; a bigger container will require the plant to expend undue energy growing new roots to fill the space, and may also cause the extra soil to stay too damp. Make sure the pot is clean, and if it is clay, immerse it in water for an hour or two before the repotting so that its porous walls do not suck water from your added soil.

2. ASSEMBLE TOOLS AND MATERIALS In addition to a trowel or spoon you may want a narrow stick for tamping down soil. Choose some crocking (potshards are best) to cover the drainage hole in the new pot, and spread newspapers over the working area for ease of cleanup later.

3. POSITION THE PLANT IN ITS NEW POT Place

crocks over the new container's drainage hole and cover them with about an inch (2.5 cm) of soil. Give your ficus a last-minute watering (its roots must not dry out during the transfer). Knock it out of its old pot again and, placing it on the new soil, check its height: the root ball should come up to about three-quarters of an inch (1.9 cm) from the top of the new container (if the root ball is very large, this can be increased to an inch (2.5 cm) or more). If it sits too low, add soil beneath it.

4. ADD SOIL If the roots encircle the root ball,

lift the ball and gently pull their ends away, pruning any that are rotted (they will be brown and spongy rather than white). Remove old crocks from the ball. Replacing the plant in the new pot and, holding it steady, dribble new soil around the edges with your trowel or spoon, gently tamping it down as you go to fill any air pockets (I poke with my fingers, but a narrow stick also works well). Do not push too hard lest you compact the soil; it should be firm but not solid. When the added soil reaches the level of the root ball's top, thump the pot on your working surface to make doubly certain no air pockets remain. Do not change the soil level in relation to the plant.

5. WATER THOROUGHLY Give the repotted

ficus a good soaking. Some devotees immerse the whole pot up to its rim in water; I merely add water until it runs out the bottom. If the watering causes parts of the surface of the soil to sink, fill the depressions with new soil. Do not fertilize at this stage — the ficus must adapt to its new environment before being fed. Once you are assured the plant is thoroughly wet, set it in its former location, but keep it out of direct sunlight for a couple of days. Do not water it again until its soil has dried out. Then water as needed. Fertilizing can be resumed when the ficus puts out new growth.

6. CLEAN THE OLD POT

Don't overlook this chore. Scrape out any old soil remaining in the pot, remove any encrustations of salts, and scrub both the inside and outside thoroughly (purists use boiling water).

Coleus from Seed

Nancy Bubel

STARTING PLANTS FROM SEED indoors can take the sting out of January's harsh weather. Coleus is a good choice for such a winter project because it can be used either as a houseplant or as a bedding plant. This colorful member of the mint family is a perennial, but because it is frost-tender, you'll find the seed listed in the "annuals" section of most catalogs.

One reason coleus is such fun to grow from seed is that even the tiny seedlings show their colors. Many of them have bicolor or tricolor leaves, with shades of cream, salmon, rose, bronze, copper, chartreuse, scarlet, and yellow. The names of the many cultivars give you some idea of the colors and patterns you can anticipate: 'Paisley Patches', 'Scarlet Poncho', 'Scarlet Dragon', 'Gaslight', 'Highland Fling'. The deep, rich hues are especially vibrant when the plant is raised under fluorescent lights.

Coleus grown as houseplants can be started at any time of the year, of course, but those intended for beds outside should be started 10 weeks before your last expected frost so the plants will be well developed when the time comes to set them out.

1. SOW THE SEEDS Prepare a flat of vermiculite or potting soil. If you use potting soil, choose a fine, fluffy, soilless mix from a garden center rather than the dense stuff that is sometimes sold as potting soil in food and variety stores. Air spaces in the vermiculite and soilless mixes encourage good root development.

Soak the planting medium well before sowing the seeds — it should be damp but not sopping wet. By watering before planting, you avoid washing the small seeds off into the corners. Always water with lukewarm water; coleus doesn't like cold soil.

Slit open the narrow end of the seed envelope and hold it over the flat, tapping lightly to distribute the seeds evenly over the moist surface. Gently press the seeds into the medium, but don't bury them under more soil. Because coleus seeds need light to germinate, they must be planted on top of the soil.

2. COVER THE FLAT The flat can be covered with any material that will let light in and retain moisture: a clean sheet of glass or acrylic, a clear plastic bag, or a piece of transparent plastic wrap. Don't envelop the flat tightly, though, because lack of air circulation may encourage damping-off disease or the development of molds.

Set the flat in a spot where light can reach it — but not in direct sunlight, or the seeds will cook. Keep it warm (at least 70°F [21°C]) with a pilot light, a hot-water heater, or a soil-heating cable. A tiny magic carpet of colored seedlings should appear in a week.

3. TRANSPLANT THE SEEDLINGS As soon as the first sprouts appear, move the flat to a place where it will receive day-long light. When the seedlings develop their first true leaves, transplant them into small individual pots or another flat, spacing them two inches (5 cm) apart.

At this point in their development, windowsill or greenhouse light will do. I've also had wonderful results using a fluorescent light cart, with which I was able to provide the young plants with 14 to 16 hours of light a day. I kept them very close to the tubes at first — about two or three inches (5 to 7.5 cm) away — by propping them up with egg cartons, which I removed when the plants became four to six inches (10 to 15 cm) tall.

4. PINCH TO PROMOTE COMPACTNESS When the plants are about six to eight inches (15 to 20 cm) high, pinch out the tip of the stem to encourage the plants to form bushy side branches. Then pinch back the branch tips when they reach a length of six to eight inches (15 to 20 cm). (The Wizard strain does not need to be pinched back, because it is naturally bushy.) Coleus bears thin wands of insignificant lavender flowers that detract from the impact of the richly colored leaves. You might want to pinch them off as well.

Outdoors, coleus leaf colors are more brilliant if the plants are set in partial to light shade. Also, compact plants are less likely to blow over in the wind. I hope you'll find, as I have, that you appreciate the colors and patterns even more after having nurtured the plants from the time when they first showed hints of what they would become.

Primulas from Seed

Thomas Fischer

APART FROM THE SATISFACTION that always comes from rearing a batch of healthy seedlings, there are a number of compelling reasons for raising primulas from seed. First, the number of primulas available commercially as plants is minuscule compared to the size of the genus, which includes about 500 species. Thus, if you want to experiment with any of the hard-to-find varieties, or to acquire some of the gorgeously colored hybrid strains, such as the Barnhavens, you'll have to start with seed.

By raising primulas from seed, you'll also be able to monitor growing conditions closely, ensuring a healthy crop of seedlings, and you'll end up with dozens of plants for a mere fraction of what they would cost at a nursery. Fortunately, the process isn't difficult, though there are a few tricks that will make success easier to achieve. This method also works well with such delicate rarities as Himalayan blue poppies (*Meconopsis* species) and ramondas, hardy alpine members of the Gesneriad Family.

1. PREPARE THE POTS FOR SOWING Begin any time from late fall through early spring, whenever you can be assured of a long stretch of cool weather. Primulas seem to germinate best and produce the most vigorous seedlings when temperatures are in the mid-50s to mid-60s (12° to 18°C). (In fact, many will not sprout at all if the temperature goes above 68°F [20°C].)

Use four-inch (10 cm) plastic pots; they are manageable and keep the medium from drying out too quickly. Fill each pot almost to the brim with any standard peat-based potting mixture. If it seems heavy, add up to one-third perlite to improve aeration.

Because primrose seedlings are susceptible to damping off, and because even supposedly "sterile" potting media can be contaminated with mold spores, you should first sterilize the medium. Set the pots in a place where they can drain freely, then soak the medium slowly and carefully with boiling water until it runs through the drainage holes. Wait for the flow to stop, then repeat the procedure two more times. Allow the medium to cool completely before proceeding. This technique, first advocated by germination expert Dr. Norman Deno, is just as effective as baking the soil in the oven, and much less smelly.

2. SOW THE SEED Sprinkle the seed sparingly over the surface of the medium so the seedlings won't be overcrowded. If you like, you can mix the fine seed with a small quantity of sand to make sowing easier. The seeds of many primulas must be exposed to light to germinate, so do not cover them with potting mix.

Next, mist the surface of the medium with a sprayer filled with tapwater that has been brought to a boil and cooled to room temperature. Label each pot, and move them all to a cool location where they will receive bright light but no direct sun. Indoor grow-lights and filtered sunlight are both acceptable. Cover the pots loosely with plastic wrap, allowing for some air circulation around each one.

3. CARE FOR THE SEEDLINGS Once the seeds begin to germinate, which may take from 10 days to two months, remove the plastic. If the seedlings' fine roots appear to be exposed to the air, sprinkle a small amount of potting mix over them until they are just covered.

At this point the seedlings are too fragile to water from above, so water from the bottom. Set the pots in a shallow tray and add an inch or two (2.5 to 5 cm) of water. When the top of the soil looks dark and wet, remove the pots, let them drain briefly, then return them to the growing area. Aim to keep the medium evenly moist but not soggy.

Feed the seedlings, also from the bottom, about once every three weeks using a balanced fertilizer diluted to one-half strength. Once the seedlings are growing vigorously, thin them if they look crowded. One four-inch (10 cm) pot can accommodate between 12 and 20 seedlings, depending on the species.

4. POT UP THE SEEDLINGS After the seedlings have produced their first true leaves and are two to four inches (5 to 10 cm) high, they may be potted up individually. Before you start, let the potting mixture get a bit dry to make it easier to disentangle the roots. Gently tap on the bottom of the pot to dislodge the soil, then tease the roots of each seedling away from the soil mass. Be sure to tug on the leaves rather than the stem, which is easily bruised. Set each plant in its own four-inch (10 cm) pot, using a standard potting mix. Water immediately from the top, and set the pots in a lightly shaded frame or nursery area.

Throughout the summer, water and feed as you would any small perennial, being careful not to let the plants dry out. By early fall, the husky young plants will be ready to assume their permanent place in the garden.

Raising Leeks

Nancy Bubel

MANY A SAVORY WINTER SOUP begins with a shivering dash to the garden to pick a wrist-thick leek from its sheltering bed. The ever-ready fortitude of the leek in winter is our reward for giving it garden space and occasional attention during its long, slow (up to 130-day) growing season. Fast-growing cultivars such as 'Titan' and 'King Richard' mature earlier, in mid- to late summer, but for winter harvest, select the much hardier traditional cultivars such as 'Large American Flag', 'Unique', 'Blue Solaise', 'Nebraska', and 'Alaska'.

The old Scottish gardener who ritually buried the laird's wool trousers under the leek row was, perhaps unwittingly, providing two of the conditions leeks like best: a deep root run and a ready supply of organic matter. For a superb stand, give the leeks deeply dug, well-drained, near-neutral or slightly acid soil rich in humus.

Young leeks are best raised to maturity in trenches. Trench planting, and the subsequent slowly rising soil level it permits, encourages the development of a longer white stem — the tender part that is so good to eat. (If you plant leeks at the surface of the ground rather than in a trench, the tougher green leaves tend to flag off from the central stem closer to the ground, limiting the amount of edible stalk.) By the time winter arrives, these exceptionally cold-hardy plants are still growing, staunchly weathering snow and ice until we harvest them for dinner.

Because the young seedlings are thready and easily overwhelmed by weeds, starting leeks from seed indoors is best. Sow seed in flats in January or February, later thinning the seedlings to stand one inch (2.5 cm) apart in each flat. Alternatively, plant leek seed directly in the ground three or four weeks before your last frost date; I've had good results from starting them in a space-saving nursery bed until they were ready for transplanting. Southern gardeners can plant leek seed in late summer for winter and spring crops.

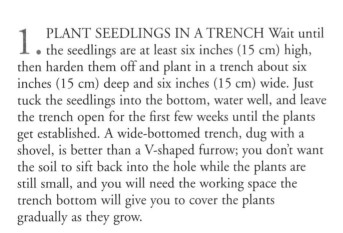

1. PLANT SEEDLINGS IN A TRENCH Wait until the seedlings are at least six inches (15 cm) high, then harden them off and plant in a trench about six inches (15 cm) deep and six inches (15 cm) wide. Just tuck the seedlings into the bottom, water well, and leave the trench open for the first few weeks until the plants get established. A wide-bottomed trench, dug with a shovel, is better than a V-shaped furrow; you don't want the soil to sift back into the hole while the plants are still small, and you will need the working space the trench bottom will give you to cover the plants gradually as they grow.

2. FILL IN THE TRENCH The object here is to keep the soil level at, or just below, the point where the leek's green leaves diverge from the stem, in order to help the plant build a longer stretch of pale stem. When the leaves are six to eight inches (15 to 20 cm) high, start to rake or hoe fine soil into the trench — only about an inch (2.5 cm) at a time — every three weeks. Keep them well watered throughout this process. To beef up the soil's humus content, substitute one inch (2.5 cm) of fine compost for one inch (2.5 cm) of fine soil on one or two of the regular trench fillings.

5. HILL UP THE BED By early fall the trench will be filled in completely, and the once slender plants will have turned into stout, muscled stalks, all the more tender because you have blanched them as they grew. Continue to pull up soil around the bases of the plants every few weeks, stopping just before the green leaf pleats begin to fan out, so that the soil won't wash down between the leaflets of the stalk. Hilling encourages the formation of additional inches of pale, tender stalk.

3. MULCH FOR WINTER Before the soil freezes hard, pile on 10 to 12 inches (25 to 30 cm) of mulch to keep the ground workable for another few weeks, and, later, to protect the leeks from extremely cold weather. If the ground freezes hard early in your area, you can replace some of the mounded-up soil with mulch to permit easier access to the plants. Straw, leaves, and aged sawdust make good weed-free mulches.

4. HARVEST Leeks are extremely hardy, but if you are concerned about deep freezing, dig some up before the ground hardens completely and store them in sand in a cold cellar. You might need to use a fork; dig from the side of the row to avoid cutting into them. Otherwise you can probably harvest the plants right into January if you've mulched the ground thoroughly before it froze.

Before cooking, rinse the leeks thoroughly to wash out soil trapped between the looser upper layers. And keep an eye on the calendar. Before long, perhaps one day after you've enjoyed a warming bowl of cock-a-leekie soup, it will be time to start another crop of leeks. You can either plant more from seed or replant the corms (small bulbs) that cluster around the base of overwintered mother plants in early spring.

Grafting a Cactus

Lee Reich

GRAFTING IS GENERALLY ASSOCIATED with fruit trees and roses, but indoor-grown cacti can be joined together using this method as well. The advantages are many. A slow-growing cactus can be attached to the more vigorous roots of another. A trailing cactus can be attached to a columnar one to create a plant with an unusual form. There are even cacti that must be grafted in order to survive. The flamboyant red- or yellow-stemmed ones, for example, lack chlorophyll and therefore need to be attached to a green rootstock. The grafting process is easy — the most difficult part about it is waiting patiently for the results.

Choose your rootstock with care. Some good candidates include species in the genera *Echinopsis*, *Eriocereus*, *Hylocereus*, *Opuntia*, and *Trichocereus*. Either buy one for the purpose or propagate one in advance from a cutting, offshoot, or seed. A rootstock must be well rooted for the project to succeed.

Almost all cacti are amenable to grafting. Just remember that not all succulent plants are cacti — milk-striped euphorbia (*Euphorbia lactea*), for example, resembles a cactus but is unrelated and cannot be grafted to one. The graft shown here, in which a slow-growing Copiapoa plant is attached to a faster-growing Trichocereus rootstock, employs a simple "saddle" graft, which could be used to join many types of cacti.

1. PREPARING THE ROOTSTOCK Make your first cut on the rootstock at the level at which you wish to attach the new piece. Hold the stem of the rootstock firmly in place against a gloved hand or a wooden backboard, and, using a sterilized, razor-sharp knife, cut the top off cleanly and squarely. Before each subsequent cut, dip the knife into rubbing alcohol to prevent microorganisms from contaminating the wounds. Next, take two downward-sloping slices from opposite sides of what is now the top of the rootstock to form a wedge.

2. PREPARING THE SCION Scion is a technical term for the piece that is to be grafted onto the rootstock. The scion doesn't have to be the same size or width as the rootstock, though a closer match has a better chance of success.

Work quickly so that neither rootstock nor scion has a chance to dry out. After cutting the scion from its own roots, slice out a wedge-shaped chip from its bottom to match the cut on the rootstock. These cuts increase the area of contact between the two pieces, and, depending on the size and type of scion, prevent the finished product from toppling over.

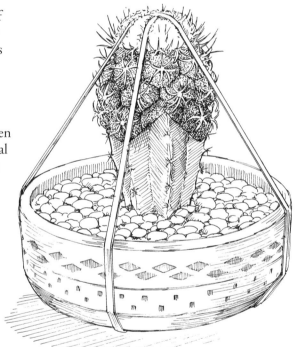

3. JOINING ROOTSTOCK AND SCION Study the cut ends of both rootstock and scion, noting the cambium of each, a barely visible ring toward the center of the stem. Line up the rings of each as closely as possible, and quickly press the pieces together. If the cambiums are of different sizes, align at least a portion of them. New cells grow from these, so aligning them guarantees a smooth flow of water and nutrients from the rootstock to the scion.

Press the parts together slightly to force out any air bubbles. Then secure the two parts firmly to allow their cells to knit. There are several ways to do this. You can loop a rubber band over the top of the scion and around the bottom of the pot (a cotton ball on top helps to relieve pressure), drape a string over the top of the scion and weight the ends with small bolts or nuts, or insert a wooden toothpick straight through both pieces.

Do not wax the union as you would when grafting other types of plants. Cacti are not likely to dehydrate, and waxing would only invite rot.

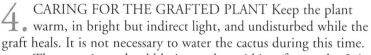

4. CARING FOR THE GRAFTED PLANT Keep the plant warm, in bright but indirect light, and undisturbed while the graft heals. It is not necessary to water the cactus during this time.

The two pieces should knit together within a few weeks. It is then safe to remove the rubber band or string. If you pinned the pieces together, simply clip off the protruding ends of the toothpick. Then move the plant to a brighter location, water it, and watch for growth to resume. Once new growth appears, resume a normal schedule of watering and fertilizing.

Making a Whip Graft

Lee Reich

GRAFTING IS A TECHNIQUE that makes it possible to add one variety of a tree to another. And of all the types of grafts, a whip graft is perhaps the easiest. It can be used on many fruit and ornamental trees, and, like all grafts, is most successful when you join closely related plants. For example, if you covet the apples on a friend's tree, you can take branches from it and use grafting to add to or completely change over an apple tree in your yard.

Do your whip grafting in late winter or early spring, just before growth begins. You will need a small knife with a razor-sharp blade. This will enable you to make smooth, clean cuts and lessens the chance of the knife slipping and causing you injury.

1. COLLECT AND STORE SCION WOOD
The "scion" is a piece of stem taken from the plant you wish to propagate. Collect scion wood while it is fully dormant, which may be weeks or even months before you actually graft. Choose shoots from the previous season's growth that are a quarter to three-eighths of an inch (.6 to .9 cm) in diameter and preferably have no flower buds. Water sprouts, or suckers, are ideal.

Cut the shoots into one-foot (30 cm) lengths, making an angled cut at the bottom of each piece and a squared-off cut at the top. This will tell you how the scion was oriented on the original tree, so you can maintain the same orientation when you graft it onto the new one.

Bundle and store your scions in a moist, cool place so they remain alive but dormant. I seal the bundle in two layers of plastic bag with a moist rag between them, and store the package in the refrigerator.

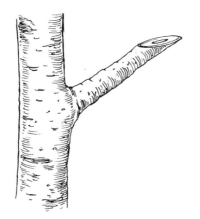

2. PREPARE THE ROOTSTOCK
Early in the season, when the buds on the rootstock tree are just starting to swell, select branches on which to perform the grafts. Look for those that originate near the trunk and have a diameter equal to or slightly thicker than that of the scions.

Make a sloping cut on each branch, one- to one-and-a-half inches (2.5 to 3.75 cm) long. Move your knife in one smooth motion because starting and stopping, or too much trimming, results in a wavy surface that makes poor contact with the scion.

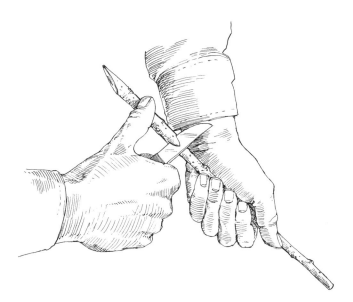

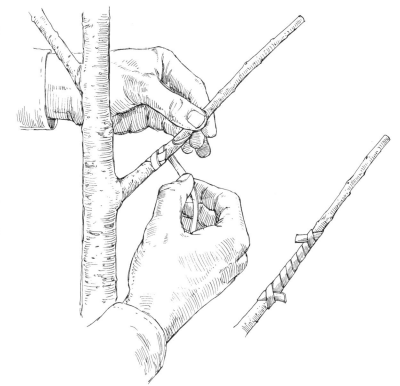

3. PREPARE THE SCIONS As soon as you finish each cut on the rootstock, prepare the scion that you want to join at that point. (If you wait too long, the cuts will dry out and the graft may not succeed.) Hold the scion firmly in one hand, with its bottom end facing you, and pull the knife toward you, making a sloping cut similar to the one that you made on the rootstock. Don't make this cut at the very bottom of the scion, where the wood may have dried out.

4. JOIN ROOTSTOCK AND SCION Between the bark and the inner wood of any branch is a thin layer of tissue called the cambium. It produces new cells that heal wounds, then forms new vessels for conducting water. So it is critical to match up the cambiums of the stock and scion as closely as possible. If the scion is thinner than the stock, line up the cambiums along one side.

Hold the two pieces together with one hand and use your other hand to wrap a cut rubber band around the graft union. (Overlap the free ends of the band as you begin and finish wrapping to prevent them from unraveling.) This will keep the scion immobile and bound to the stock while the graft heals.

Cover the graft union with sealant to prevent it from drying out. I use black tree-wound dressing, but grafting wax or a strip of plastic food wrap will do the job. Add a dab of sealant to the top of the scion to prevent it from losing moisture there.

5. AFTER CARE The next day, check to be sure that the union is still well covered with sealant. Reapply if necessary, covering any cracks that formed overnight or spots you may have missed. Over the next few weeks, rub off any sprouts that appear on the stock just below the graft. Once the scion is growing strongly, use a razor blade to slit the rubber band longitudinally and prevent it from strangling your plant.

Pruning a Large Tree Limb

Oliver E. Allen

THE BEST TIME to remove a limb from a tree is winter, except in the cases of maples, birches, and other trees that produce copious sap. For such trees summer is a better time (in subtropical climates the end of the dry season is preferred). If you can easily reach the limb with a ladder, there is no reason not to tackle the job yourself. However, if you're thinking about climbing up into the branches to remove a limb, don't. This is a dangerous task best left to professionals who have the proper training and equipment.

You can ensure your own safety by following a few precautions. Be certain your ladder rests on a firm base; if the ground is soft, set the ladder on some planks. Lash taller ladders to the tree and have someone hold the base of the ladder while you work. But keep other spectators away. And note where the limb will fall, making sure its drop won't injure people or plants. If its fall might damage a valued shrub, for instance, tie a rope around it, pass the rope over another limb higher in the tree, and lower the cut limb slowly to the ground.

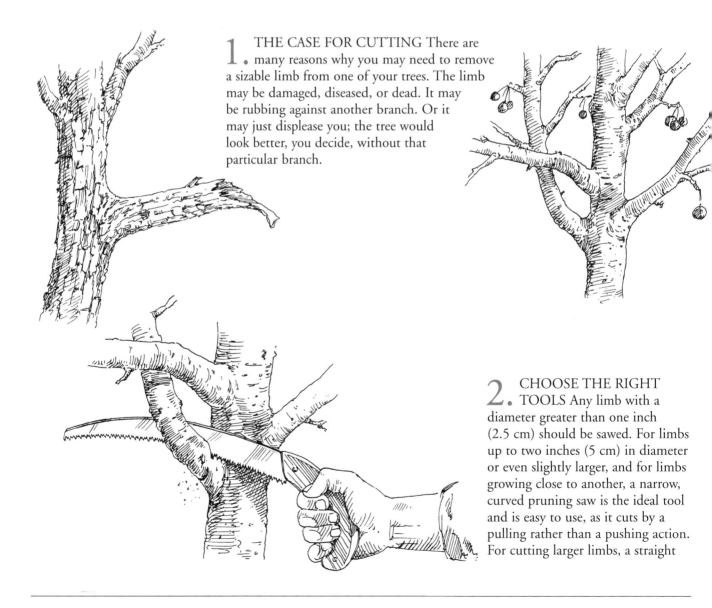

1. THE CASE FOR CUTTING There are many reasons why you may need to remove a sizable limb from one of your trees. The limb may be damaged, diseased, or dead. It may be rubbing against another branch. Or it may just displease you; the tree would look better, you decide, without that particular branch.

2. CHOOSE THE RIGHT TOOLS Any limb with a diameter greater than one inch (2.5 cm) should be sawed. For limbs up to two inches (5 cm) in diameter or even slightly larger, and for limbs growing close to another, a narrow, curved pruning saw is the ideal tool and is easy to use, as it cuts by a pulling rather than a pushing action. For cutting larger limbs, a straight

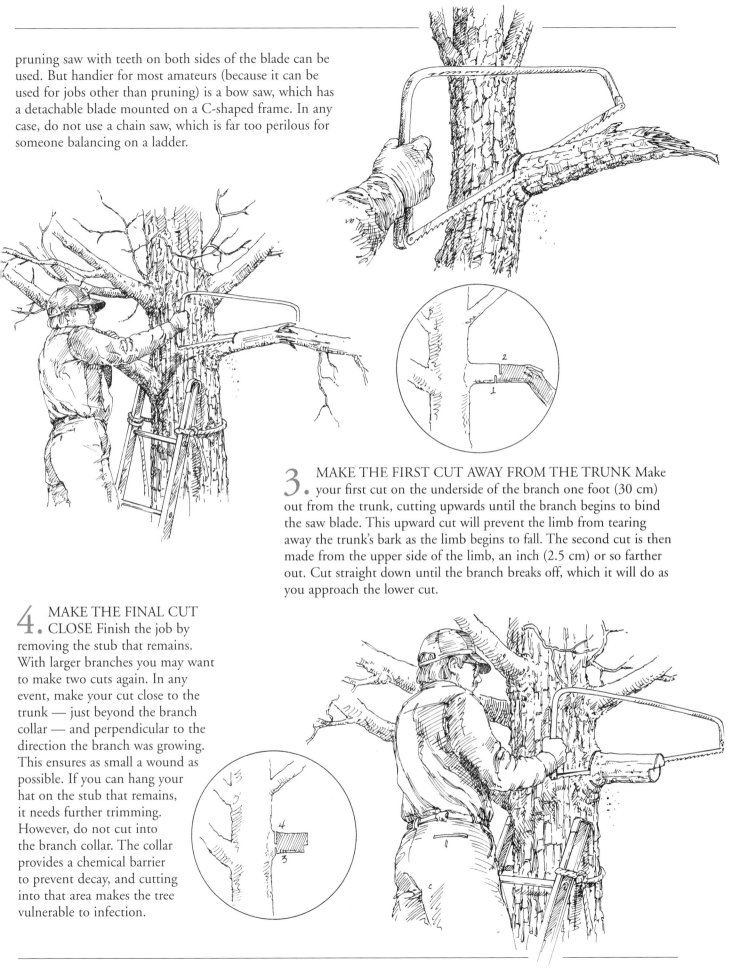

pruning saw with teeth on both sides of the blade can be used. But handier for most amateurs (because it can be used for jobs other than pruning) is a bow saw, which has a detachable blade mounted on a C-shaped frame. In any case, do not use a chain saw, which is far too perilous for someone balancing on a ladder.

3. MAKE THE FIRST CUT AWAY FROM THE TRUNK Make your first cut on the underside of the branch one foot (30 cm) out from the trunk, cutting upwards until the branch begins to bind the saw blade. This upward cut will prevent the limb from tearing away the trunk's bark as the limb begins to fall. The second cut is then made from the upper side of the limb, an inch (2.5 cm) or so farther out. Cut straight down until the branch breaks off, which it will do as you approach the lower cut.

4. MAKE THE FINAL CUT CLOSE Finish the job by removing the stub that remains. With larger branches you may want to make two cuts again. In any event, make your cut close to the trunk — just beyond the branch collar — and perpendicular to the direction the branch was growing. This ensures as small a wound as possible. If you can hang your hat on the stub that remains, it needs further trimming. However, do not cut into the branch collar. The collar provides a chemical barrier to prevent decay, and cutting into that area makes the tree vulnerable to infection.

Making a Moss-Lined Basket

Thomas Christopher

MY CONSERVATISM may be the despair of my wife, who tires of chinos, loafers, and button-down shirts, but it suits hanging plants just fine. They'll survive in plastic baskets, all right, but they flourish in old-fashioned wire baskets lined with sphagnum moss. This technique was popular among Victorian gardeners, who knew that a moss basket's permeable skin guarantees perfect drainage while allowing air to reach the plants' roots. The moss also acts as a reservoir, absorbing excess water and releasing it back into the soil as needed. Even the water that evaporates from the moss's outer surface is not wasted. By boosting the humidity around the plants' foliage, the evaporation protects the greenery against the desertlike aridity of winter's hot, stuffy, indoor atmosphere.

Such a homemade container does require a bit more work, but at this season of the year, I'm generally looking for employment. For me, though, the most persuasive argument in favor of an old-fashioned basket is aesthetic. When I potted up a basket of spearmint for the kitchen recently, I planted not only in the top but through the side walls. A couple of weeks' growth was all that was needed to turn that basket into an unbroken sphere of sweetly aromatic foliage.

1. SELECT AND PREPARE THE PLANTS Though I chose spearmint for my most recent basket, there are any number of foliage and flowering plants that adapt well to the treatment. Your local nursery can help with suggestions.

Buy rooted cuttings, since these smaller specimens are easier to insinuate through the basket's walls. Commonly, cuttings are grown three or four together in a two-and-a-half-inch (6 cm) pot. Water well, and allow the cuttings an hour or two to fill with moisture. Then slip each root ball from its container, and separate the plants by cutting their roots apart with a knife.

2. LINE THE BASKET Although plastic containers are widely available, a good garden center, especially one that doubles as a florist, will still stock the hemispherical wire nests that serve as the skeletons for moss-lined baskets. A wire nest 12 inches (30 cm) in diameter is a handy size for an indoor basket. Larger baskets are available, but I find them more appropriate for outdoor displays. Ordinary unmilled sphagnum will serve for lining the basket, but it is easier to handle when rolled into a sheet. The garden center should stock this "sheet moss" too, or at least be able to order it for you. Simply soak the moss in warm water, then press it into place along the inside of the wire form; if more than one piece of moss is required to complete the job, be sure to overlap adjoining edges.

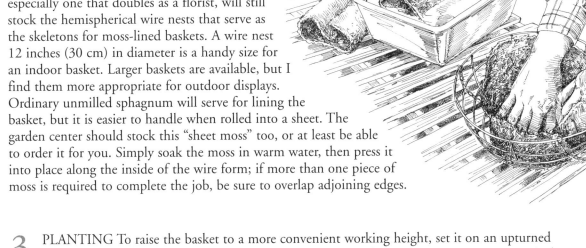

3. PLANTING To raise the basket to a more convenient working height, set it on an upturned bucket. Then pour an inch (2.5 cm) of ordinary potting soil into the moss nest, tamping it down lightly with the bottom of a small flowerpot. With a knife, poke a hole in the moss wall at a point just above the soil level. Choose a healthy cutting, and ease its root ball in from the outside, between the wires, through the hole, and into the basket. Move four or five inches (10 to 12.5 cm) farther along the circumference of the basket and repeat this process, carrying on until you've ringed the basket with plants.

Add enough soil to the basket's interior to bury the cuttings' roots about an inch (2.5 cm) deep, tamp down gently, and plant again, staggering the second tier of cuttings so that none lie directly over any of those in the lower ring. Add yet another layer of soil to bring the level to within two inches (5 cm) of the basket's lip, and plant the top. Space four or so cuttings evenly over the basket's surface, and sift soil in among the roots, firming it down with your fingertips. Leave the soil's surface slightly concave so that water will soak in rather than run off.

4. WATERING AND CARE The care this type of hanging basket requires is much the same as that of any other, except that since moisture evaporates through the sides, it needs more frequent watering. Which brings us to the moss basket's one liability: It leaks. I set a bucket below these containers when I water and leave it in place for 20 minutes afterward while the basket drains. But still, I do not hang moss baskets over hardwood floors. My basket of mint rests safely over a tiled kitchen floor. A bathroom is another good alternative, as is a sun porch finished with indoor/outdoor carpeting. Or hang the basket in a window, protecting the sill with a tray of pebbles. Any spillage there is an extra dividend, another source of humidity to help your houseplants through winter's artificial drought.

Testing for Germination

Nancy Bubel

AS THE SUN GRADUALLY GROWS stronger, we gardeners start to shuffle through our packets of seed. Sometimes we find ourselves with leftovers from other years, seeds of flowers, herbs, and vegetables that we never got around to trying. Except for the short-lived seeds of lettuce and parsnips, most year-old seed should still be fine for planting this year — if it has been stored in a cool, dry place. But what about older seeds, the envelopes that get shunted, once again, to the bottom of the pile because you're not sure they're still viable? What about the heirloom seeds you want to plant every few years to keep the strain alive? Or the undated seeds you've received free? (I was once given a packet of marigold seeds by a local political candidate on election day.) With a new growing season quickly approaching, perhaps you would like to give some of these seeds a try.

You can avoid wasting time and garden space in spring (if the seeds are indeed duds) by testing them for germination now, while there's still time to replace them if necessary. Seed with a low germination rate can still produce a worthwhile stand of plants if you sow thickly. The following steps are a homegrown version of the test that seed companies use.

1. PREPARE A MOIST BASE Professional testers often use a base of superabsorbent felt or blotting paper, but for home testing double layers of paper towels work fine. You'll also find scoring easier if you mark off the paper towel into one-inch (2.5 cm) squares with a ball-point pen. Then fit the paper towels into the bottom of a shallow pan or cookie sheet. Dampen the towels with warm water until they are moist but not soggy.

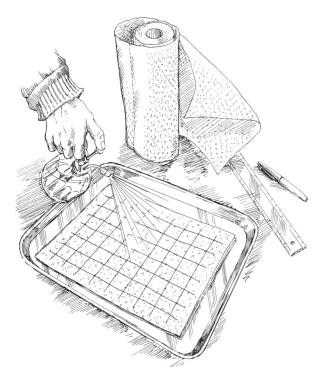

2. COUNT OUT THE SEEDS Professionals usually test 100 seeds at a time, but 50 is plenty for the home gardener. If your seed supply is limited, as few as 20 should give you an adequate test, if not a completely accurate one. In any event, a good rule of thumb is to use less than 20 percent of your supply. Remember that it is easier to calculate germination percentages from round numbers. Now, place a seed in the center of each marked square. Seal the remaining seeds in their container or packet, and return them to storage in a cool, dry place.

3. INCUBATE THE SEEDS For vegetables, herbs, and most flowers, cover the seeds with two layers of damp paper towel or newspaper and slide the whole arrangement into a large plastic bag. Some seeds — mostly flowers, among them ageratum, lobelia, primroses, and Shasta daisies — need light to germinate. Leave these seeds uncovered, and enclose the pan in a clear plastic bag. In either case, seeds need air as well as moisture to germinate, so don't close the bag tightly.

Because the most rapid germination occurs when the seeds are in the 70° to 80°F (21° to 27°C) range, place the bagged tray in a consistently warm place — atop a hot-water heater or refrigerator, near a wood stove, or perhaps on a high shelf near a hot-air vent. For light-sensitive seeds, choose a place where they will receive indirect light, or they will get the life steamed out of them. For slower-germinating seeds, be sure the paper towels remain damp. Gently sprinkle warm water on the paper if it shows signs of drying.

4. CHECK FOR GERMINATION Take your first peek at the seeds after two or three days. Most viable seed will germinate within two or three weeks, and some will sprout much sooner. Seeds of plants in the cabbage family will often sprout in two days, cucumbers and zucchini in three or four. Seeds of parsley, carrots, and related plants can take up to three weeks to germinate. Zinnias and marigolds are often up within a week; coleus two weeks, dusty miller and astilbe three weeks. Consult the seed packet or a seed-starting guide so you know what to expect.

If 40 out of 50 seeds sprout, the seeds are definitely worth planting. Even a germination rate of 50 percent means there are still enough viable seeds for a decent stand. Jot down the test date and germination rate on the seed packet or label so you'll remember to plant them more thickly. In the cases of some food crops and bedding plants, a germination rate this low should preclude planting. A germination rate lower than 25 percent of any seed should persuade you to order fresh replacements.

Keep in mind also that these results were obtained under near-ideal conditions. If you have reservations about the germination rate of your seeds after this test — whether you plan to start a flat of zinnias indoors or sow hard-to-transplant root vegetables outdoors — you can stack the deck in your favor. Plant the seeds with a heavy hand, use only fine soil, and keep your flats or beds well-watered even before the seedlings appear. In other words, give the seeds every bit of encouragement.

Starting Broccoli Seedlings

Janet H. Sanchez

OF ALL THE BRASSICAS, or members of the cole family (Cruciferae), delicious, tender broccoli is the easiest to start indoors. But you must start it early, as the heads need time to mature before hot weather arrives. Broccoli planted too late becomes strongly flavored and bolts prematurely into flower. If you sow seeds indoors in pots in late winter, however, you will have sturdy seedlings by the time the weather begins to warm up. Indeed, you can even plant them in the garden two or three weeks *before* the last frost. Check with your cooperative-extension agent or a local nursery for the average last frost date in your area. Then calculate backwards, and plan to sow about six weeks before you want to transplant.

1. SOW THE SEEDS It is most convenient to start broccoli seeds in pots that are large enough to accommodate the plants from sowing right through to transplanting. Use two- or three-inch (5 or 7.5 cm) plastic pots or household items of similar size, such as disposable cups, to give the roots plenty of room to grow. Punch several drainage holes in the bottom of containers that lack them, for seedlings will die if water collects around their roots. If you are reusing old pots, scrub them out and rinse them with a mixture of one part bleach to nine parts water to destroy any lurking disease organisms.

Use a soilless mix for potting, as these mixes are weed-free and have a light, fluffy texture that encourages quick growth. Pour the mix into a bucket and stir in enough water to make it damp but not soggy. Fill each pot to within a half inch (1.25 cm) of the top, tapping the pot gently to firm the mix.

Now, use a pencil to make a furrow an inch (2.5 cm) long and half an inch (1.25 cm) deep across the center of each pot. Sow four or five seeds, cover them with more mix, and press down gently. Be sure to label each container with the variety name and sowing date. Freezer tape works well.

Arrange the pots in a tray (an old roasting pan is fine), and cover them loosely with transparent plastic wrap to retain moisture. To speed germination, place the tray in a warm spot such as the top of the refrigerator or television, or near a wood stove.

2. EXPOSE THE SEEDLINGS TO LIGHT As soon as you spot green leaves arching out of the potting mix (usually within four to eight days), remove the plastic wrap and move the seedlings into bright light. Without adequate light, they will become spindly and weak.

Gardeners living in sunny climates can raise seedlings on a south-facing windowsill, giving the pots a quarter-turn daily so that all sides receive equal amounts of light. If early spring is cloudy in your area, or if you lack a south window, keep the seedlings under fluorescent lights. You can either make your own light units using standard 48-inch (1.2 m) shop fixtures, or order one of the ready-to-use units offered in many seed catalogs. The tubes should be only an inch or two (2.5 or 5 cm) above the plants' top leaves. Keep them on for about 14 hours a day.

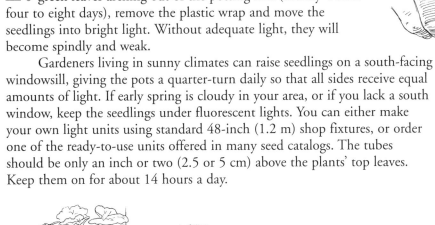

3. CARE FOR THE SEEDLINGS Young broccoli seedlings become too soft and lush if grown at high temperatures. Try to keep them relatively cool (60° to 65°F [15.5° to 18°C] during the day, 10 degrees cooler at night). Provide ventilation if the room is too warm, but don't let cold drafts hit the plants.

Water gently so that the young roots aren't disturbed. Use a thin stream from a small watering can, or place the pots in a tray and allow water to soak in from the bottom. In either case, add a liquid 5-10-5 fertilizer to the water, diluted to half strength, once a week.

Gradually thin the seedlings, removing the weaker ones with small scissors. By the time the plants are about two inches (5 cm) tall, you should have only one plant growing in each pot.

4. HARDEN OFF THE SEEDLINGS A sudden move from cozy indoor quarters to harsh outdoor life can seriously shock young broccoli plants, slowing growth and decreasing the eventual harvest. Hardening off forces the seedlings to become tough enough to survive and grow in the cooler temperatures, bright sun, and chill wind of the early-spring garden.

To harden the seedlings off, stop fertilizing them about two weeks before your transplanting date. Wait an extra day or two between waterings, but don't let the plants become so dry that they wilt. A week into this leaner regimen, place the seedlings in a well-ventilated cold frame or on a patio or porch. Shade them from bright afternoon sun and either bring them in at night or cover the cold frame to protect them from frost. Expose the seedlings to increasing amounts of sun and cold each day, watering when the soil surface feels dry. By the time you are ready to plant them out, the seedlings — now four to six inches (10 to 15 cm) tall — should be ready for life in the garden.

Restoring a Grapevine

Lee Reich

Few GARDEN SIGHTS are as sorry as an untended grapevine. Its branches become so tangled that sunlight and air no longer dry them readily, making the plant prone to disease. The grapes become difficult to harvest because they are out of reach. But even a vine that has been neglected for years can be coaxed into bearing good crops once again. Proper pruning will bring the vine back to a manageable size and enable it to channel energy into making fewer but larger bunches of fruit.

It sometimes takes several seasons to get a vine back into shape, depending on how long it has been neglected. For an extremely overgrown specimen, it may be necessary to lop the entire plant back to the ground, then select trunk, canes, and spurs over the next two or three seasons. Prune in late winter when buds are plump but before bud break.

When pruning the branches, leave a short stub so the vine can heal. A half-inch (1.25 cm) stub is fine in most cases; on larger branches, leave a stub equal to half the diameter of the wood. Also, avoid making a cut too near to a bud you wish to save, for a bud too close to a wound will dry out. Grapevines commonly bleed sap when cut, but this does not harm the plant.

1. FORMING A TRUNK The first step toward taming your neglected grapevine is to create a trunk. Choose one healthy vertical branch arising from the base of the plant. It needn't be the oldest or biggest one; indeed, a slightly younger trunk is often more vigorous. (In northern areas, choose two trunks to provide insurance in the event that winter kills one trunk to the ground.) Then cut away all other low shoots. The tangle will now be much reduced.

2. SELECTING FRUITING CANES Grapevines produce fruit each year on shoots that grow off the previous year's branches, called canes. Canes are easily recognized by their smooth, tan bark; the bark of older wood is dark and peeling.

Select four canes that originate as close to the trunk as possible, two growing horizontally in opposite directions at about waist height, and two growing horizontally

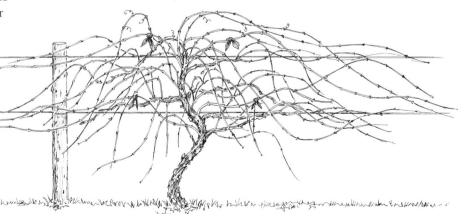

in opposite directions at about head height. The most fruitful canes are pencil-thick with about six inches (15 cm) of space between buds. Mark the four you've chosen with a ribbon, but don't cut them yet.

3. SAVING RENEWAL SPURS
Renewal spurs furnish buds that will grow into canes this season and produce next season's fruit. In order to keep future fruit within reach, the spurs must originate near the trunk. Choose four branches at about the same height as your chosen canes. The age of these branches is not critical, but be sure that there are buds visible near their bases. Cut each branch back to two buds.

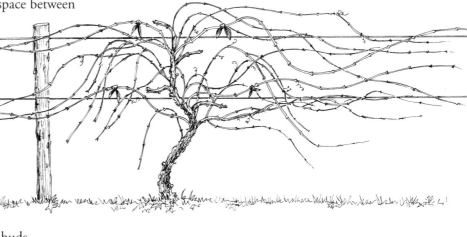

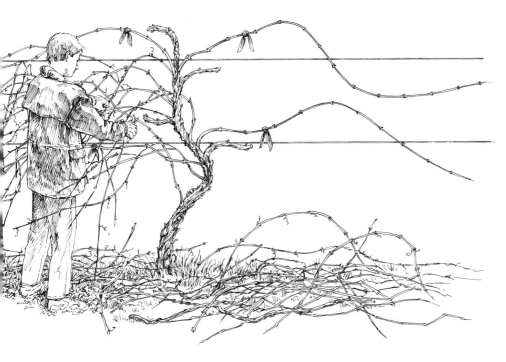

4. REMOVING UNNEEDED WOOD
Completely cut away all remaining wood except for the four renewal spurs and the four tagged fruiting canes. Much of the remaining growth on the plant will probably be long and tangled, so you'll have to remove branches in pieces. After you cut each piece, give it a tug to release it from clinging tendrils, then slide it free. Shorten the trunk to just above the top canes or spurs.

5. SHORTENING FRUITING CANES Now that your fruiting canes are free from the tangle, shorten them. Leave about 10 buds on each cane (not counting those clustered at the base), or about 40 buds per plant. Leave more buds on vigorous vines, less on weak vines. Twist the shortened canes around the trellis wire, if it is still intact, or tie them loosely to some other type of support.

For continued production, repeat this process each winter, selecting and shortening new fruiting canes, leaving renewal spurs, and removing all other wood except for the trunk.

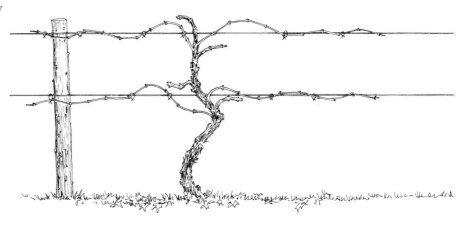

Pruning a Fruit Tree

Lee Reich

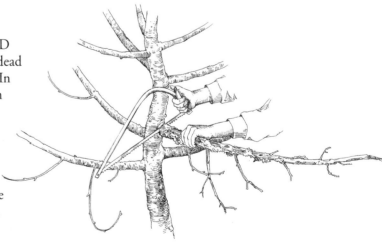

A FRUIT TREE that has reached its mature size and is yielding fruit requires regular pruning. Such maintenance keeps the tree healthy and within its allotted space and opens its branches to sunlight so that they stay productive. Although you'll remove some fruit buds and, hence, potential fruits as you prune, the quality of those that remain will be better. In addition, pruning maintains a balance between fruiting and nonfruiting growth. After you prune, the tree will respond with a flush of leafy shoots that provide new bearing wood and nourish developing fruits.

How much you cut out depends on the type of tree. Trees that flower on year-old wood, such as peaches, benefit from a more severe pruning than trees that flower on old wood, such as apples and pears. Some trees, such as plums and cherries, bear fruit on both year-old and older wood. With adjustments for fruit-bearing habits, the instructions that follow for an apple tree's annual pruning can also be applied to other fruit trees.

The best time to prune a tree is from the time it goes dormant until its blossoms open in spring. Where winters are severely cold, wait until after midwinter. That way you'll avoid cold damage in the cut area, plus you'll be able to identify any wood that is dead or weakened. Depending on the size of a branch, make your cuts with sharp pruning shears, loppers, or a pruning saw.

1. **REMOVE DEAD, BROKEN, AND DISEASED BRANCHES** Always begin by cutting back all dead or broken branches to the trunk or to healthy buds. In addition to being unsightly, such branches provide an entryway for disease. Dead wood is obvious in late winter or spring because it appears shriveled and its buds remain lifeless while buds on healthy wood are swelling.

Next, check twigs or branches for telltale evidence of disease, such as dark, sunken lesions or the black specks of fungal spores. Cut off infected wood a half-foot (15 cm) back from the diseased area.

2. CUT LARGE BRANCHES As a tree ages, the highest branches tend to grow most vigorously, shading the lower ones. With time, a tree also may grow out of bounds in height or spread. Periodically removing some large limbs will both contain your tree and open it to light. Remove large limbs at their origin or shorten them back to small, healthy side branches. This is also an opportune time to cut out branches that should have been removed when they were young and to remedy other past pruning mistakes.

Sawing off a large limb can be tricky. Keep the job safe and neat by first shortening the branch to about a foot (30 cm). To avoid stripping the bark, undercut the branch slightly before sawing it from above. Then saw off the stub, leaving a slight collar to promote good healing. It is not necessary to use a wound sealant.

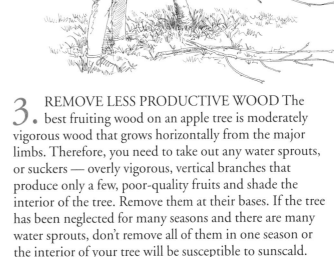

3. REMOVE LESS PRODUCTIVE WOOD The best fruiting wood on an apple tree is moderately vigorous wood that grows horizontally from the major limbs. Therefore, you need to take out any water sprouts, or suckers — overly vigorous, vertical branches that produce only a few, poor-quality fruits and shade the interior of the tree. Remove them at their bases. If the tree has been neglected for many seasons and there are many water sprouts, don't remove all of them in one season or the interior of your tree will be susceptible to sunscald.

Branches that droop downward tend to be too weak for good fruiting. If they're still young, shorten them to stimulate growth from buds just below the cuts. If they are old, shorten them to side branches growing in near-horizontal positions. Finally, remove any twiggy branches growing from the undersides of limbs, as these are particularly weak.

4. THINNING SPURS Apples and pears bear most of their fruit on long-lived spurs — fat, stubby growths that elongate less than an inch (2.5 cm) per year. With age, these become weak and overcrowded. Invigorate individual spurs by cutting them back to strong buds. If they are crowded, remove a few so that fruit will be evenly distributed, but not crammed, along the branches. (This step does not apply to other fruit trees.)

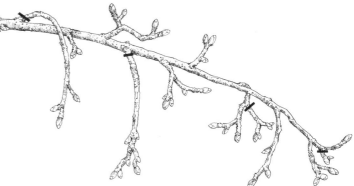

New Peperomias from Stem Cuttings

Oliver E. Allen

A SURPRISING NUMBER of houseplant owners are unaware of how easy it is to propagate new plants from old ones by making stem cuttings. Indeed, the task used to be a bit tricky, as the need to keep the cuttings moist required constant supervision or elaborate misting devices. But the advent of plastics, specifically that great kitchen marvel the clear plastic food-storage bag, changed all that. And the introduction of hormone rooting powders made the process virtually infallible. So whether you want to produce duplicates of your favorite houseplant — for example, a peperomia — to give to your friends or make a new, younger plant to replace one that is overgrown or otherwise marred, vegetative reproduction (cloning) could well be the answer. A cutting dusted with a rooting powder, imbedded in a soilless mix, enclosed in plastic, and put aside for a couple of weeks will make strong roots that take readily to actual soil.

The best time to take cuttings is when a plant is in active growth and forming strong new shoots — usually in the spring. Peperomias, however, like many stalwart houseplants, are almost constantly in new growth and will yield fine "slips," as cuttings used to be called, at virtually any time.

You will need the following materials:

A container; any small pot will serve, its size depending on how many cuttings are to be made. I have had good luck using a small plastic flat, which I line with newspaper to keep the perlite from leaking out. The newspaper is hardly permanent, but it is simple to install and it does the job.

Perlite and peat moss; the former for drainage, the latter for holding moisture. Vermiculite can be substituted for perlite but may not be so readily reused. Sharp sand is another time-honored alternative.

A hormone powder such as Rootone F, available at most garden centers.

A plastic bag at least as large as a food-storage bag.

Some heavy wire; a coat hanger will work nicely.

1. GETTING READY The night before you take cuttings, water the parent plant. The next day, fill the container with equal amounts of perlite and peat moss, mixing them well, until they come to about an inch (2.5 cm) from the top of the container. Add water until it runs freely out the bottom, then set the container aside to drain any excess, leaving the mix thoroughly moist.

2. **MAKE THE CUTTINGS** Choose the youngest, most vigorous new shoots on your peperomia and make cuttings three to four inches (7.5 to 10 cm) long from the ends. Use a very sharp knife, or, better yet, a single-edged razor blade, and make the cut just below a node or leaf joint (that's where adventitious roots form most readily). Strip off the bottom leaves from the shoot and perhaps the next as well; the object is to reduce the number of leaves on this miniplant and thereby the rate of transpiration, and also to avoid having leaves buried when the shoot is set into your mix; but keep at least two leaves on it. Place cuttings temporarily in a glass of water so they will not dry out as you work.

3. **INSERT INTO MIX** Using a pencil or narrow stick (I use a miniature screwdriver), make a hole about an inch deep in the moist mix. Dip the lower end of the cutting in the hormone powder, shake off the excess, insert the cutting into the hole (making sure it reaches the bottom and is in firm contact with the mix), and firm the mix around it. It must not rock or teeter. Add other cuttings to the pot or flat as desired, but make sure their leaves do not touch each other, as this may cause rot.

4. **COVER WITH PLASTIC** Cut lengths of wire to fashion two hoops for holding the plastic safely above the cuttings and insert these as needed in the flat or pot. Slide the container (with its cuttings and hoops) into the plastic bag, lightly mist the cuttings, then close the bag securely with a twist-tie or rubber band. Set it in a bright spot but out of direct sunlight. Tiny droplets of moisture will probably coat the plastic after a day or so, which is to be expected; but if large drops appear, open the bag for a couple of hours to reduce the humidity, then reclose it.

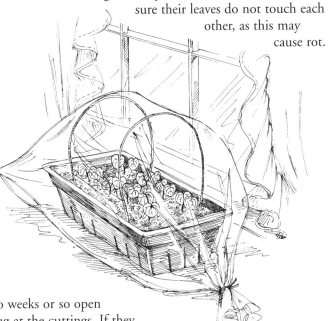

5. **TRANSPLANTING** After two weeks or so open the bag, reach in, and gently tug at the cuttings. If they have formed roots, they will stoutly resist your efforts and will be ready for transplanting to genuine houseplant soil. If instead they do not resist but lift easily, reinsert them into the mix and then mist them once more. Close the bag and give them another week or so. Most houseplant cuttings will root in two or three weeks, though some may take up to two or three months before they resist strongly enough to justify transplanting.

Some devotees insist the new plants must be weaned from their enclosed environment by being allowed to sit in the mix for several days without the plastic cover before being transplanted. I have never found this necessary. It is important, however, to avoid bruising the young roots. Pry up the new root structure using a spoon handle or flat stick to keep it intact, bringing up with it any perlite that may adhere, and set it gently into a hole prepared for it in its new pot. Firm the soil around it carefully. Use only sterilized soil mixes, and avoid fertilizing for several weeks to allow the plant to adapt.

Forcing Belgian Endive

Lee Reich

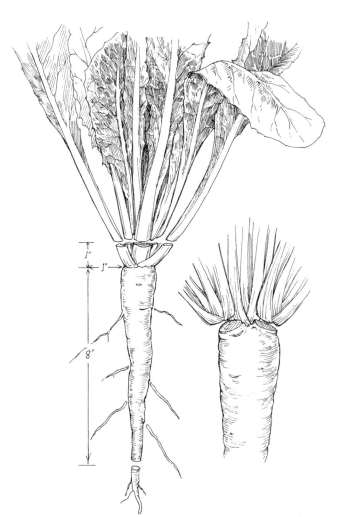

F RESH SALAD is a special treat in early spring, particularly if you can raise your own ingredients. One salad green that is especially easy to grow indoors is Belgian endive. With very little soil and no light, you can harvest its tasty leaves all winter long.

Belgian endive *(Cichorium intybus)*, sometimes called witloof or French endive, is actually a type of chicory. It is related to, but a different species from, curly endive and escarole, both of which are grown and harvested in the garden for their loose, leafy heads. When you force Belgian endive indoors, the leaves are blanched in the process, making them less sharp tasting than those of its outdoor-grown relatives. Delicious varieties that have been developed specifically for winter forcing are 'Large Brussels' and 'Witloof Improved'.

To harvest this green in winter, you must plan ahead and sow seeds in the garden in late spring. Refrain from harvesting any leaves over the course of the summer so the plants can develop the sturdy roots needed for winter forcing.

1. PREPARING THE ROOTS Before the ground freezes solid in autumn, dig up your plants' roots and save those that are straight and an inch or two (2.5 or 5 cm) thick at the top. Roots thicker than that are unsuitable because they produce multiple heads, while those less than an inch (2.5 cm) across do not have sufficient stored energy to make good heads.

Cut the leafy tops to within an inch (2.5 cm) of the crowns. If more than one rosette of leaves is growing off a root, snap off all but the centermost rosette. Next, use a sharp knife to trim the roots to a manageable size for forcing. Cut off all side roots, and shorten each root to about eight inches (20 cm).

If you want a prolonged harvest, store extra roots in a perforated plastic bag in the refrigerator (just as you would store carrots) and remove a few at a time as needed.

2. PLANTING THE ROOTS Select a box that is about 18 inches (46 cm) deep. (The other dimensions depend on the number of roots you intend to plant in it.) You can make a suitable box from scrapwood, but even a cardboard box will hold together for the relatively short time needed to force Belgian endive. In any case, be sure to punch drainage holes in the bottom.

Fill the box with several inches of well-drained garden soil, sand, or new or used potting soil. The mix's fertility is unimportant because the roots rely on stored energy for growth; the medium's function is simply to support the roots and to supply them with moisture. (Don't use readily decomposable organic matter, such as fresh compost or manure, as the roots may rot.)

Poke the roots into the mix so they stand upright almost shoulder to shoulder, with their tops at the same level. Sift additional mix around the roots to just below the point where the leaves grow from the crowns, then water thoroughly.

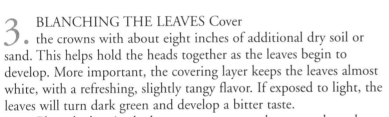

3. BLANCHING THE LEAVES Cover the crowns with about eight inches of additional dry soil or sand. This helps hold the heads together as the leaves begin to develop. More important, the covering layer keeps the leaves almost white, with a refreshing, slightly tangy flavor. If exposed to light, the leaves will turn dark green and develop a bitter taste.

Place the box in the basement or some other spot where the temperature is in the low 60s (mid teens C). Periodically check to make sure the medium around the roots is still moist by lifting the box to feel how heavy it is or by rapping it with your knuckles and listening for a dull thud. If the mix seems dry, poke a few holes down through the layer of soil or sand that is covering the heads and pour water into these holes. This wets the bottom layer of growing mix but keeps the developing heads dry and less prone to rot.

4. HARVESTING THE HEADS After three or four weeks the heads will have elongated enough so that their tips just peek through the top layer. Pull away the covering and cut each head, leaving a short piece of root attached.

Belgian endive takes longer to force if the box is stored in a place cooler than the recommended temperature. Conversely, it will grow faster if the box is kept warmer.

It is sometimes possible to force a root twice. After harvest, try covering the roots again for another few weeks.

Appendices

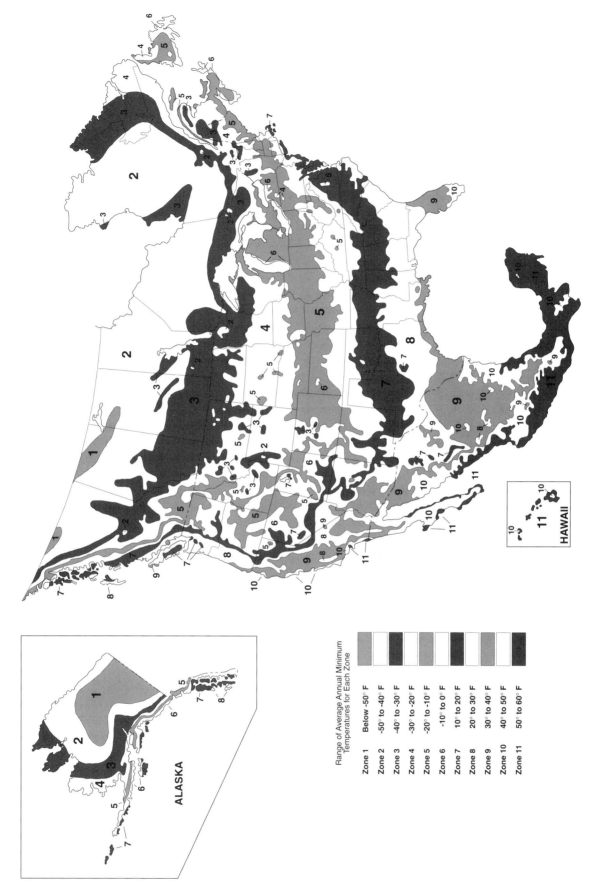

USDA Hardiness Zone Map

Range of Average Annual Minimum
Temperatures for Each Zone

Zone 1   Below -50° F

Zone 2   -50° to -40° F

Zone 3   -40° to -30° F

Zone 4   -30° to -20° F

Zone 5   -20° to -10° F

Zone 6   -10° to 0° F

Zone 7   0° to 10° F

Zone 8   10° to 20° F

Zone 9   20° to 30° F

Zone 10   30° to 40° F

Zone 11   40° to 50° F

             50° to 60° F

HAWAII

ALASKA

Source: *Fertilizers for Free*, Editors of Garden Way Publishing

The pH Scale

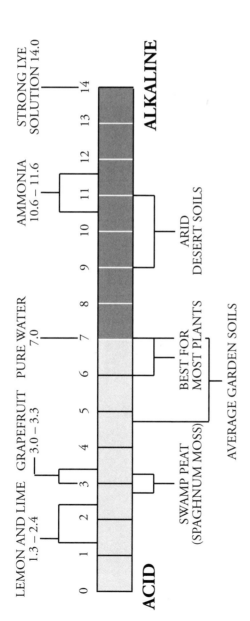

LEMON AND LIME 1.3 – 2.4
GRAPEFRUIT 3.0 – 3.3
PURE WATER 7.0
AMMONIA 10.6 – 11.6
STRONG LYE SOLUTION 14.0

ALKALINE

ACID

SWAMP PEAT (SPAGHNUM MOSS)
AVERAGE GARDEN SOILS
BEST FOR MOST PLANTS
ARID DESERT SOILS

Source: *Let It Rot!* Stu Campbell

How to Raise pH Value
1 Unit

Soil	Ground Limestone, Marl, or Oyster Shells (Lbs. Per 100 Sq. Ft.)	Burnt Lime (Lbs. Per 100 Sq. Ft.)	Hydrated Lime (Lbs. Per 100 Sq. Ft.)
Light sandy soil	3	2	2½
Sandy loams	4½	2½	3⅓
Loams	6¾	3¾	5
Silt loams and clay loams	8	4½	6

Note: For soils low in organic matter, reduce the above amounts by 25%; for soils high in organic matter, increase by 100%.
Source: *Succesful Small Food Gardens*, Louise Riotte

How to Lower pH Value
1 Unit

Soil	Sulphur (Lbs. Per 100 Sq. Ft.)	Aluminum Sulphate (Lbs. Per 100 Sq. Ft.)	Iron Sulphate (Lbs. Per 100 Sq. Ft.)
Light sandy soil	½	2½	3
Silt loams and clay loams	2	6½	7½

Source: *Fertilizers for Free*, Charles Siegchrist

Organic Fertilizers

FERTILIZER	NUTRIENTS	APPLICATION RATE	USES
Blood meal	N 15% P 1.3% K 7%	Up to 3 lbs. per 100 sq. ft. (more will burn plants)	Readily available nitrogen. Speeds decomposition of compost.
Bonemeal	N 3% P 20% K 0% Ca 24-30%	Up to 5 lbs. per 100 sq. ft.	Raises pH. Excellent source of phosphorus. Good for fruit, bulbs, flowers.
Cow manure	N 2% P 1% K 1%	40 lbs. per 50-100 sq. ft.	If fresh, will burn plants. Because slow releasing, a valuable soil additive.
Cottonseed meal	N 6% P 3% K 2%	2-5 lbs. per 100 sq. ft.	Acidifies soil. Lasts 4-6 months.
Fish emulsion, Fish meal	N 5-8% P 4-6% K 0-1%	Meal: Up to 5 lbs. per 100 sq. ft. Emulsion: 20:1	In early spring, as a foliar spray. Lasts 6-8 months.
Gypsum	Ca 23-57% S 17%	Up to 4 lbs. per 100 sq. ft.	When both calcium and sulfur are needed and soil pH is high. Helps loosen clay soils.
Kelp meal, Liquid seaweed	N 1% P 0% K 12% Trace minerals	Meal: Up to 1 lb. per 100 sq. ft. Liquid, dilute 25:1	Contains natural growth hormones. Use sparingly. Lasts 6 months.
Sulfur	S 100%	1 lb. per 100 sq. ft. to lower pH 1 point. As fungicide, 3 tablespoons per 1 gallon of water.	Lowers pH in alkaline soils. Increases crop protein. Ties up excess magnesium.

NUTRIENT SYMBOLS N Nitrogen Ca Calcium
P Phosphorus S Sulfur
K Potash

Source: *The Able Gardener*, Kathleen Yeomans, R.N.

Approximate Composition of Natural Fertilizer Materials

MATERIAL	PERCENT NITROGEN (N)	PERCENT PHOSPHORIC ACID (P)	PERCENT POTASH (K)
ROCK POWDERS			
Basic slag	–	8.0 - 17.0	–
Greensand (Glauconite)	–	1.4	4.0 - 9.5
Hybro-tite	–	.002	4.5
Rock phosphate (apatite)	–	38.0 - 40.0	–
VEGETATIVE & ANIMAL CONCENTRATES			
Bonemeal, steamed	2.0	22.0	–
Castor pomace	6.0	1.9	.5
Cocoa shell meal	2.5	1.5	2.5
Cottonseed meal	6.0	3.0	1.0
Dried blood meal	13.0	1.5	.8
Fish meal	10.0	6.0	–
Fish scrap	5.0	3.0	–
Garbage tankage	1.5	2.0	.7
Hoof & horn meal	12.0	2.0	–
Sewerage sludge	2.0	1.4	.8
Sewerage sludge, activated	6.0	3.0	.1
Soybean meal	7.0	1.0	.1
Tankage, animal	9.0	6.0	–
Tankage, processed	7.0	1.0	.1
Tobacco dust and stems	1.5	.5	5.0
Wood ashes	–	1.8	5.0

MATERIAL	PERCENT NITROGEN (N)	PERCENT PHOSPHORIC ACID (P)	PERCENT POTASH (K)
BULKY ORGANIC MATERIALS			
Alfalfa hay	2.5	.5	2.0
Bean straw	1.2	.3	1.2
Grain straw	.6	.2	1.0
Olive pomaces	1.2	.8	.5
Peanut hulls	1.5	–	.8
Peat	2.3	.4	.8
Sawdust	.2	–	.2
Seaweed (kelp)	.6	–	1.3
Timothy hay	1.0	.2	1.5
Winery pomaces	1.5	1.5	.8
MANURES			
Bat guano	10.0	4.5	2.0
Cow manure, dried	1.3	.9	.8
Cow manure, fresh	.5	.2	.5
Hen manure, dried, w/litter	2.8	2.8	1.5
Hen manure, fresh	1.1	.9	.5
Horse manure, fresh	.6	.3	.5
Pig manure, fresh	.6	.5	.4
Sheep manure, dried	1.4	1.0	3.0
Sheep manure, fresh	.9	.5	.8

Source: *Down-to-Earth Vegetable Gardening Know-How*, Dick Raymond

Mulch Materials

MATERIAL	APPEARANCE	INSULATION VALUE	RELATIVE COST	THICKNESS	WEED CONTROL	WATER PENETRATION	SOIL MOISTURE RETENTION	DECOMPOSITION SPEED	COMMENTS
Aluminum foil	Poor	Fair; reflects sun's heat	Very high	1 layer	Good	Poor, unless perforated	Excellent	No decomposition	Aphids shy away from foil-mulched plants. Should be removed and recycled.
Asphalt	Poor	Fair	High	½–1 in.	Fair	Fair	Fair-good	Decomposes in about 1 year	Complicated for home gardener to apply.
Bark, mixed	Good	Good	Moderate	2–3 in.	Good	Good	Good	Slow unless composted before use	Must be replaced only every two years. Can be stringy, difficult to manage.
Bark, redwood	Excellent	Good	High	2–3 in.	Fair	Fair; repels water in some places	Fair	Very slow; add nitrogen to application	Earthworms avoid redwood. May act as an insect repellent.
Buckwheat hulls	Good	Good	High	1–1½ in.	Good; may sprout	Excellent	Fair	Slow	Easy to handle. May be blown around in high wind or splashed by rain.
Burlap	Poor	Fair	Moderate	1 layer or more	Poor	Excellent	Fair	Slow	Excellent for preventing erosion on slopes. New grass grows right through it.
Cocoa hulls	Good-excellent	Good; absorbs heat from sun	High in most areas	1 in.	Good	Good unless allowed to mat	Good	Slow; adds nitrogen to soil	Sawdust can be added to improve texture and increase water retention. May develop mold. Has chocolatey smell.
Coffee grounds	Good	Fair	Low but not plentiful	Never more than 1 in.	Good	Fair; may cake	Good	Fairly rapid	Use carefully. May prevent ventilation. Best used in container gardens.

continued

Mulch Materials (continued)

MATERIAL	APPEARANCE	INSULATION VALUE	RELATIVE COST	THICKNESS	WEED CONTROL	WATER PENETRATION	SOIL MOISTURE RETENTION	DECOMPOSITION SPEED	COMMENTS
Compost	Fair	Good	High; supply usually limited	1–3 in.	Good	Good if well rotted	Good	Rapid; adds nutrients	Partially decomposed compost is an excellent feeding mulch.
Cork, ground	Fair–good	Excellent	High	1–2 in.	Good	Good	Good	Very slow; has little effect on soil nitrogen	Odorless. Stays in place nicely once it has been soaked.
Corncobs, ground	Good	Good	Low in Midwest	2–3 in.	Excellent	Fair; should be well soaked before applying	Excellent	Nitrogen fertilizer should be added	Avoid close contact with stems of plants because of heat generation.
Cottonseed hulls	Good	Good	Low in the South	1–2 in.	Good	Good	Good	Fairly rapid	Will blow in wind. Has fertilizer value similar to cottonseed meal.
Cranberry vines	Good	Fair	Low in some areas	3–4 in., 2 in. if chopped	Fair–good	Good	Good	Fairly rapid	Excellent winter cover mulch. Pea vines have similar characteristics.
Evergreen boughs	Poor	Good; recommended for wind protection	Low	1 to several layers	Fair	Good	Fair	Slow	Good for erosion control. Should be removed from perennials in spring.
Felt paper (tar paper)	Poor	Good; absorbs heat from sun	High	1 layer	Excellent	Poor, unless perforated	Good	Extremely slow if at all	Difficult to manage, tears. Must be carefully weighted and removed each fall.
Fiberglass	Poor	Excellent	High	3½–6 in.	Excellent	Fair; will get soggy and mat	Good	No decomposition	Unpleasant to handle. Totally fireproof. Mats are better than building insulation.

continued

Mulch Materials (continued)

MATERIAL	APPEARANCE	INSULATION VALUE	RELATIVE COST	THICKNESS	WEED CONTROL	WATER PENETRATION	SOIL MOISTURE RETENTION	DECOMPOSITION SPEED	COMMENTS
Grass clippings	Poor if not dried. Can have unpleasant odor.	Good	Low	1 in. maximum	Fair	Good if not matted	Fair	Rapid; green grass adds nitrogen	Can be mixed with peat moss. After drying can be spread thinly around young plants. Could contain herbicides. If very fresh, could heat up enough to damage plants.
Geotextiles	Poor, without a cover mulch	Poor	High	Single layer	Good	Fair	Good	Rapid with exposure to sunlight; slower with use of cover mulch	Use of a cover mulch highly recommended.
Green ground covers (cover crops)	Fair	Good once there is a heavy sod	Low	Allow to grow to full height	Good	Good	Good	Decomposing legumes and cover crops are rich in nitrogen	Should be harvested or tilled directly into the soil.
Growing green mulch	Excellent	Fair	Moderate	1 layer	Fair	Good	Good	Will live from one year to the next	Includes myrtle, pachysandra, etc. Use where you are not going to walk.
Hay	Poor unless chopped	Good	Low, if spoiled	6-8 in., 2-3 in. if chopped	Good	Good	Good	Rapid; adds nitrogen	Second- or third-growth hay that has not gone to seed is ideal.
Hops, spent	Fair	Fair; heats up when wet	Low where available	1-3 in.	Good	Good	Good	Slow; rich in nitrogen and other nutrients	Avoid close contact with trunks and stems because of heating.
Landscape fabric	Poor	Good	High	1 layer	Good	Good	Good	Slow; can last several years	Use in permanent beds. Cover with attractive top mulch.

continued

Mulch Materials (continued)

MATERIAL	APPEARANCE	INSULATION VALUE	RELATIVE COST	THICKNESS	WEED CONTROL	WATER PENETRATION	SOIL MOISTURE RETENTION	DECOMPOSITION SPEED	COMMENTS
Leaf mold	Fair	Good	Low	1½ in.	Fair-good	Fair; prevents percolation if too thick	Good	Rapid	An excellent feeding mulch. Use like compost.
Leaves	Fair	Good	Low	4-6 in.	Good	Fair; likely to mat	Good	Fairly slow; adds nitrogen	Contributes many valuable nutrients. Can be chopped and mixed with other things.
Manure	Poor-Fair	Good	Moderate-high	As thick as supply allows	Fair	Fair-good	Good	Rapid; adds nitrogen; packaged mixes may have harmful salts	Should be at least partially rotted. Supplies many nutrients.
Muck	Poor	Fair	Moderate	1-2 in.	Fair	Good, but will splash and wash away	Fair	Rapid	Very fertile. Can be mixed with other materials to improve texture.
Newspaper	Poor	Good	Low	2 layers	Excellent	Fair	Good	Lasts 1 season	Cover with hay or other top mulch to hold in place. Use between rows and on paths.
Oak leaf mulch	Good	Good	Low	2-4 in.	Good	Good	Good	Slow	Recommended for acid-soil plants. Has only slight influence on soil pH.
Oyster shells, ground	Good	Fair	High	1-2 in.	Fair	Good	Good	Slow	Works like lime. Will raise soil pH.
Paper	Poor; can be covered with soil	Fair	Low, but specialized mulch paper is expensive	1-several layers	Good	Poor unless perforated	Good	Slow, unless designed to be biodegradable	Can be shredded and used effectively.

continued

Mulch Materials (continued)

MATERIAL	APPEARANCE	INSULATION VALUE	RELATIVE COST	THICKNESS	WEED CONTROL	WATER PENETRATION	SOIL MOISTURE RETENTION	DECOMPOSITION SPEED	COMMENTS
Paper pulp	Poor	Fair	Moderate	in.	Fair	Fair	Good	Rapid, nitrogen-rich as side-dressing	Requires special equipment. Useful in deep-planting operations. Good way to recycle.
Peanut hulls	Good	Good	Low where plentiful	1-2 in.	Good	Good	Good	Rapid; adds nitrogen	Can be mixed with other material for superior appearance. Might splash in rain.
Peat moss	Good	Good	Moderate-high	1 in.	Good	Poor; absorbs much water	Poor; draws moisture from soil	Very slow	Adds little or no nutrients to soil. Valuable only as a soil conditioner.
Pine needles	Good-excellent	Good	Low	1-1½ in.	Good	Excellent	Good	Slow; very little earthworm activity	Often used with acid-soil plants, cut can be used elsewhere.
Plastic	Poor, but can be covered	Fair; some colors absorb heat	Moderate-high	1-6 mil.	Excellent	Poor unless perforated	Excellent	No decomposition	Contributes nothing to the soil. Must be handled twice a year. Various colors available. Can use black plastic to warm soil before planting heat-loving crops.
Poultry litter	Poor	Fair	Low-moderate	½ in.	Fair	Good	Fair	Very rapid; adds nitrogen	Should not be used unless mixed with dry material. Excellent fertilizer.
Pyrophyllite	Fair	Fair	High	1-3 in.	Fair	Good	Fair	Extremely slow	Should be considered a permanent mulch.
Salt hay	Good	Good	Moderate, unless you gather it yourself	3-6 in.	Good; contains no seed	Good, does not mat	Good	Slow	Can be used year after year. Is pest-free. Good for winter protection.
Sawdust	Fair-good	Good	Low	1-1½ in.	Good	Fair	Fair	Slow unless weathered; robs soil of nitrogen	Has high carbon content. Does not sour soil. Very little earthworm activity.

continued

Mulch Materials (continued)

MATERIAL	APPEARANCE	INSULATION VALUE	RELATIVE COST	THICKNESS	WEED CONTROL	WATER PENETRATION	SOIL MOISTURE RETENTION	DECOMPOSITION SPEED	COMMENTS
Seaweed (kelp)	Poor	Good; recommended as a winter mulch	Low in coastal areas	4-6 in.	Excellent	Fair	Good	Slow; adds nitrogen and potash	Provides sodium, boron, and other trace elements. Excellent for sheet composting.
Stone	Excellent	Good; dark stone retains heat, light stone reflects	High	2-4 in.	Fair, except shale	Good	Fair	Extremely slow	Should be considered permanent mulch. Contributes some trace elements through leaching.
Straw	Fair, unless chopped	Good	Low-moderate	6-8 in., 1-2 in. if chopped	Good; avoid oat straw for weed control	Good	Good	Fairly slow; nitrogen fertilizer is helpful	Should be seed-free if possible. Straw is highly flammable.
Sugarcane (bagasse)	Poor-fair	Good	Moderate	2-3 in.	Good	Good	Good	Rapid due to sugar content	Needs to be replenished often. Has fairly low pH. Mix with lime.
Vermiculite	Excellent	Excellent	High	½ in.	Good	Good	Good	Extremely slow	Totally sterile. Recommended for hothouse use. Will blow and splash outdoors.
Walnut shells	Excellent	Good	Low where plentiful	1-2 in.	Good	Good	Good	Very slow	Will furnish good trace elements. Resists fire.
Wood chips	Good	Good	Moderate	2-4 in.	Good	Good	Good	Fairly slow; little effect on soil nitrogen	May contain carpenter ants, but does not retain tree diseases.
Wood shavings	Fair	Fair	Low	2-3 in.	Fair	Good	Fair	Very rapid; will use up soil nitrogen.	Hardwood shavings are better than pine or spruce. Chips or sawdust make better mulch.

Source: *The Mulch Book*, Stu Campbell

When to Prune Shrubs

SHRUBS TO BE PRUNED AFTER BLOOMING

The best time to prune these shrubs that bloom on year-old wood is just after the blossoms have faded. Then the shrub will grow new branches and form the buds that will bloom the following year.

Akebia	Chionanthus (white fringe)	Jasminum (jasmine)	Rhododendron
Amelanchier (shadblow)	Cornus (dogwood, without berries)	Kalmia (laurel)	Ribes (flowering currant)
Azalea	Cotinus coggyria (smoke tree)	Kerria japonica (Japanese rose)	Rosa
Benzoin (spicebush)	Crataegus oxyacantha (English hawthorn)	Kolwitzia amabilis (beautybush)	Spirea (bridal wreath)
Berberis (barberry)	Cydonia (Japanense quince)	Lonicera fragrantissima (bush honeysuckle)	Spirea thunbergii
Buddleia alternifolia (butterfly bush)	Cytisus (broom)	Magnolia	Spirea van Houtei
Calycanthus floridus (sweet shrub, strawberry shrub)	Daphne (garland flower)	Philadelphus (mock-orange)	Syringa (lilac)
Caragana (Siberian pea)	Deutzia	Physocarpus (ninebark)	Tamarix (spring-flowering)
Celastrus (bittersweet)	Exochorda (pearlbush)	Pieris (andromeda)	Viburnum carlesi, V. lantana (snowball)
Cercis (Judas tree, redbud)	Forsythia (goldenbell)	Potentilla (cinquefoil)	Viburnum opulus (highbush cranberry)
Chaenomeles (flowering quince)	Hydrangea hortensia	Prunus (flowering almond, cherry, plum)	Weigela

continued

When to Prune Shrubs (continued)

SHRUBS TO BE PRUNED BEFORE THE BUDS SHOW GREEN

Shrubs that form flowers on wood grown the same season should be pruned when the plant is dormant

Abelia grandiflora	Cephalanthus (buttonbush)	Hypericum (St. Johnswort)	Salix (willow)
Abelia schumannii	Clethra (sweet pepper bush)	Indigofera (indigo)	Salvia greggii (autumn sage)
Acanthopanax (five-leaved aralia)	Cytisus nigricans (broom)	Kerria	Sambucus canadensis (American elder)
Althea, shrubby (Rose of Sharon)	Diervilla sessilifolia (bush honeysuckle)	Lagerstroemia (crape myrtle)	Sorbaria (false spirea)
Amorpha (indigo bush)	Euonymus kiautschovica (spreading euonymus)	Lespedeza (bush clover)	Spiraea (all summer-blooming spirea)
Aralia elata (Japanese angelica)	Fatsia japonica (Japanese fatsia)	Ligustrum (privet)	Staphylea (bladdernut)
Artemisia (sagebrush, southernwood, wormwood)	Franklinia alatamaha (Franklin tree)	Lilac japonica (tree lilac)	Stephanandra
Baccharis (groundsel shrub)	Garrya (silk-tassel)	Lonicera (berried honeysuckle)	Symphoricarpos (coralberry, snowberry)
Berberis (barberry)	Hamamelis virginiana (witch hazel)	Lycium (matrimony vine)	Tamarix odessana (late-flowering tamarisk)
Buddleia (butterfly bush, except for B. alternifolia)	Hibiscus	Rhamnus frangula (alder, buckthorn)	Viburnum (berry-bearing)
Callicarpa (beautyberry)	Holodiscus discolor (ocean-spray)	Rhus (sumac, smoke tree)	Vitex (chaste tree)
Caryopteris (bluebeard)	Hydrangea arborescens 'Grandiflora'	Roses (garden bush varieties)	
Ceanothus	Hydrangea paniculata 'Grandiflora'	Rubus odoratus (flowering raspberry)	

Sources: *Pruning Trees, Shrubs and Vines*, Editors of Garden Way Publishing, *Pruning Simplified*, Lewis Hill

Pruning Guide for Selected Fruit Trees and Shrubs

TYPE OF TREE	WHEN	HOW
Apple	Winter or early spring	Train tree for low head. Prune moderately. Keep tree open with main branches well spaced around tree. Avoid sharp V-shaped crotches.
Blackberry	After bearing and summer	Remove at ground canes that bore last crop. In summer cut back new shoots 3 feet high.
Raspberry	After bearing and in fall	Remove at the ground canes which bore last crop. Remove weak new canes and thin to no closer than 6 inches apart. In fall head back canes 4 or 5 feet.
Cherry	Winter or early spring	Prune moderately, cut back slightly the most vigorous shoots.
Currant	Early spring	Remove old unfruitful growth. Encourage new shoots.
Gooseberry	Early spring	Same as currant. Cut back new shoots at 12 inches high and side shoots to two buds.
Grape	Late winter or early early spring, before sap starts	Requires heavy pruning of old wood to encourage new bearing wood. Remove all old branches back to main vine. Cut back the previous year's new growth to four buds.
Peach	Early spring	Prune vigorously – remove one-half of the previous year's growth, keep tree headed low, and well thinned-out.
Plum	Early spring	Remove dead and diseased branches, keep tree shaped up by cutting back rank growth. Prune moderately.
Quince	Early spring	Cut back young trees to form low, open head. Little pruning of older trees required except to remove dead and weak growth.

TYPE OF SHRUB	WHEN	HOW
Barberry	Early spring	Little pruning required except to remove a few old branches occasionally to encourage new growth. Head back as necessary to keep plant in shape.
Butterfly Bush	Early spring	Cut out all dead wood. Remove some old branches and head-in as necessary to keep plant properly shaped.
Clematis	Depends on flowering time	Spring-blooming types should be cut back after bloom, if shaping is desired. Early-summer-blooming types should be cut back 6-8" to a pair of strong buds in March, if shaping is desired. Summer-and-fall-blooming types should be cut back to 12" from ground every March.
Crabapple	Early spring	Prune moderately. Cut out dead and broken branches and suckers.

continued

Pruning Guide for Selected Fruit Trees and Shrubs (continued)

TYPE OF SHRUB	WHEN	HOW
Deutzias	After flowering	Remove a few older branches and all dead wood. Do not let growth get too dense.
Dogwood, Flowering	After flowering	Remove dead wood only.
Dogwood, Other	Spring	Varieties grown for colored twigs should have the old growth removed to encourage bright-colored new shoots.
Elderberry	After fruiting	Prune severely. Remove one-half of season's growth.
Forsythia	After flowering	Remove a few older branches at the ground each year and head back new growth as necessary.
Honeysuckle, Bush	After fruiting	Cut out some old branches. Keep bush open.
Hydrangea	Early spring	Hills of Snow variety: cut back to ground. Others: remove dead and weak growth, cut old flowering stems back to two buds.
Laurel, Mountain	After flowering	Prune very little. Remove a few old branches at the ground from weak, leggy plants to induce growth from the roots.
Lilac	After flowering	Remove diseased and scaly growth, cut off old flower heads, and cut out surplus sucker growth.
Mock-Orange	After flowering	Cut out dead wood and a few old branches to thin out plant.
Rhododendron	After flowering	Treat same as Laurel, Mountain.
Roses, Climbing	After flowering	Cut out about one-half of old growth at the ground and retain the vigorous new shoots from the root for next year's flowers. Head back as necessary.
Roses: Tea, Hybrid, Perpetual	Spring after frosts	Cut away all dead and weak growth and shorten all remaining branches or canes to seven or eight buds.
Rose of Sharon	When buds start	Cut out all winter killed growth back to live wood.
Snowberry	Early spring	Thin out some old branches and cut back last season's growth of that part remaining to three buds.
Trumpet Vine	Early spring	Prune side branches severely to the main stem.
Weigela	After flowering	Prune lightly, remove all dead, weak growth and head in as necessary. Cut out a few old branches at the ground to induce new growth.
Wisteria	Spring	Cut back the new growth to the spurs at the axils of the leaves. This can be repeated in midsummer.
Viburnum	Early spring	Prune lightly. Remove all dead, weak and a few of the old branches.
Virginia Creeper	Spring	Clip young plants freely. Older plants require little pruning except to remove dead growth and some thinning.

Source: *Pruning Trees, Shrubs and Vines*, Editors of Garden Way Publishing

Pruning Ornamental Trees

BOTANICAL NAME	COMMON NAME	SPECIAL REMARKS
Amelanchier	shadbush	Prune only to shape, as either bush or tree
Carpinus betulus	European hornbeam	Prune to tree form
Carpinus orientalis	Oriental hornbeam	Prune to tree form
Cassia fistula	golden-shower, senna	Cut back season's growth to short spurs after blooming
Cercis	redbud	Prune after blooming if necessary
Cornus florida	flowering dogwood	Prune as little as possible, heals slowly
Cornus Kousa	Kousa dogwood	See Cornus florida
Cotinus obovatus	American smoke tree	Prune to grow as bush or small tree, cut off fading flowers
Crataegus	hawthorn	Prune to shape in late winter, renew branches if necessary
Elaeagnus	Russian olive	Prune only to control size if necessary, in late winter
Euonymus atropurpurea	burning bush	Prune in late winter, only if necessary
Franklinia alatamaha	Franklin tree	Prune to tree form
Halesia monticola	silver-bell	Needs pruning rarely
Hydrangea paniculata 'Grandiflora'	peegee hydrangea	Prune in late winter
Koelreuteria paniculata	golden rain tree	Prune to shape when young
Laburnum anagyroides	golden-chain	Prune after blooming
Magnolia	magnolia	Prune just after blooming
Malus	flowering crab apple	Prune to shape, renew old wood if necessary
Myrica cerifera	wax myrtle	Prune to remove winter injury, or to shape, in late winter
Myrica pensylvanica	bayberry	Prune to remove suckers, winter injury
Oxydendrum arboreum	sourwood	Needs pruning early
Prunus	flowering almond, apricot, cherry, peach, plum	Prune to shape in late winter
Rhamnus davurica	buckthorn	Prune to shape in late winter
Sorbus	mountain ash	Prune to tree form, in late winter
Symplocos paniculata	sweetleaf	Prune to shape, renew old branches
Syringa reticulata	Japanese tree lilac	Prune right after blooming, if necessary
Viburnum	cranberry bush, nannyberry, black haw	Prune in late winter only, as necessary

Source: *Pruning Simplified*, Lewis Hill

Indoor Plant Diseases

DISEASE	SYMPTOM	CURE
Bacterial infection	Graying and yellowing leaves. Crown rot.	Use antifungal spray. Water from the bottom.
Botrytis blight	Gray mold on all parts of the plant.	Avoid overcrowding, overfeeding, and overwatering. Provide good air circulation. Spray with antifungals. Dispose of infected plants.
Edema	Plants rapidly absorb water, but transpiration is slow and cells burst. Swelling on leaves and corky ridges.	Increase temperature and lower humidity. Allow soil to dry out before watering.
Fungal diseases	Stem and root rot.	Increase air circulation. Decrease humidity.
Powdery mildew	Leaves covered with white powder.	Use antifungal spray. Let dry between waterings. Usually can't be saved.
Virus	Mottled, yellowing leaves. Leaf curl. Spotted flowers. Stunted growth.	Remove and destroy infected plant promptly. Watch out for the insects that spread these diseases!

Source: *The Able Gardener*, Kathleen Yeomans, R.N.

Indoor Plant Pests

PEST	DESCRIPTION	SYMPTOM	CURE
Aphids or plant lice	(3 mm): White, red, green, or black, these small, softbodied insects suck plant juices and carry fungus and disease.	Foliage deformation. Sticky, curled, or yellowed leaves. Sometimes a sooty mold.	Remove aphids with an alcohol-dipped cotton swab. Rinse plant in a soapy solution and then in lukewarm water. Spray with pyrethrin, if necessary.
Mealybugs	(6 mm): These white, oval, hairy-looking insects with a cottony appearance suck plant juices.	Pale foliage. Leaf drop. Stunted growth.	Remove mealybugs with an alcohol-dipped cotton swab. Wash with soapy water. Spray only if necessary.
Mites	(7 mm): Very hard to see without a magnifying glass, mites suck plant juices.	Leaf curl. Leaf drop. Stunted growth. Blackened buds. Grayish, dusty look to the plant. Webs on the underside of the plant.	Very difficult to eradicate. Try soapy water. Remove from the rest of your plants. Spray with insecticide. Put plant outside. High humidity sometimes helps.
Scales	(3 mm): Hard-shelled lumps on stems and leaves attach so tightly they sometimes look like part of the plant.	Yellowed foliage. Dropping leaves.	Scrub off with alcohol-soaked swab. Rinse in soapy water. Spray as necessary. Very difficult to eradicate if the infestation is heavy.
Whiteflies	(1.60 mm): White, wedge-shaped winged insects that suck plant juices and spread diseases, especially viruses.	Yellowing leaves. Dropping leaves. Swarms when plant is disturbed.	Wash with strong water spray. Difficult to eradicate. Sometimes a hot pepper spray solution helps. Quarantine the plant.

Source: *The Able Gardener*, Kathleen Yeomans, R.N.

Summer-Flowering Bulbs

FLOWER	HEIGHT	PLANTING TIME	PLANTING DEPTH	SPACING
Acidanthera	20"	Early spring	2"	5"
Anemones de Caen, St. Brigid	18"	South, Sept.-Jan. North, Early spring	2"	3"
Dahlia large varieties	48"	After last frost	4"	24"
dwarf varieties	12"		4"	6"
Galtonia	40"	April-May	5"	10"
Gladiolus large flowering	60"	April-mid June	3-4"	6"
small flowering	30"		3-4"	6"
Lily	3-7'	Fall or early spring	8"	8"
Montbretia	24"	April-end of May	4"	4"
Ranunculus	12"	South, Sept.-Jan.	2"	8"
Tigridia	16"	Early spring	3"	6"

Spring-Flowering Bulbs

FLOWER	HEIGHT	BLOOMING TIME	PLANTING DEPTH
Snowdrop	4-6"	Early spring	4"
Crocus	3-5"	Early spring	3-4"
Anemone blanda	5"	Early spring	2"
Grape hyacinth (Muscari)	6-10"	Early spring	3"
Early tulips	10-13"	Early spring	6"
Hyacinth	12"	Early spring	6"
Daffodil	12"	Midspring	6"
Darwin hybrid tulips	28"	Midspring	6"
Crown imperial	30-48"	Midspring	5"
Late tulips	36"	Late spring	6"
Dutch iris	24"	Late spring	4"
Allium giganteum	48"	Late spring	10"

Source: *Landscaping with Bulbs*, Ann Reilly

Glossary

ACID SOIL. Soil that tests to a pH of less than 7. True acid-soil plants prefer soil at pH 6.5 or lower and thrive at a pH of 4 to 6.

ALKALINE SOIL. Soil, often called "sweet," that tests to a pH of more than 7. Is usually found in limestone country and is associated with hard water.

ANNUAL. A plant that is sown, flowers, sets seeds, and dies all within one season.

AXIL. The angle formed by a branch, leaf stalk, or flower stalk, with the stem or another branch.

BALLED-AND-BURLAPPED. A plant that has been dug up with the soil carefully maintained around its roots and wrapped in burlap (or plastic-backed burlap).

BARE-ROOT. A plant that has been dug from its growing place and is usually shipped or sold wrapped in cardboard or plastic with roots protected with something like damp sphagnum moss.

BASAL. The base or bottom of a plant.

BIENNIAL. A plant that takes two years to complete its growing cycle from seed; usually flowers, fruits, and dies during its second season.

BORDER. A planting at the edge of an area.

BRACT. A small modified leaf with or without a stem, particularly one of the smaller scalelike leaves in a flower cluster.

BROADCAST. Scatter seeds freely over the entire seedbed.

BT. *(Bacillus thuringiensis)* A bacterium that causes disease in a variety of pest larvae, but is safe to humans, birds and pets, and plants; marketed under such tradenames as Biotrol, Dipel, and Thuricide.

BUILDER'S SAND. Inexpensive substitute for horticultural sand. Available at hardware stores and home centers, it is used to aerate and increase drainage when mixed with potting soil.

BULB. The fleshy root of plants such as lilies, tulips, and similar plants.

BULBIL. A small bulblike bud or bulblet, usually produced in the axil of a leaf or place of the flower, and capable of developing into a new plant when planted.

CALLUS. A growth of tough protective tissue developed over or around a wounded surface, such as that formed over the end of a cutting, and from which roots develop, or over a smooth wound caused by a pruning.

CALYX. The outer set of small, leaflike parts that, with the corolla, comprises the perianth or floral envelope of a flower.

CAMBIUM. The layer of living tissue just below the bark, whose growth results in the increase in thickness of stems and perennial roots.

CLAY SOIL. A soil containing from 30 to 100 percent clay; fine-textured and sticky when wet.

COMPOST. A rich, porous mixture composed of decaying or decayed organic matter.

CORM. A modified, swollen stem filled with food storage tissue; a fleshy root similar to a bulb, but not solid.

CROWN. The area of a seed plant where the root and stem merge.

CULTIVAR. A cultivated variety, usually unique and an improvement in the species, created by the successful cross-pollination of two different plants within a species.

CUTTING. A method of plant propagation whereby a piece of plant is cut from a parent plant and inserted into a growing medium to encourage root development, thus forming a new plant.

DAMPING-OFF DISEASE. A fungus disease carried in unsterile soil; causes young seedlings to wither and die.

DEADHEAD. To pick or cut off flowers as soon as they fade in order to encourage continued bloom on the plant.

DECIDUOUS. Term describing trees, shrubs, and vines that shed their leaves in winter.

DIBBLE. A pointed tool used to make holes in soft ground for planting bulbs or setting small plants.

DIVISION. A method of plant propagation whereby a plant (including its root system) is dug and cut or pulled apart; the resulting plants can be replanted.

DORMANCY. A period of time during which plant growth and other activity ceases temporarily because of unfavorable weather.

DRILL. A shallow furrow into which seed is sown.

ERICACEOUS. Plants of the Heath Family, a large important group of shrubs and small trees.

EVERBLOOMING. Plants that bloom more or less continuously throughout their growing season.

FIBROUS ROOT. A fine, young root.

FLAT. A shallow, topless box with drainage holes in the bottom; used for germinating seeds, growing young transplants, or propagating cuttings.

FORCE. To grow plants outside their natural seasons, most often used to speed up the maturation of a plant.

FROND. The entire leafy portion of any fern.

FROST-FREE DATE. The approximate date of the last killing frost of spring.

FUNGICIDE. Material used to protect plants against or to inactivate or kill fungi, primarily those that cause plant diseases.

GENUS. A group of plants constituting a subdivision of a family, and containing groups of species more or less closely related and having certain obvious structural characteristics in common.

GERMINATION. The sprouting of seeds.

GIRDLING. To remove a strip of bark all around the stem of a plant, thus cutting its circulation of water and nutrients. Also, to remove a similar bark strip on a limb to induce rooting in air layers or for putting on a patch bud.

GRAFT. Process whereby a part (scion) taken from one plant is made to unite with and grown upon another part of a plant (stock).

GRANULAR FERTILIZER. Low-release nutrient granules usually used for top or side-dressing.

GREEN MANURE. A cover crop that is grown to improve nitrogen availability in the soil and, when it is turned into the soil, to add humus to the soil.

GREENSWARDS. Turf verdant with growing grass.

GROUND COVER. Plant adapted for covering the ground, especially where grass is unwanted or doesn't thrive.

HARDENING OFF. The process of subjecting seedlings that were begun indoors to increasing amounts of light and outdoor temperatures prior to transplanting them into the garden.

HARDPAN. A layer of impervious soil, sometimes found just below the surface or topsoil

HARDWOOD CUTTING. Cutting taken from a dormant plant.

HARDY. A plant that withstands frost and thus can be planted outdoors in early spring or left out late into fall.

HEELING IN. A technique whereby plants that cannot be immediately planted are lain on their sides in a shallow trench, with their roots covered with about 6 inches of soil.

HERBACEOUS. Plant in which the part above the ground has a soft stem and does not become woody.

HERBICIDE. A chemical used for killing plants, usually weeds.

HORMONE ROOTING POWDER. Chemical in liquid or powder form that aids in the development and growth of roots on cuttings.

HUMUS. The brown substance that results following the breakdown of organic materials by various soil organisms.

HYBRID. A new plant created by the successful cross-pollination of two plants of two different species, thus with different genetic traits.

INDIRECT SUNLIGHT. Diffused light, as opposed to the direct rays of the sun, such as that on the north side of a rock or in the shade of thick woods.

INOCULANT. A powder that contains live bacterial of the Rhizobium genus.

INSECTICIDAL SOAP. A specially prepared, biodegradable soap made from natural fatty substances that kills many insects on contact without damaging plants or harming people, animals, or beneficial insects.

INSECTICIDE. A chemical or organic agent used for insect control.

LAYERING. A method of plant propagation whereby a long, flexible stem of a woody plant is secured to, or slightly under, the ground to encourage root development at the point of contact with the ground, thus forming a new plant.

LEADER. The main or terminal shoot of a tree.

LEAF MOLD. Decayed leaves.

LIME. A compound of calcium, often used to alter chemical solutions or soil conditions.

LOAM. A soil consisting of about a 50–50 mixture of sand and clay.

MANURE TEA. Manure and fertilizers dissolved in water, resulting in liquid manure.

MICRONUTRIENTS. An element essential in minute amounts for the proper growth and health of plants.

MULCH. A protective covering, such as bark chips or sawdust, spread over the ground to reduce evaporation, maintain an even soil temperature, prevent erosion, control weeds, and enrich the soil.

NATURALIZE. To establish plants as if native.

NODE. The part of the stem at which leaves and buds have their origin.

OFFSETS. A plant that develops at the base of a "mother" plant.

OPEN-POLLINATED. Plants pollinated by movement, wind, or insect activity, not controlled by man.

ORGANIC MATERIAL. Naturally occurring plant and animal resources in soil, compost, or humus.

PEAT MOSS. Compacted plant debris, including sphagnum moss.

PERENNIAL. A plant that lives from year to year, usually flowering and setting seed in spring and summer, dying to the ground in winter, and regrowing the following spring.

PERLITE. Porous, hard white material formed from lava, used to improve drainage and aeration and reduce the weight of the soil.

PETAL. One of the inner series of floral leaves that together make up the corolla.

pH. The relative acidity and alkalinity of a soil on a scale of 1 to 14; a soil with a pH of 7 is considered neutral.

PHOTOSYNTHESIS. The process by which the green leaves of plants, with the aid of sunlight, manufacture sugars and starches from air, water, and raw food materials taken in by the roots.

PINCHING; PINCHING BACK. The technique of pinching out the growing tip of developing plants in order to encourage bushiness.

POLLEN. The male sex cells of flowering plants.

POLLINATION. The transfer of pollen from one flower (cross-pollination), or part of a flower (self-pollination), to another; a critical step in plant fertilization.

POTTING MIX. Pre-packaged ready-to-use soil mixture that may include sand, compost, vermiculite, and peat moss.

PRESSURE-TREATED WOOD. Impregnated with preservatives to resist decay.

PROPAGATE. To multiply plants by one of a variety of techniques. See also Cutting; Division; Layering.

PRUNING. The process of removing dead, diseased, or unwanted parts of a tree so that those parts that remain are benefitted.

RAISED BED. Elevated garden bed offering better drainage and aeration and warmer soil than a conventional bed.

RHIZOME. Underground or rootlike stem, from the joints (nodes) of which spring true roots and stems of new plants.

ROCK PHOSPHATE. Mined phosphate used to furnish phosphorous, which is essential to plant growth.

ROOT. The descending axis of a plant that penetrates the soil, absorbs moisture and nutrients, and acts as support and anchor for the stem.

ROOT BALL. The mounded mass of roots and soil that cling to a plant, tree, or shrub when it is removed from a pot or dug from a bed.

ROOT CUTTING. Small pieces of roots that have been cut up for the purpose of starting new plants asexually.

ROOT PRUNING. The reduction of root length as a horticultural operation, for example to remove damaged roots and encourage growth or to check vegetative growth.

ROOTING HORMONE. A natural or synthetic compound, in liquid or powder form, that aids in the development and growth of roots on cuttings.

ROOTSTOCK. The root on which a scion is grafted.

ROSETTE. A cluster of leaves or other plant organs arranged in a tight circle.

RUNNER. A long, slender, trailing stem that may take root and produce new plants wherever its leaf and bud parts come in contact with the soil.

SANDY SOIL. A soil with from 50 to 100 percent fine sands, as well as coarse sands with 35 to 100 percent fine gravel and some fine sand. Although sandy soil can be formed into a ball when wet, the ball will break easily when touched.

SCARIFY. Nick or break seed coat slightly with a small file or scissors in order to facilitate the entrance of water into the seed.

SCION. The branch or bud that is grafted or bud-grafted onto a rootstock.

SEEDLING. A young plant grown from seed.

SELF-POLLINATION. The use of a plant's own pollen upon its own stigmas to produce self-fertilized progeny.

SHADE CLOTH. Woven material used to shade and protect plants.

SHARP SAND. Used in rooting mixtures, a sand that is identified by its coarse, "sharp" feeling when rubbed between the fingers.

SIDE-DRESSING. Fertilizer applied to a plant once it is growing.

SILICA GEL. A desiccant used to dry flowers for craft use.

SLIP. A cutting.

SLOW-RELEASE FERTILIZER. A fertilizer formulated to be inactive until released by water or temperature and to activate slowly over a period of time (e.g., 3-month or 6-month formulations).

SOD. The surface layer of a lawn or other stretch of closely mown grass.

SOFTWOOD CUTTING. A cutting made early in the season, from new growth.

SOIL AMENDMENT. Ingredients such as sand, peat moss, or compost that are added to soil to improve its texture.

SOIL-TESTING. Measuring the nitrogen/phosphorus/ potassium, trace elements, minerals, salts, and pH levels of the soil. Gardeners can test their own soil with soil testing kits, or send soil samples to the local Cooperative Extension Service office.

SOILLESS MIX. Growing medium often containing materials such as perlite, vermiculite, and peat moss, but no grit soil. Holds water and nutrients well.

SPECIES. The basic division of the living world, consisting of distinct and similar individuals that can breed together to produce offspring similar to themselves.

SPHAGNUM MOSS. Moss commonly found in bogs, harvested and used in soil mixtures to increase water retention.

SPORE. A body of microscopic size that serves to disseminate and reproduce fungi, ferns, and club-mosses, corresponding to seed in the higher plants.

SPUR. A modification of one or more petals or sepal so that they are fused to form a tubelike structure, as in larkspur or columbine.

STANDARD. A plant form whereby the strongest stem is selected and all other stems and lower foliage are pruned away, thus allowing the plant to fill out and bloom only at the top, like a small tree.

STERILE SOIL. Soil heated to more than 180 degrees F to kill weed seeds and bacteria.

STOCK. Rootstock.

SUBSPECIES. A distinct, often geographically isolated subdivision of a species.

SUCCULENT. Fleshy plant whose leaves are able to store water, including many cactus species.

SUCKER. A short or subordinate stem springing from a bud at the summit of the root.

TAPROOT. The main root of a plant.

TENDRIL. A very slender, flexible appendage that serves to support a plant by clinging to or winding around some other object.

THIN. To remove the weakest seedlings to prevent crowding of plants.

TILL. To work the soil by cultivating or digging it.

TOPSOIL. The surface layer of soil, consisting of good loam and organic matter.

TRANSPIRATION. The process by which water is given off by the leaves of a plant.

TRANSPLANT. To remove plants from one place and reset them in another.

TUBER. A short, swollen, underground stem gorged with reserve food.

USDA ZONE. U.S. Department of Agriculture classifications according to annual minimum temperatures and/or lengths of growing seasons. Also referred to as hardiness zones.

VARIETY. A plant that is different from the true species occurring in nature.

VERMICULITE. Lightweight, highly water-absorbent material resulting from the expansion of mica granules under high temperatures; used in potting medium.

WHIP GRAFT. Graft in which the scion and rootstock are locked together tighter than in ordinary grafting.

Index

Page references in *italics* indicate illustrations; page references in **bold** indicate tables.

Other Storey Titles You Will Enjoy

The Big Book of Gardening Secrets, by Charles W.G. Smith. Provides scores of professional secrets for growing better vegetables, herbs, fruits, and flowers. 352 pages. Paperback. ISBN 1-58017-000-5.

The Big Book of Gardening Skills, by the Editors of Garden Way Publishing. A comprehensive guide to growing flowers, fruits, herbs, vegetables, shrubs, and lawns. 352 pages. Paperback. ISBN 0-88266-795-5.

Caring For Perennials, by Janet Macunovich. Leads the home gardener through month-by-month maintenance program for the perennial garden. 200 pages. Paperback. ISBN 0-88266-957-5.

Carrots Love Tomatoes: Secrets of Companion Planting for Successful Gardening, by Louise Riotte. Explains how to put vegetable relationships to work for you in your garden to produce a bountiful crop. 244 pages. Paperback. ISBN 1-58017-027-7.

Contained Gardens, by Susan Berry and Steve Bradley. Covers step-by-step techniques for creating dozens of designs, color themes, groupings, and using unique planters. 160 pages. Hardcover. ISBN 0-88266-889-4.

Easy Gardening 101, by Pat Stone. Outlines the basic principles of gardening and demystifies the gardening process, making working in the garden fun and accessible to all. 192 pages. Paperback. ISBN 1-58017-041-2.

From Seed to Bloom, by Eileen Powell. Easy-to-understand plant-by-plant format which includes information on hardiness zones, sowing seeds indoors and out, germinating times, spacing, light and soil needs, care, and propagation techniques. 320 pages. Paperback. ISBN 0-88266-259-7.

Let It Rot! The Gardener's Guide to Composting, by Stu Campbell. Simplifies the technical terminology to make composting easy, and provides information on selecting and combining the right materials. 160 pages. Paperback. ISBN 1-58017-023-4.

Pruning Made Easy: A Gardener's Visual Guide to When and How to Prune Everything, from Flowers to Trees, by Lewis Hill. From Storey's Gardening Skills Illustrated Series. 224 pages. Paperback: ISBN 1-58017-006-4. Hardcover: ISBN 1-58017-007-2.

Roses Love Garlic: Companion Planting and Other Secrets of Flowers, by Louise Riotte. Provides secrets to successful "companion planting" and offers lore and growing advice for hundreds of flowers. 256 pages. Paperback. ISBN 1-58017-028-5.

Secrets to Great Soil: A Grower's Guide to Composting, Mulching, and Creating Healthy, Fertile Soil for Your Garden and Lawn, by Elizabeth P. Stell. From Storey's Gardening Skills Illustrated Series. 224 pages. Paperback: ISBN 1-58017-008-0. Hardcover: ISBN 1-58017-009-9.

Seed Sowing and Saving: Step-by-Step Techniques for Collecting and Growing More Than 100 Vegetables, Flowers, and Herbs, by Carole B. Turner. From Storey's Gardening Skills Illustrated Series. 224 pages. Paperback: ISBN 1-58017-001-3. Hardcover: ISBN 1-58017-002-1.

Tips for the Lazy Gardener, by Linda Tilgner. Contains hundreds of valuable suggestions for every gardener who wants to cut down on weeding and enjoy gardening more. 128 pages. Paperback. ISBN 1-58017-026-9.

These books and other Storey books are available at your bookstore, farm store, garden center, or directly from Storey Books, Schoolhouse Road, Pownal, Vermont 05261, or by calling 1-800-441-5700. www.storey.com